THE FILMS OF BONG JOON HO

Global Film Directors

Edited by Homer B. Pettey, Professor of Film and Comparative
Literature at University of Arizona, and R. Barton Palmer, Calhoun
Lemon Professor Emeritus of English at Clemson University

Volumes in the Global Film Directors series explore cinematic innovations by
prominent and emerging directors in major European, American, Asian, and
African film movements. Each volume addresses the history of a director's *oeuvre* and its influence upon defining new cinematic genres, narratives, and techniques. Contributing scholars take a context-oriented approach to evaluating
how these directors produced an identifiable style, paying due attention to those
forces within the industry and national cultures, that led to global recognition of
these directors. These volumes address how directors functioned within national
and global marketplaces, contributed to and expanded film movements, and
transformed world cinema. By focusing on representative films that defined the
directors' signatures, these volumes provide new critical focus upon international directors, who are just emerging to prominence or whose work has been
largely ignored in standard historical accounts. The series opens the field of *new
auteurism* studies beyond film biographies by exploring directorial style as influ-
encing global cinema aesthetics, theory, and economics.

Recent titles in the Global Film Directors series:

Nam Lee, *The Films of Bong Joon Ho*
Jim Leach, *The Films of Denys Arcand*

Bong Joon Ho with Oscar (Credit: Mark Ralston/AFP, Getty Images).

THE FILMS OF BONG JOON HO

NAM LEE

RUTGERS UNIVERSITY PRESS
New Brunswick, Camden, and Newark, New Jersey, and London

Library of Congress Cataloging-in-Publication Data

Names: Lee, Nam, author.
Title: The films of Bong Joon Ho / Nam Lee.
Description: New Brunswick, New Jersey : Rutgers University Press, [2020] | Series:
Global film directors | Includes bibliographical references, filmography, and index.
Identifiers: LCCN 2020004583 | ISBN 9781978818910 (cloth) | ISBN 9781978818903
(paperback) | ISBN 9781978818927 (epub) | ISBN 9781978818934 (mobi) | ISBN
9781978818941 (pdf)
Subjects: LCSH: Pong, Chun-ho, 1969—Criticism and interpretation. | Motion picture
producers and directors—Korea (South) | Motion pictures—Korea (South)—History.
Classification: LCC PN1998.3.P6625 L44 2020 | DDC 791.4302/33092 [B]—dc23
LC record available at https://lccn.loc.gov/2020004583

A British Cataloging-in-Publication record for this book is available from the
British Library.

♾ The paper used in this publication meets the requirements of the American
National Standard for Information Sciences—Permanence of Paper for Printed
Library Materials, ANSI Z39.48–1992.

www.rutgersuniversitypress.org

Manufactured in the United States of America

For Kun Soo, Yong Oh, and Yong Jae Chung

CONTENTS

ILLUSTRATIONS

PREFACE

While this book was in production in February 2020, Bong Joon Ho stunned the world by sweeping the Academy Awards with his film *Parasite*, winning Oscars for Best Picture, Best Director, Best Original Screenplay, and Best International Feature. It was truly a historic moment in film history. Not only was it the first time a South Korean film had been nominated for an Oscar—let alone had won any—but it was also the first time a foreign-language film won Best Picture. *Parasite* has overcome the "subtitle barrier" to win the hearts of American movie-goers as well as Academy Awards voters. Furthermore, *Parasite* became the first film since *Marty* (1955, dir. Delbert Mann, U.S.) to receive both the Best Picture Oscar and the Palme d'Or at the Cannes Film Festival.

While the Academy Awards honor "quality films" made within the Hollywood industry, the Cannes Film Festival tends to favor director-driven works. And because of the different nature of the two awards, *Parasite*'s Best Picture win was even more surprising and utterly unexpected. Palme d'Or winners have not been favored or even considered possible candidates for Best Picture unless they are English-language Hollywood films. *Parasite* has shattered that convention. This rare achievement of winning both the Palme d'Or and several Oscars seems to be a fitting recognition of Bong Joon Ho's unique filmmaking, which seamlessly combines Hollywood genres and auteur cinema.

Bong's Palme d'Or and Oscar awards posed some "pleasant" challenges to the writing of *The Films of Bong Joon Ho*. Indeed, one of the difficulties I faced during the production of this book stems from the fact that I was writing about a living director who not only keeps making films but also keeps making history! The book was first conceived in 2013, when *Snowpiercer* was released in Korea, and the first draft of the manuscript was completed in 2017. However, then *Okja* premiered at the Cannes Film Festival against the backdrop of a Netflix scandal, and I had to revise the manuscript to add an analysis of the film. Then while the manuscript was going through a review process, *Parasite* became the first Korean film to win the Palme d'Or in May 2019, and so the book had to include an analysis of it too, because it would be missed if not. So I rewrote the conclusion to add a much-needed analysis of that film. However, this was not the end, as you can see: I am currently sitting at my desk rewriting this preface to bring the book up to date on the significance of Bong's achievements. It gives me some sense of security and relief to know that Bong Joon Ho will not be releasing any new films before the book's publication, although I most eagerly await his next film.

The first time I sat down with director Bong Joon Ho to talk about his films was in November 2011, when I organized the second Busan West Film Festival at Chapman University's Dodge College of Film and Media Arts, where I teach film studies. (I had met him twice before in Los Angeles, but both were brief meetings at postscreening receptions for his films.) The Busan West Film Festival was hosted biannually by Dodge College in partnership with South Korea's Busan International Film Festival (BIFF) with the aim of introducing the latest Asian films. In 2011, Bong was invited as the main guest filmmaker and the recipient of the Busan West Icon Award. He stayed on campus for three days and offered a master class, audience Q&As, and lunch meetings with students to talk about his films and filmmaking. The festival's opening film was the 3D version of *The Host*, which had just been converted from 2D and premiered at the BIFF a month prior. The festival also included a miniretrospective of Bong's films, including his debut feature, *Barking Dogs Never Bite* (2000); *Memories of Murder* (2003); his Korean Film Academy thesis film, *Incoherence* (1994); and the mockumentary short film *Influenza* (2004). His latest film, *Mother* (2009), had already screened at the inaugural Busan West two years earlier. So basically, Chapman students and the audience had the opportunity to see all of his feature films to date.

At the time, Bong was attracting international attention as an emerging Korean director. *The Host* and *Mother* had been released in the United States and elsewhere to critical acclaim, but his fame and popularity had not reached the level he now enjoys. *Barking Dogs Never Bite* was released in Korea in 2000, after I had left to study film in the United States, which meant I had to watch his movies on Korean DVDs or at the film festivals held in Los Angeles. When I started teaching film studies at Dodge College in 2008 and began offering new courses on Korean and Asian cinema, I included Bong's films in my syllabi. Of all the Korean and Asian films I screened and discussed in class, Bong's were always the students' favorites and the ones that prompted the liveliest discussions. Students were fascinated by his unique ways of bending genre conventions and his films' tonal shifts and unexpected plot twists, and they were baffled by his endings, which offered no resolution. His films also proved to be the most popular subjects for final paper assignments.

The students' reactions to Bong's films were the main motivations behind my inviting him to the Busan West Festival; however, another reason—a personal one—was that I myself was particularly attracted to his films. I was intrigued and impressed by the ways in which he dealt with the 1980s in *Memories of Murder* and *The Host*. The decade was one of the most crucial periods in contemporary Korean history, one in which the democratic movement continued and intensified, culminating in the June Struggle of 1987, which finally brought an end to the military regime. Korean films made during the 1980s and how the period is represented in contemporary Korean cinema were my main research topics at the time.

How are the 1980s remembered and portrayed in New Korean Cinema? Bong's *Memories of Murder* and *The Host* were excellent examples with which to explore this question. *Memories of Murder* is based on a real-life serial rape and murder case in the 1980s that remained unsolved at the time of production. The film was unique because instead of focusing on the killer, it examined the crime within the wider context of its time. I was impressed by the ways in which the film pointed to the oppressive military regime as the main reason behind the detectives' inability to catch the killer.

During the postscreening Q&A of *Memories of Murder*, I asked Bong about his different approach to crime thrillers and learned that he had thoroughly researched the case for six months before writing the script. He spent thousands of hours reading newspaper articles in archives and interviewing people involved in the case, including the detectives. He became obsessed with the case to the point that he imagined meeting the killer and even composed a list of questions to ask him. He explained that the idea of making the film a story about the 1980s military regime occurred to him during his newspaper research. The newspaper articles on the case were surrounded on the page by other articles on a range of different subjects, so this allowed him to identify the wider political and social atmosphere of the time. I could see he was very perceptive and amazingly thorough.

His next film, *The Host*, comments on the legacy of the 1980s student movement through the former student activist character of Park Nam-il, and it features many iconic images of the 1980s democratic movement, including some that allude to the May 1980 Kwangju Massacre (discussed in the introduction), which remains the most traumatic event in contemporary Korean history. *The Host* fascinated me because I thought it was arguably the first film to allegorize the tragic Kwangju Massacre in a popular genre—the monster movie—instead of in a serious drama. Thus it was the most interesting film to explore the question of the representation of the 1980s in New Korean Cinema.

Chapter 3 of this book is the product of my inquiry on the representation of the 1980s in Bong's films. Given that it was the first chapter I completed and it paired two films under the theme of the 1980s, it was logical to organize other chapters and films by theme: *Barking Dogs Never Bite* and *Mother* under the theme of moral ambiguity and *Snowpiercer* and *Okja* under the theme of global politics and neoliberal capitalism.

In addition to the thematic categories adopted in this book, other combinations are possible. *Mother* can be analyzed as a sequel to *Memories of Murder*, as they are both crime thrillers set in a rural town twenty years apart; the portrayal of the police in *Mother* and in *Memories of Murder* is quite different because *Mother* is set in the postdemocratic era. Furthermore, in October 2019, the serial rapist and murderer of the 1980s was finally identified, thirty-three years after his last murder. It caused a sensation in Korea, and Bong and *Memories of Murder* attracted renewed interest in the mass media. The killer's mother adamantly denied the possibility that her son had committed such terrible crimes, given his gentle and quiet nature. Her reaction inevitably reminds us of the mother in *Mother*. It is uncanny that as the real killer was caught, the fictional mother of *Mother* was summoned back. Thus it is not a stretch to say that *Mother* is a sequel to *Memories of Murder*. Then *The Host* and *Okja* can be paired in terms of the giant CGI imaginary creatures they feature, while *Snowpiercer* and *Parasite* can be compared and contrasted in terms of class polarization and catastrophic imagination, since both films end in a catastrophe as a result of a class conflict.

Although Bong has not been a prolific filmmaker, releasing a new film every three or four years, *Parasite* was released only two years after *Okja*, which is a welcome change for both the director and audiences alike. Despite the completion of this manuscript having to be postponed in order to keep up with Bong's filmmaking, it is better—even fortunate—that *Parasite* is included, because as I write in the conclusion, it is a film that both summarizes his previous films and one that lets us see the new direction Bong seems to be taking. Perhaps we could say that the seven feature films discussed in this book compose the first half of Bong's filmmaking career. I am curious to see his next film.

The process of writing this book included watching Bong Joon Ho grow from a promising local film director to a global auteur. It was also a process of witnessing the effects of globalization—which Bong's films so precisely capture—as the films themselves came to be shared by audiences worldwide. Bong's films are a testament to how the most local issues can also be the most global in our era of neoliberal capitalism. I would like to thank him for his unique oeuvre that inspired me to write this book. I also thank him for offering his generous time to sit down with me for interviews whenever I visited Korea.

Many people and institutions have inspired and helped me at various stages of this project, and I would like to express my sincere gratitude for their support and encouragement. My heartfelt gratitude goes to David Desser for his valuable advice during the entire process of writing this book. His willingness to give his time so generously to read my work in progress has been instrumental in completing this book. I would like to give special thanks to my dear friend Linda Robinson, the first reader of many versions of my draft and whose proofreading and editing greatly improved my manuscript. I am particularly grateful to film critic and longtime friend Lim Jae-cheol for his insightful comments and suggestions in the final stage of this project and for thought-provoking conversations on the art of cinema.

I have been privileged to receive thorough support and encouragement from David E. James, who has been a mentor to me during my academic career over the years. His insightful comments and encouragement helped me refine my ideas. Namhee Lee, whose book on the 1980s *minjung* (people's) movement in Korea was inspirational in my analysis of *Memories of Murder* and *The Host*, also read parts of my manuscript and enthusiastically supported my project. I thank Kathy Kleypas for her constructive suggestions in the early stages of the project. I also appreciate the rigorous readings of the anonymous manuscript reviewers that helped strengthen my approaches in analyzing Bong's films. I also acknowledge the mentorship and inspiration from professors when I studied at University of Southern California: Dana Polan, the late Anne Friedberg, Peggy Kamuf, and Marsha Kinder.

I am fortunate to have joined a welcoming community of colleagues at Dodge College of Film and Media Arts at Chapman University. I am particularly grateful to former dean Bob Bassett for his support for my research and teaching of Korean and Asian cinema. He spearheaded the launch of the Busan West Film Festival, which brought Bong to our campus in 2011. I also extend my gratitude to associate deans Michael Kowalski and Pavel Jech for their support for film studies faculty research. It allowed me opportunities to present early versions of this work at conferences, where I had thought-provoking discussions that enriched this book. I thank my colleagues at Dodge College's film studies program. I am grateful to Bill Dill for offering me generous time out of his busy schedule to discuss cinematography in Bong's films. His keen analytical eye helped me refine my own reading of the films in terms of their visual construction. I was also blessed to have Korean cinematographer Kim Hyung Koo visit my "Korean Cinema Today" class in fall 2015 to discuss his work on *Memories of Murder* and *The Host* with my students. A special thanks to the Korean Cultural Center, Los Angeles, for sponsoring Kim's guest visit. I also thank my Korean cinema students whose creative curiosity and fresh perspectives inspired me to write this book.

A number of people offered information and intellectual encouragement through conversations and correspondences. In particular, conversations or seminars with Inyoung Nam, Hyangjin Lee, and Hyun-seon Park, all scholars of Korean cinema, were inspirational in expanding the theoretical framework in analyzing Bong's films. The seminars I had with Inyoung and Hyun-seon on Jacques Rancière and Alain Badiou were crucial in constructing my reading of *Snowpiercer*. I also thank Inyoung for inviting me to the Forum Busan 2019 to present my chapter on *Parasite*. I am also grateful for the many discussions I had with Jeon Chan-il, film critic and former Korean film programmer of Busan International Film Festival, on Bong's films. He also helped me organize Busan West Film Festivals.

Chapman colleagues Stephanie Takaragawa and Jan Osborn have been extremely supportive of my work throughout the process. I deeply appreciate their willingness to discuss my research and writing, to listen to my queries, and to lend a hand whenever I need them. I extend my thanks to my fellow members of the Irvine Cultural Forum, a Korean book club in Orange County, who watched Bong Joon Ho films to discuss my work in progress in two of their monthly meetings. I benefitted from their comments and observations from a non–film studies point of view in my effort to make this book accessible to a wider readership.

I would like to acknowledge two Korean institutions—the Academy of Korean Studies (AKS) and the Korea Foundation (KF)—that provided me with generous funding to conduct field research in Korea. The AKS Junior Fellowship Program allowed me to begin archival research and conduct interviews with Bong in Korea in the summer of 2013. While the AKS fellowship was instrumental in shaping my project in its early stages, KF's Fellowship for Field Research in fall 2019 supported a fruitful sabbatical semester of research and writing to bring the manuscript to completion. I am also grateful to Chapman University for granting me a sabbatical semester during this final stage to add a new chapter on *Parasite* and to finish the edits of my manuscript.

My sincere thanks go to editor Nicole Solano, Global Film Directors series editors Homer B. Pettey and Richard Barton Palmer, and the staff at the Rutgers University Press for their guidance and help in bringing this book to fruition.

Last but not least, I thank my extended family in Korea for their many years of support and love. First, to my dear parents, Sang Ho and Jung Hee Lee, for their unconditional love and support throughout my life. They helped me raise my two kids during my most difficult times as a working mom in Korea. I would not be where I am today if not for their unwavering belief in me. My siblings, Young, Young Jin, and Hyun, and my sister-in-law, Mikyung, always make my stay in Korea comforting and full. I thank them for their heartwarming support across the Pacific Ocean, particularly my little sister, Hyun, who looked after me when I injured my knee during the sabbatical period in Korea. Without her care, I would not have had the peace and stability to work on completing the manuscript. My deepest gratitude and love goes to my husband, Kun Soo Chung, whose remarkable patience, love, and devotion have sustained me throughout the years in Korea and California. His belief in me never falters. Finally, I send my love and thanks to my two sons, Yong Oh and Yong Jae, and my daughters-in-law, Connie and Monica, for numerous fun times of board games, movies, and travels. I thank you for being who you are.

A NOTE ABOUT ROMANIZATION

The romanization of Korean names and terms in this book follows the McCune-Reischauer system. Exceptions to this rule are the names of the people quoted from other sources, such as the Korean Movie Database (KMDb), or where there is already a widely accepted romanization. In compliance with the Korean practice, Korean names are presented with the last name preceding the given name, except for names printed otherwise in English-language publications. Previously, Bong Joon Ho's romanized name has been *Bong Joon-ho* with a hyphen in order to indicate that Joon Ho is his first name; however, *Bong Joon Ho* without a hyphen is Bong's preferred romanization. All translations from Korean-language references are mine unless otherwise noted.

THE FILMS OF BONG JOON HO

INTRODUCTION

When Bong Joon Ho announced a monster movie, *The Host*, as his new project in 2004, many if not all Korean film industry insiders were skeptical, despite Bong's great success—both critical and commercial—with his feature film *Memories of Murder* the year before. Nobody could predict the record-breaking blockbuster phenomenon the film was to become in 2006. Upon its release on July 27, the film broke the opening-day record, set a new domestic record by selling more than ten million tickets in twenty-one days,[1] and became the highest-grossing film of all time with more than thirteen million tickets sold. It maintained this record for the next eight years. *The Host* was successful not only domestically but also internationally: it screened at the 2006 Cannes Film Festival to critical acclaim and earned Bong international recognition.[2]

The reason this project was initially met with strong skepticism was, in large part, because monster movies have never before been popular with Korean audiences. Unlike Japanese cinema, which has established a unique *kaiju* (strange beast) genre, South Korean cinema does not have a strong monster genre tradition. The 1960s saw a few notable *kaiju*-influenced films, but for the most part, they were considered children's movies and were not taken seriously; moreover, their special effects were poor.[3] Thus Bong's plan to make a monster movie that required significant use of sophisticated visual effects was considered reckless, and some tried to dissuade him from attempting the project.

Of course, skepticism about his film projects was nothing new to Bong Joon Ho. In fact, industry insiders had scornfully predicted that his first three feature films would be disasters. The story told in his debut film, *Barking Dogs Never Bite* (2000), of dogs that go missing in a small apartment complex, was deemed too trivial for a feature film, and *Memories of Murder* (2003) was scorned as commercial suicide because it was a crime thriller in which detectives fail to capture the killer. At the time, the Korean domestic film market was dominated by romantic comedies with happy endings, so Bong was advised to change the film's ending so the mystery was solved satisfactorily. However, Bong kept the original conclusion because it was based on an actual unsolved serial murder case, and he wanted to remain true to the real story. Some investors even pulled out after seeing the edited film. Bong was an unknown young director at the time, but he could make these films as he had originally conceived because of the unusual support he received from his producer.[4]

The fact that, from the outset of his career, Bong has maintained the original conception of his films against all odds is crucial to understanding his approach to filmmaking. Although he makes mainstream commercial films, he does not abide by the accepted rules or conventions of established genres. He has always been a self-conscious auteur who refuses to compromise his own vision and integrity as a filmmaker. Instead, he tweaks, turns, and inverts conventions and even turns them upside down. Still, he completely snubs the skepticism that clouded his new projects every time and pulls off great box-office successes and movies that receive critical acclaim. In his films, the guilty get away with murder, literally and/or figuratively. His genre films—whether a crime thriller, monster movie, or science fiction—do not give audiences the reassurance offered by their Hollywood counterparts. Rather, his films usually end without a clear sense of resolution, leaving the audience puzzled, if not bewildered. The absence of the Hollywood "happy ending" constitutes one of the most prominent elements of genre subversion in Bong's films: the dog killer gets away in *Barking Dogs Never Bite*; the detectives fail to capture the serial killer in *Memories of Murder*; the family cannot save their daughter from the monster in *The Host*; the real murderers are set free in *Mother* (2009); the world comes to a bleak end in *Snowpiercer* (2013); the girl saves her giant pig, but the horror of the slaughterhouse continues in *Okja* (2017); and all four members of the poor family succeed in getting jobs with the wealthy family, but their successful scheme only leads to a total catastrophe in *Parasite* (2019).

Even so, Bong's films are immensely popular among Korean audiences, and with the success of *Snowpiercer*, *Okja*, and *Parasite*, which received the Palme d'Or at the 2019 Cannes Film Festival as well as four major awards at the Oscars in 2020, he has become the most sought-after director on a global stage as well. Bong's unique achievement as a filmmaker lies in his successful foray into what I would describe as "political blockbuster" filmmaking. The "political" in his films is not overt or didactic but effortlessly blends into his films' entertainment. Instead, the films are political in their aesthetics of subverting the conventions of blockbuster films and in the sense that they draw our attention to the world we live in and encourage us to ponder the social and political issues we identify with in his films. In certain ways, his films provide a cultural forum where important and pressing social issues are mobilized and discussed by the audience. For example, *Okja* prompted online discussion about the modern meat industry and, as the *Foodbeast* blog reported in July 2017, inspired some people to go vegan.[5] Similarly, as will be discussed in detail in chapter 5, *Snowpiercer* opened up public discussions on the issue of global warming. *Parasite*, which became Bong's second film after *The Host* (2006) to surpass ten million ticket sales in Korea, saw a proliferation of interpretations of the various themes in the film, mostly the issue of class polarization in our own era.

Whether set in South Korea (hereafter Korea) or in an imaginary space, the stories in Bong's films are grounded in the realities of the world and address issues that affect everyday lives. And these stories are always told from the perspective of ordinary people. Indeed, Bong's films pay particular attention to the socially weak. The protagonists of his films are unlikely heroes—a dim-witted father in *The Host*; a poor, middle-aged single mother and her mentally disabled son in *Mother*; a young girl from remote rural Korea in *Okja*—who are thrown into situations in which they have to battle a powerful system (whether political or corporate) in order to save their loved ones. And it is the plight of the socially weak that seems to resonate with audiences both locally and globally.

LEITMOTIF OF MISRECOGNITION

With seven feature films between his debut in 2000 and 2020, Bong has established himself as a rare film director who garners both critical acclaim and commercial success while maintaining full control over his work. He has successfully balanced entertainment and social commentary, as the issues embedded in the stories do not overshadow the cinematic enjoyment they provide. Bong achieves this by cleverly using the leitmotif of "misrecognition" or "misconception"—an inability to recognize an object or a person, mistaking it for another or holding inaccurate expectations about it—as the main trigger of the narrative. This leitmotif is most evident in his thrillers, a genre that lends itself to this theme when based on a mystery-plot structure in which the protagonist is chasing an unknown criminal. In Bong's thrillers, protagonists often fail to recognize the criminal or perceive the wrong person to be the criminal and fail to capture the culprit.

In *Barking Dogs Never Bite*, the protagonist, desperate to stop a neighbor's dog from barking, kidnaps and hides it in the basement of his apartment building, only to learn that he has stolen the wrong dog. Before he can release it, however, the building's janitor kills and cooks the dog; thus, this initial misrecognition triggers the film's horror subplot. The plot of *Memories of Murder* is a series of one misrecognition after another, and the primary question the narrative raises—what is the identity of the serial killer who is preying on the young women of this rural village?—is never answered. A young girl is captured by the river monster in *The Host* only because her father, running away from the monster, grabs the hand of another girl, leaving his daughter behind to be snatched away by the monster's tail. Moreover, the characters in *The Host* never learn what has created this monster, although its origins are revealed to the audience in the film's prologue.

Mother is the story of a woman trying to prove her son's innocence when he is charged with murder, and this murder charge is the misconception that sets the story in motion. The mother mistakes two other men as the real killers before learning she is the one who has been laboring under a misconception all along; rather than the innocent victim she believes him to be, her son is, in fact, the murderer. At the same time, detectives misread blood found on another boy's shirt as proof of his guilt and charge him with the murder in the film's final misrecognition.

The very premise on which the story of *Snowpiercer* is built is a misconception. In this film, the remnants of the world's humanity circle the earth in a perpetually running train, believing the ice age blighting the planet has made it uninhabitable. At the film's end, however, this belief is revealed to be false; following a revolt within the train during which an explosion derails it and frees its inhabitants, the survivors of the crash venture out, possibly to start human civilization anew. An earlier misconception is revealed when the leader of the revolt confronts the train's owner and operator, only to learn that the train is run not by mechanics alone but is dependent on child labor.

In *Okja*, the protagonist Mija's mission of saving her superpig Okja begins when the pig is taken away by the Mirando Corporation, which genetically engineers superpigs for food consumption. Mija was unaware of the fact that Okja was an engineered pig and that she is to be taken away to the United States by the Mirando Corporation to be publicly revealed as the winner of their superpig competition. Thus when Dr. Johnny Wilcox, a zoologist, a well-known TV show host, and the brand ambassador of the Mirando Corporation, arrives at her house with a filming crew, she misrecognizes him as just filming one of his TV episodes. That is why she leaves the house to the filming crew without any suspicion to visit her parents' grave with her grandfather. Also, one of the climactic scenes in the film rests on an intentional mistranslation. After the Animal Liberation Front (ALF) has helped Mija reunite with Okja, the ALF leader, Jay, wants to ask Mija if she will agree to their next mission, which is to take Okja to New York to penetrate the Mirando Corporation and take them down from the inside. If she does not agree, they will not pursue their mission. The Korean American member K acts as an interpreter between them. Mija replies that she does not agree and she just wants to take Okja back to the mountain. At this critical moment, however, K decides to give a deliberate mistranslation and tells the ALF members that she agrees. This triggers the narrative forward to New York and subsequently to the slaughterhouse. Thus *Okja*'s narrative is built upon three misunderstandings or misrecognitions: first, Mija thought Okja was a pet she could keep; second, she misrecognized Dr. Johnny Wilcox only as the famous TV personality; and lastly, she did not even know that her answer was mistranslated, which was why they go to New York.

Parasite takes this motive of "misrecognition" to a new level. While the misrecognitions in the previous films were not intentional ones, the protagonists in this film actively use them. The four members of the Kim family succeed in getting hired by the rich family all by pretending to be somebody else, presenting false identities and résumés. They also pretend to be strangers to one another. The whole film is triggered by their pretensions. (The film even has a scene in which the son, Ki-Woo, asks Da-Hae, whom he is tutoring, to compose an English paragraph using the word *pretend* at least two times.)

Alfred Hitchcock is the greatest master of the "wrong man" motif, and the plots of his films are often structured on misrecognition. Bong effectively appropriates Hitchcock's motif of misrecognition to express the absurdities of Korean realities and global issues. In *Barking Dogs Never Bite*, *Memories of Murder*, and *Mother*, characters are wrongfully accused or convicted of crimes; however, unlike various Hitchcockian protagonists wrongfully identified, pursued, and—in the case of *The Wrong Man* (1956)—charged with a crime, Bong's characters are often not cleared or set free, or at least not until after having experienced violence or torture. Further, Bong's narrative structures are more complex than Hitchcock's. For instance, *Mother* has dual narrative strands consisting of two murders committed by two separate individuals; moreover, both murderers go free while the audience knows—although the police in the film do not—that a wrongfully convicted man remains in prison. The complexity of this dual structure and the layering of mismatched knowledge are more effective than a straightforward mystery in conveying the peculiar realities of Korean society. Bong uses the leitmotif of misrecognition because, it seems, it provides the most effective tool to reveal the multiple layers of social absurdities of contemporary Korean society. Korean citizens (including the characters in his films) expect that the system that governs the nation will protect and save them from disasters or crises, but their expectations are always betrayed.

Indeed, the five Bong films set in Korea capture his idea of "Koreanness." Before expanding his filmmaking to a global level with *Snowpiercer* and *Okja*, his aim was to appeal exclusively to Korean audiences. He has stated that *The Host*, which enjoyed international success, "was acclaimed at Cannes, but they do not understand this film 100 percent. The film is full of humor and comedy only Koreans can understand."[6] But he added that he was "happy to see that Korean sentiment and sensibilities also worked in the West."[7] Specifically, Bong localizes "conventional" (i.e., Hollywood) genres within Korean stories, realities, and sensibilities. And it is this localization that makes the subversion of genre conventions inevitable, as chapter 3 will demonstrate. Unlike Americans, whose collective trust and belief in their governmental system and authority are usually reflected in mainstream Hollywood films, Koreans generally are suspicious of their government or authorities. And these two opposing tendencies or sensibilities clash within Bong's films to create his unique adaptation of Hollywood genres.

KOREANNESS AS SOCIAL ABSURDITY

The notion of Koreanness can be interpreted in different ways. So how, precisely, does Bong define the Koreanness that informs his filmmaking? For Bong, Koreanness does not lie in the traditional Korean culture of the premodern era. In this, he differs from veteran director Im Kwon-Taek, whose films are often associated with the uniquely Korean notion of "han." This is a concept that has no English equivalent, but it refers to unresolved grief, grudges, or regrets, a sentiment that has accumulated in the hearts of Koreans throughout the country's tumultuous history. In contrast, in Bong's films, Koreanness lies, in his own words, in the absurdities or irrationalities (*pujoris*)[8] in everyday life. In his films, the social *pujoris* are the result of the widespread political corruption, social injustices, and anomie of contemporary Korean society, and these *pujoris* are the key to understanding Bong's films. For instance, these *pujoris* are the reasons his films lack clear resolutions. They also account for his films having narratives that result in failure.

This element, which I call the *narrative of failure*, can be explained by Korea's discourse of "failed history." Specifically, after liberation from thirty-six years of Japanese colonial rule in 1945, Korea experienced postwar U.S. occupation, national division, civil war (i.e., the Korean War), and then almost three decades of successive military dictatorships that came to an end only in the late 1980s after an intense struggle for democracy. However, pride in achieving democracy turned into increasing confusion and cynicism after a financial crisis in 1997 and an International Monetary Fund (IMF) bailout that mandated the adoption of neoliberal measures, which, in turn, intensified the economic inequalities and social injustices.

One cause of the persistent social injustices and political corruption in Korean society can be traced to Korea's failure to identify and prosecute collaborators and perpetrators of Japanese imperialism and military dictatorships, particularly those involved in the Kwangju Massacre in May 1980, during which Korean paratroopers turned their weapons on civilian protesters demanding democracy. Even after democratization in 1987, no substantial change has been achieved in Korea's system of corruption and *pujoris*. Thus today a sense of despair, anger, and cynicism is widespread in Korea. Man-made disasters occur frequently, and the government and other authorities often fail to protect ordinary citizens; these are the historically accumulated sentiments that Bong's films capture and that strike a chord with Korean audiences.

Bong's observations on the workings of Korean society are so keen and accurate that they are almost prophetic. In *The Host*, a monster emerges from the Han River and attacks people along the shore. However, government authorities in the film are bent on chasing a family victimized by the monster rather than on containing or killing it. Furthermore, the authorities continue to pursue the family as carriers of a monster-borne virus even after learning that the virus does not exist.

Six years after its release, the film was summoned back to public discourse in the aftermath of the worst ferry disaster in history. On the morning of April 16, 2014, the ferry *Sewol* capsized and sank off Korea's south coast, killing 304 people. The victims were mostly high school students on their way to Cheju Island for a school excursion. The nation watched the *Sewol* sink in real time on live TV broadcasts as government rescue efforts failed to arrive in time to save the passengers. Most viewers identified with the horror the students' parents must have felt as they watched helplessly, unable to save their children. President Park Geun-hye was conspicuously absent while the boat was sinking; it was revealed later that poor oversight by regulatory bodies had contributed to the disaster, and the government was accused of a cover-up. The victims' families and other members of the public engaged in protests, but the government refused to investigate and has never explained why rescue services were late in responding to the disaster. Further, instead of investigating what went wrong, the government began to accuse the protesting families of politicizing the event, going so far as to label them "North Korean sympathizers" bent on disrupting the nation.

The striking similarity between the *Sewol* ferry disaster and the monster attack in *The Host* became an immediate topic of discussion on social media, as reflected in these sample Twitter posts: "Is Bong Joon Ho's film *The Host* a prelude to the Sewol disaster? The nation's incompetence; the families', especially the father's, desperate struggle; and the victimized young child. It seems that the fathers' desperate struggle will continue in this monsterized society" (@ell65, August 22, 2014); "Watching Bong Joon Ho's *The Host* again and this is completely identical. Director Bong has incredible insight" (@hanjovi21, July 15, 2014). The comic writer Lee Jae-suk wrote, "On second viewing, [*The Host*] is a film about Korea and the Sewol disaster . . . Bong Joon Ho's *The Host* is not an SF fantasy film" (@kkomsu10000, July 5, 2014). This evocation of *The Host* in the wake of the *Sewol* ferry disaster is a testament to the extent to which Bong's films provide a keen insight into contemporary Korean society. His films are in a way a study of the social ills and their effects on the lives of ordinary Korean people.

Therefore, his films can be best understood through an examination of the Korean realities that serve as their subtexts. Specifically, the chronotope[9] of his films is the transitional period in Korean history between the military dictatorship of the 1980s and the democracy and neoliberal capitalism of the twenty-first century. His films probe the dire consequences of the rapid economic growth Korean society experienced in the forty years after the Korean War (1950–1953)—known as an "economic miracle"—during which Korea transformed itself from one of the world's poorest nations to one of the world's largest economies. Politically, Korea transitioned within twenty-six years from a military dictatorship in 1961 to a democratic society in 1987. In economic terms, the transition from military dictatorship to a democratic society was a journey from state-planned economic growth to neoliberal capitalism.

While *Memories of Murder* looks back at the dark era of the 1980s military dictatorship, *Barking Dogs Never Bite*, *The Host*, and *Mother* dig beneath Korea's postwar economic miracle and explore the ways in which its consequences drove individuals, especially the socially weak, into disastrous situations. Bong interrogates the superficiality of the parliamentary democracy and reveals how the preexisting system of social ills and corruption has been maintained and has even intensified in postdemocratic Korean society.[10]

Bong stands out among contemporary Korean film directors for his politically and socially conscious approach to filmmaking; perhaps alone among his cohorts, he maintains a critical gaze toward Korean society while also making popular films. His works explore the problems of Korea's social system, reveal political and moral corruption and social injustice, and (in)directly address unresolved issues in Korean history. Uniquely, however, his work remains squarely in the realm of commercial entertainment, achieving wide appeal through his appropriation of Hollywood genres. Thus his films differ from those of other well-known and critically acclaimed Korean directors, such as Lee Chang-dong, Hong Sang-soo, and Kim Ki-duk, whose film styles are more radical and whose works circulate mostly in the art cinema / film festival circuit.

At the same time, Bong is different from Park Chan-wook, who also works within a genre tradition. While Park's films manifest auteur consciousness through their highly stylized aesthetic, Bong's films are more realistic, both visually and thematically. They are also more mass oriented than Park's, with playful subversions of genre conventions and blockbuster spectacles, whereas Park's films tend to be more serious and philosophical, with twisted stories that unfold around the theme of revenge. Bong's films are more sociological than philosophical. However, this does not mean Bong is not conscious of being an auteur. Rather, he strongly defends his integrity as an auteur to such a degree that he is willing to risk commercial success to maintain full control over his work, as his struggle with Harvey Weinstein over the U.S. release of

Snowpiercer demonstrates.[11] Rather than conforming to the distributor's request to cut twenty minutes of his film to guarantee a wider release, Bong opted for the limited release of the uncut version. This decision reinforces the idea that Bong often goes against suggestions for wider audiences; instead, he pushes forward his original vision for his films. Two weeks into a limited theatrical release, *Snowpiercer* went on a streaming service concurrently and became one of the most watched of his films there, which in turn led the distribution company to increase the number of screens in the theaters.

Bong's tremendous global success offers an interesting case study of making films that are at once nationally specific and universally appealing. It is fair to say that this transnational appeal of his films is related to economic globalization and the spread of neoliberal capitalism worldwide. Since the late 1990s, Korea has been at the forefront of neoliberal capitalism, and Bong's films capture the various social ills intensified by the neoliberal policies of deregulation of government measures to control markets, privatization of public assets, cutback of social welfare, and de-unionization, all of which engender corporate greed and widen the gap between the rich and the poor. As these neoliberal measures spread with the global market economy, the consequences are shared globally as well. Thus although Bong's films portray specifically Korean realities, the underlying social problems and issues are universal. As he ventured into English-language global filmmaking with *Snowpiercer* and *Okja*, his scope of social inquiries also expanded to include global issues. These two films are global versions of his Korean-language films in terms of their interrogation of social systems and their biting critique of neoliberal capitalism. *Snowpiercer* is an allegory of the ever-widening gap between the rich and poor while raising the global issue of climate change; *Okja* deals more directly with corporate greed, the issues of genetically modified food, and the cruelty of animal factory farms.

By combining Hollywood genres and local politics, Bong opens up what Homi Bhabha terms a "third space"[12] of enunciation in which the cultural differences between postcolonial society and the West are translated and articulated. Bhabha posits that recognition of this third space opens the way to "conceptualizing an *inter*national culture, based not on the exoticism or multiculturalism of the diversity of cultures, but on the inscription and articulation of culture's *hybridity*." Bong Joon Ho's films can be considered the product of this hybrid filmmaking, standing as he does between Hollywood filmmaking on one hand and Koreanness on the other. The contemporary Koreanness in his films is rooted in the various historical, social, political, and cultural abnormalities Korea is faced with as a postcolonial society. By bringing together elements from each, he creates something new and uniquely his own.

However, it is not the goal of this book to trace the uniqueness of Bong's films solely to his cinematic genius or to link them to the romantic notion of an auteur whose intentions provide the keys to understanding the meaning of his films. Rather, the book takes French sociologist Pierre Bourdieu's idea that a work of art is not a product of some sort of inspiration from God but a social phenomenon shaped by concrete social and historical processes. Bourdieu's concept of a "field of cultural production"—the idea that understanding a work of art involves looking not only at the art itself but also the conditions of its production and reception—provides a tool to overcome the opposing approaches to studying a work of art: the internalist approach that focuses on the work's formal qualities and structural determinism that claims that art is a mere reflection of social structures.[13] His claim that "scientific analysis of the social conditions of the production and reception of a work of art, far from reducing it or destroying it, in fact intensifies the literary experience"[14] supports the aim of this book to provide concrete historical, social, and cultural context—the field of production—to enhance the pleasure of discovering the rich subtext in Bong's films. While recognizing his creative agency, the book acknowledges that all forms of culture, including films, are shaped by social practices and that the creators are also cultural products.

Bong Joon Ho himself can be described as a "cinematic sociologist" whose films are embedded in concrete social realities of both Korean society and neoliberal capitalism at large. His films are about individual lives—in particular, the marginalized of Korean society. However, they are always positioned within the larger social, political, and economic context. In this sense, his films realize what American sociologist C. Wright Mills termed as "sociological imagination," a creative way of understanding the private troubles by looking at them within larger social realities and public issues.[15] All of Bong's films are about the plight of ordinary, disadvantaged people, and in the process of portraying the difficulties they face, his films reveal and suggest to the audience the root cause of their predicaments. This will be analyzed in detail in the subsequent chapters; however, for example, *Memories of Murder* places the serial murderer and the incompetent police within the larger context of the 1980s military dictatorship; in *The Host*, the root causes of the tragedy of the Park family are the postcolonial conditions of Korea: its subservient relationship to the United States and the corrupt authorities. The moral corruption of the protagonists in *Barking Dogs Never Bite* and *Mother* is not depicted as caused by the individuals' monstrous nature but rather by the harsh social and economic conditions forced upon the weak. In *Snowpiercer* and *Okja*, Bong's cinematic sociology becomes more overtly political to indict the global phenomenon of neoliberal capitalism, which allows corporate greed to disregard dire issues of global warming and animal cruelty. *Parasite* brings a renewed attention to the issue of class, the polarization of the rich and the poor under a neoliberal capitalist society in which upward mobility is no longer attainable for those who have fallen through the cracks.

Thus the chapters of this book are structured thematically in terms of the Korean context of the specific social ills and corruption the aforementioned leitmotifs of misrecognition and misconception aim to reveal.

Chapter 1, "A New Cultural Generation," provides a brief biography of Bong Joon Ho, summarizing the diverse and hybrid cultural influences on his work. It analyzes his short films and the films he worked on as a screenwriter before becoming a director. With this background, the chapter then positions Bong Joon Ho and his films within the context of New Korean Cinema. Characterized by the emergence of cinephile filmmakers and audiences, New Korean Cinema burst onto international movie screens in the late 1990s. Among the most popular and influential of these films, which demonstrate Korea's powerful popculture presence, were *Shiri* (1999), *JSA* (2000), *My Sassy Girl* (2001), and *Oldboy* (2003). Of all these films, however, the most popular by far was *The Host* (2006). A record-breaking blockbuster in Korea, the film also achieved acclaim internationally with serious movie fans and cult audiences alike.

Chapter 2, "Cinematic 'Perversions': Tonal Shifts, Visual Gags, and Techniques of Defamiliarization," focuses on Bong's formal techniques and visual expression. It closely examines how Bong's focus on Koreanness is communicated visually and formally. Specifically, I discuss Bong's major filmic techniques of genre bending and tonal blending; his realist aesthetics, analogous to the tradition of the "real-view landscape" in Korean painting; and his defamiliarization of everyday spaces. I borrow the Russian formalist and literary critic Viktor Shklovsky's notion of *defamiliarization*—making familiar objects appear unusual or new to the viewer/reader—to explain Bong's use of space in his films. Bong tends to use spaces that are often overlooked, such as the basement of an ordinary apartment in *Barking Dogs Never Bite* and the sewage of the Han River in *The Host*. His films turn these everyday places into spaces of horror.

Chapter 3, "Social *Pujoris* and the 'Narratives of Failure': Transnational Genre and Local Politics in *Memories of Murder* and *The Host*," focuses on and analyzes the ways in which Bong utilizes specifically Korean politics in the narratives of the crime movie (*Memories of Murder*) and the monster movie (*The Host*) to subvert and reinvent genre conventions. Bong has shaped these films with specifically Korean narrative forms I identify as *narratives of failure*. These narratives of failure reflect the self-perception of a "failed history" that characterizes the collective experience of Korean society since the mid–twentieth century, beginning with its liberation from three decades of Japanese colonial rule in 1945 and concluding with the neoliberal capitalism of the twenty-first century. Both films position the 1980s as the crucial transitional period in Korea's postwar history that created Korean society as it exists today.

Chapter 4, "Monsters Within: Moral Ambiguity and Anomie in *Barking Dogs Never Bite* and *Mother*," explores these films' representation of the social effects of Korea's experience of compressed economic growth. The rapid economic growth the nation experienced following the Korean War transformed Korea, in a matter of decades, into an urban, industrialized nation, bringing about great social confusion and disruption of moral values. Both films portray the emotional struggle ordinary Koreans faced with moral dilemmas arising from Korea's adoption of neoliberal policies in the late 1990s. In these films, the socially weak are portrayed not as mere victims of the system but as driven to succumb to moral corruption by their desperate situations. In these films, the line between good and evil is blurred, and the films illustrate the manner in which moral confusion and anomie have intensified in the lives of the individual as a result of the major political, industrial, and financial shifts Korea has experienced in the late twentieth and early twenty-first centuries.

Chapter 5, "Beyond the Local: Global Politics and Neoliberal Capitalism in *Snowpiercer* and *Okja*," situates these two films within the context of global filmmaking and illustrates their radical politics by examining, first, how the train in *Snowpiercer* and the Mirando Corporation in *Okja* symbolize a microcosm of the current neoliberal capitalist system and, second, how the films' transnational appeal can be located in the global expansion of this neoliberalism. The films create a new "political space" Nancy Fraser argues for in order to raise issues of global injustice and inequality as well as environmental issues. The radical politics of the tail section's revolt in *Snowpiercer* is analyzed in terms of Jacque Rancière's redefinition of politics and his notion of the "distribution of the sensible," and *Okja* is analyzed in terms of the relationship between film and activism, focusing on the fact that *Okja* initiated among its audience a movement to go vegan.

Chapter 5 is followed by the conclusion, "*Parasite*—a New Beginning?," and a detailed filmography of all Bong Joon Ho's films. The analysis of his latest film, *Parasite*, offers a wonderfully fitting conclusion to the book as it is at once Bong's return to Korean realities and a departure to a new level of his idiosyncratic approaches to genre filmmaking. The film summons his previous films in various ways but at the same time departs from them in its focus on sociological aspects of emotion, which has been considered as something individual and personal. The film shows how the feelings of humiliation are built up in the poor and the deprived in contemporary Korean society and how they can trigger a total catastrophe in which nobody is a winner. Filmography includes short- and feature-length films Bong directed as well as those he did not direct but produced, wrote, or acted in. Detailed synopses of each film will allow those readers not familiar with them to obtain the necessary information to help follow the analyses in this book.

By grounding the films of Bong Joon Ho securely within the sociopolitical transformation of Korean society since democratization in 1987 and the global expansion of neoliberal capitalism in the twenty-first century, this book aims to illustrate the ways in which his films are reflections of a growing sense of injustice and failure among Koreans in the age of neoliberal globalization, a sentiment global audiences may identify with as well. Films cannot be isolated from the cultural system that generated them. Placing Bong's films in the dual context of the transition from military dictatorship to democracy in Korean history and the simultaneous changes in the Korean film industry will clarify to the non-Korean readers the rich subtext crucial to a full understanding of the films of Bong Joon Ho.

1 · A NEW CULTURAL GENERATION

In 2015, a documentary short made by three high school students caught the attention of the Korean film community, garnering awards at a number of youth and short film festivals. Titled *Searching for Bong Joon Ho*,[1] the film follows these students as they try to meet the filmmaker Bong Joon Ho, whom they idolize. Their almost impossible quest begins when their parents dismiss their dream of becoming filmmakers, given the harsh realities of the Korean film industry. In response, they decide to search for Bong by any means necessary to seek his advice. As the voice-over narration explains, the student filmmakers "go wild at director Bong's films. Wouldn't he be able to give [us] helpful advice, given that he made it big despite the difficult conditions [of the film industry]?" The students use social media, email, and phone calls to reach out to people who have worked with Bong, but most of them refuse to help. Finally, the students are exhilarated when Hong Kyung-pyo, the director of photography who worked with Bong on *Mother* and *Snowpiercer*, helps set up a meeting with him.

This short documentary is noteworthy in two respects. First, it attests to Bong Joon Ho's success and popularity among aspiring filmmakers in Korea. Second, it demonstrates how Bong's approach to filmmaking influences these young filmmakers. Consciously or not, the documentary resembles Bong's films in its playfulness, its conception of the powerless pursuing a seemingly impossible task, and most of all, in its final unexpected twist with a bittersweet ending. They finally succeed in meeting with Bong, but instead of giving the students the support and encouragement they expected, Bong discourages them from pursuing a career in filmmaking.

The students' interview with Bong is oddly funny. When they ask him for any fond memories he had when making his films, he had to stop and think for a moment. Finally, he tepidly offers, "Visiting Korean rural areas was enjoyable."

Then they ask about the hardships he has encountered as a filmmaker, and he replies, "Everything. You can say everything is hard." If, however, they choose to ignore his advice and continue to pursue a filmmaking career, he urges them not to cater to anyone but themselves, to make films that make *them* happy. At the film's end, undeterred, the students are still intent on becoming filmmakers. It turns out that the most encouraging advice came not from Bong Joon Ho but from Hong Kyung-pyo, who was the one to urge them not to give up trying to find Bong from the beginning.

As this student film testifies, Bong Joon Ho has become one of the most significant directors to come out of New Korean Cinema that emerged in the late 1990s. Among the Korean directors who gained national and international recognition, Bong is arguably the only one whose filmmaking is unequivocally commercial and whose name is considered a guarantor of box office success. Bong is both a role model for aspiring filmmakers and a brand that is known and marketed around the world,[2] despite his relatively brief filmography. He has made seven feature films—*Barking Dogs Never Bite* (2000), *Memories of Murder* (2003), *The Host* (2006), *Mother* (2009), *Snowpiercer* (2013), *Okja* (2017), *Parasite* (2019)—and six short films: *White Man* (1993), *Memories of My Frame* (1994), *Incoherence* (1994), *Influenza* (2004), *Sink & Rise* (2004), and *Shaking Tokyo* (2008). With the exception of his debut feature, *Barking Dogs Never Bite*, all his feature films dominated the box office and garnered numerous awards. *The Host* and *Mother* made the Korean Film Archive's 2014 list of the "100 Greatest Korean Films," and *Memories of Murder* ranked seventh in the all-time best ten, the only film released in the 2000s to be included in the list.[3] The critical and commercial success of *The Host, Mother, Snowpiercer, Okja*, and *Parasite* in the United States and elsewhere established Bong's international reputation as one of the most innovative genre filmmakers working today.

As Christina Klein argues, Bong's approach to genre filmmaking is not mere "Copywood" but local interpretations and reinventions of dominant cultural forms.[4] His films exemplify what Arjun Appadurai refers to as a "multiplicity of localized events" that brings different cultures into contact.[5] And this process of cultural hybridization, Homi Bhabha argues, creates something different and new that opens up "a new area of negotiation of meaning and representation."[6] This negotiation includes subversion, transgression, and reformulation. Bong's films are products of diverse cultural influences, and they subvert and reformulate Hollywood genres. By combining elements of different cultures and various film traditions in his work, Bong has opened up new possibilities of creative filmmaking in a postcolonial context.

Specifically, Bong's films demonstrate a new cultural practice of appropriating global genres and film styles to inscribe the local—Koreanness—into them. Bong's filmic world reflects a keen interest in the Korean way of life, local politics, and social systems while unfolding stories about the everyday lives of ordinary Korean citizens, particularly the socially disenfranchised. Bong utilizes local subjects and politics to open up new forms of genre filmmaking that confront and challenge the global force of Hollywood cinema. In so doing, Bong has pioneered a "third space" for world cinema. And in this third space, Bong Joon Ho never relies too much on either Korean or Hollywood styles and themes but always finds a happy middle ground between the two. Of course, as previously stated in the introduction, filmmakers and films do not exist independently of the social conditions and cultural system in which they exist but are in constant interaction or struggle with them within what Pierre Bourdieu terms "the field of cultural production." Conversely, through films, we can read the society and the system that produced both the auteur and his or her films.

What, then, are the internal and external forces that shape Bong Joon Ho's filmic world? What are the material conditions that enable Bong to create blockbuster films? What are the cultural influences that inform his creativity and cultural hybridity? How are we to position his cinema in relation to the politics, cultures, and cinemas of Korea and of the world? This chapter aims to answer these questions by examining the individual and institutional conditions involved in Bong's filmmaking: his formative years as a filmmaker, the significance of the "386 generation" both in Korea's political landscape and its cultural production, the Korean film industry's struggle against Hollywood domination and the subsequent rise of New Korean Cinema, Korea's democratization and achievement of the freedom of expression, and Korea's financial crisis and the implementation of various neoliberal economic policies. Thus while recognizing the creative agency that renders Bong's approach to filmmaking distinct to him, this chapter examines the various conditions—historical, political, social, and cultural—that shaped the structure or social formation within which he has made his films.

This chapter pays particular attention to the diverse and intercultural influences reflected in Bong's films: Hollywood films, European and Asian films, Japanese manga, and the strong tradition of critical or social realism in Korean cinema. Bong represents a new generation of filmmakers who grew up watching Hollywood movies and Japanese cartoons on TV, participated in film clubs in the 1980s and 1990s, and attended film schools. Thus this chapter positions Bong Joon Ho and his films in the context of the rise of New Korean Cinema led by this new generation in the 2000s. It explores the ways in which changes in the Korean film industry gave this group of filmmakers the opportunity to make films that, in turn, brought about the further transformation of the industry and its mode of production while simultaneously putting Korean cinema on a world map.

BONG JOON HO AND FILM AUTHORSHIP

A study on a director inevitably raises the question of authorship in film. The traditional notion of the auteur—the claim that the director is, or should be, the author of his or her films, advanced by young critics of the film journal *Cahiers du cinéma* in 1950s France—has been much contested, especially with respect to the Hollywood studio system, where a director's creative control was limited. Indeed, unlike literary work, cinema is an inherently collaborative enterprise, which makes it difficult to attribute the role of the "author" to one person. However, despite the continuing debate on its validity, auteur or director studies persist. Recent auteur studies have increasingly focused on filmmakers on the margin of mainstream filmmaking, such as women, diasporic, avant-garde, and other non-Hollywood directors. In addition, the scope of the "auteur" has broadened to include producers, screenwriters, stars, and even the Hollywood production system itself.[7] Academic and critical attention has also shifted to reception studies or audience studies that reject the idea that the author is the sole originator of the text's meaning. Increasingly the "author" is considered only one of many voices that create the meaning of texts.[8]

Film authorship then can be thought of in terms of the auteur's agency. Janet Staiger locates this agency in the choices directors make and brings attention to the ways in which subjects in minority positions, such as women, peoples of the LGBTQ community, and people of color, have practiced methods of self-expression that would be described as "'transcending,' 'defamiliarizing,' 'subverting' or 'resisting.'"[9] Seung-hoon Jeong and Jeremi Szaniawki see the need to reassess the film auteur in the age of globalization as the "global auteur," whose authorship is expressed through film directors capturing the zeitgeist. Thus the auteur is an agent who "subjects itself to sociohistorical ideologies, cultural voices, technological conditions through which meaning is motivated, rationalized, mediated or reconstructed between an auteur and an audience."[10] We can say that Bong Joon Ho is a prime example of such an agent.

In addition, Bong can be appropriately examined as an auteur because of the extent to which he maintains control over his work. His nickname, in fact, is Bong-tail, combining Bong Joon Ho and the word *detail*, reflecting his close attention to all aspects of his films. He has written or cowritten all his films and is known for demanding the right to the final cut. In Hollywood, however, directors are not usually given such a right. This is why, unlike Park Chan-wook and Kim Jee-woon, who came to Hollywood to make their first English-language films, Bong turned down offers from Hollywood studios and instead made his first global film, *Snowpiercer*, with funding from the Korean company CJ E&M. However, *Snowpiercer* was not free from Hollywood intervention.

The release of *Snowpiercer* in the United States and other English-language territories was delayed almost a year after its Korean release in July 2013 due to the conflict between Bong and Harvey Weinstein, the American distributor of the film. Weinstein, the owner of the Weinstein Company, requested twenty minutes be cut out because "midwesterners are too stupid to understand the movie as it is."[11] In addition, Weinstein considered adding opening and closing voice-overs for further explanation of the story. Bong was "reportedly furious about the Weinstein English-version cuts."[12] Non-English-speaking countries including France, Taiwan, and Japan had released Bong's original version.

Interestingly, this conflict between Bong and Weinstein sparked an online debate and even a "Free *Snowpiercer*" petition campaign led by a film activist. The petition points out Americans' long anticipation of the film and the film's potential to raise urgent issues to the American society: "social classes and the dangers of elitism."[13] Eventually, an agreement was reached to retain Bong's original version, but it meant forsaking a wide release. The film's distributor was switched to Radius-TWC, a boutique label from the Weinstein Company that releases films on multiplatform video-on-demand (VOD) services and in theaters. The film was finally released in the English-language territories on June 27, 2014, in eight theaters. However, with overwhelmingly positive reviews and word of mouth, the film finally achieved a wide release in more than 150 theaters nationwide. Also, the film was released on VOD two weeks into the theatrical release, making it the first film to be available on streaming service while still playing in theaters. Thus *Snowpiercer* left its mark on the history of online distribution in the United States.

Three years later in 2017, another of Bong Joon Ho's films became the center of controversy, this time on the issue of online streaming services. *Okja*, his first non-Korean film in terms of financing, was met with fierce resistance from local exhibitors in France and Korea. *Okja* was produced as a Netflix original movie. Netflix offered Bong $50 million and total creative freedom, which was important to him. The only restriction was the choice of format. While he wanted to shoot the film in 35 mm, Netflix required that all their original movies be shot and archived in 4K.[14] Thus *Okja* became his first film to be shot on digital. It was also his first film to be invited to the Competition section at Cannes International Film Festival. (Both *The Host* and *Mother* were screened out of competition.) However, *Okja*'s entry prompted protests from French distributors and exhibitors who were furious that Cannes had selected a film that was not set for theatrical release in France. During the premiere screening, the audience booed when the Netflix logo appeared on the screen, although the critical reception of the film was overwhelmingly positive. This incident led the Cannes Festival to issue a new rule that all future competition titles have to be released in French theaters. So unintentionally, Bong Joon Ho's film was at the center of a controversy surrounding the new distribution format of online streaming. It was in a way the price he had to pay in exchange for total creative freedom.

The controversy and uproar did not stop in France. *Okja* was also met with resistance from the Korean theater chains as well. CGV, Lotte Cinema, and Megabox—the top three theater chains in Korea, composing 93 percent of the nation's movie theaters—boycotted *Okja* over the simultaneous release on Netflix, citing that it violates the three-week window between theatrical release and streaming availability.[15] Through his choices, Bong was able to keep his cinematic vision intact; however, in the process, his work demonstrated the tensions created by innovations in film distribution, laying bare the unresolved obstacles to the coexistence of online streaming and theatrical release. He inadvertently stood at the forefront of the new changes in digital distribution. While Netflix provides non-Hollywood filmmakers like Bong the ability to make a studio-quality movie with a creative control not offered by studios, it also limits the film's consumption to primarily laptop screens and home televisions, which is a problem for blockbuster movies like *Okja*.

Bong's growth as an auteur was supported by the change in the industrial climate of the Korean film industry during his formative years. From the mid-1990s to early 2000s, the traditional Korean film industry—known as the Chungmuro, after the name of the street in Seoul where film production companies were concentrated—began to hand over the reins to large conglomerates.[16] Giant corporations such as Samsung and Daewoo set up their own movie business subsidiaries and began investing and producing films. This change would eventually allow individual directors like Bong to plan and produce films by dealing directly with conglomerates for funding.

Furthermore, the French film culture and its notion of the auteur exerted strong influence at the time, creating an environment in which directors are usually given full control over their work. (Hence the impetus for Bong's choice to have *Snowpiercer* produced by a Korean rather than Hollywood studio.) Indeed, in the 1990s, the Korean film industry used auteurism as a strategy to raise its international status. For instance, the Busan International Film Festival, which was launched in 1996 and has contributed to bringing international attention to Korean cinema, is deliberately and consciously director centric. Indeed, the rise of New Korean Cinema is attributable to this strategy of making the director the center of creativity in film.

BONG JOON HO AND NEW KOREAN CINEMA

The start of Bong Joon Ho's film career coincides with the emergence of New Korean Cinema, which burst onto international movie screens in the new millennium. Yet of all these films, the most popular one in the 2000s was, by far,

The Host (2006). The film broke records in Korea and also struck it big internationally with serious movie fans and cult audiences alike. While the film works marvelously as both a horror film and a black comedy, a sociopolitical agenda is clearly visible beneath the waves of the monster's watery home. Just what that agenda is—how the film responds to Korean-U.S. relations, the image of the Korean military, and family and generational conflicts—may seem a bit murky to non-Korean audiences; nevertheless, it was an international breakthrough film for the young Bong Joon Ho. It is symbolic that Bong's first feature film, *Barking Dogs Never Bite*, was released in 2000, the year that celebrated the new millennium. It was as if to announce that Bong is going to become one of the leading lights of New Korean Cinema. Indeed, Bong's trajectory corresponds to the success story of the Korean cinema itself.

The changes the Korean film industry was going through since the mid-1990s were revolutionary in all aspects. The production system, government policies, and the mode of distribution and exhibition underwent a drastic shift; new film media, especially film magazines, attracted new readers and film audiences; and international film festivals boomed. The artistic and technological quality of the films were greatly improved as well. This period is often referred to as the "renaissance of Korean cinema," following a dark period from the 1970s to the 1980s in which Korean cinema suffered heavy political censorship under military dictatorship. The renaissance of Korean cinema was spearheaded by a new generation of filmmakers, including producers, directors, cinematographers, production designers, and so on. They constituted the first generation of film school graduates, technically sophisticated with new cinephile sensibilities.

Described by Chris Berry as a "full service cinema," the Korean film industry achieved success in a "full range of modes of production and consumption."[17] Art films began making a mark in international film circuits, while the commercial films, so-called Korean-style blockbusters, were having huge success in the domestic market. The share of home-produced films in the domestic market was a mere 15.9 percent in 1993, but it rose to more than 50–60 percent in the twenty-first century.[18] Korea remains one of the few nations whose home-produced films dominate over Hollywood films in the domestic market. The rise of this New Korean Cinema was made possible by Korea's achievement of democracy in the early 1990s, which in turn freed filmmakers from the political censorship that plagued the industry during the 1970s and 1980s. Film censorship was deemed unconstitutional by a Constitutional Court of Korea ruling in 1996. This freedom of expression opened the door for the creative power of a new generation of filmmakers to explode on to the world scene, and Bong is one of them, arguably the most successful filmmaker to emerge from this newly found freedom.

The term *New Korean Cinema* refers to the creative and commercial resurgence Korean cinema experienced during the late 1990s and early 2000s.[19] It ushered in the "renaissance of Korean cinema" on both the domestic and the international level. In Korean context, the terms *Korean New Wave* and *New Korean Cinema* are used to indicate two separate periods and two distinct film styles, although the latter inherits the former's legacy of critical realism or social realism. Korean New Wave cinema's period roughly falls between 1988, when Park Kwang-su's debut feature, *Chilsu and Mansu* (*Chilsu wa Mansu*), was released, and 1995, when Park released his fifth feature film, *A Single Spark* (*Aleumda-un cheongnyeon Jeon Taeil*). Korean New Wave films were much more politically oriented, whereas New Korean Cinema was focused more on commercial viability and transnational appeal. While Korean New Wave films dealt with social issues, New Korean Cinema was prompted by the idea of borrowing Hollywood's concept of blockbuster and localizing it in order to win back the audience from the massive onslaught of Hollywood blockbusters.

The filmmakers of Korean New Wave, such as Park Kwang-su, Jang Sun-woo, and others who were born in the 1950s, suffered under harsh political censorship; however, the filmmakers of New Korean Cinema were free from such restrictions. Also, while the Korean New Wave filmmakers were inspired by the prodemocratic political movement and the underground independent film movement of the 1980s, New Korean Cinema filmmakers were the first cinephile generation of filmmakers in Korea who were inspired by Hollywood genre movies and art cinema of Europe and Asia. For Korean New Wave filmmakers, cinema was an art for social critique and a tool for social change; for New Korean Cinema filmmakers, it was more of an entertainment and self-expression. Bong Joon Ho's films are significant in that they merge the two different approaches to filmmaking: the commercial entertainment aspect of cinema and the social commentary on injustices and social ills.

With the onset of the financial crisis in 1997, the Korean film industry was faced with numerous challenges that threatened its foundation. First of all, conglomerates began to exit from the film industry, shutting down their film-related wings, which caused the film industry to face its own financial crisis. To make matters worse, in the following year, the 1998 bilateral trade agreement (BIT) between Korea and the United States posed a serious threat to the screen quota system. The United States demanded the elimination of the system in exchange for more imports of Korean products such as cars and electronics into the U.S. market. Typically, a screen quota system is a legislative measure for governments to protect their domestic film industry. It requires every screen to set aside a certain number of days to domestic films so that foreign films—mostly Hollywood—do not dominate the theaters. At the time, every screen was required to show Korean films up to 146 days a year.

This threat to eliminate the screen quota was palpable to the Korean film community. It was truly a life-and-death problem. A massive resistance ensued.

Major filmmakers even shaved their heads in protest to the government's disregard for the cultural value of cinema. In December 1998, the Screen Quota Emergency Committee was formed, encompassing "various groups in and out of the Korean film industry: mainstream filmmakers, producers, KIFA [Korean Independent Film Association], Screen Quota Watchers, and numerous civil movement organizations."[20] This committee led the massive protests against the elimination of the screen quota system in 1998 and 1999. This strong resistance succeeded in pressuring the Korean government to take the screen quota negotiation off the table, although eventually it was reduced to seventy-three days per year in 2006.

The sense of urgency surrounding the screen quota struggle stimulated the Korean film community to devise ways to survive and possibly win back the audience from Hollywood domination. Filmmakers and critics were actively discussing what would be the best way to bring about the resurgence of Korean cinema. Should they follow the auteur-centered European model and make their mark in the international film festivals? Should they adopt more Hollywood-like commercial films? How could they compete with the big-budget Hollywood blockbusters? They cannot compete in terms of budget, so it should be something that only the Korean film community can produce. The resulting idea was what is referred to as the "Korean-style blockbuster," the idea that they should adopt the Hollywood style of narrative structure that audiences are familiar with but make stories that are uniquely Korean.

A new generation of producers was at the forefront of creating and establishing the Korean-style blockbuster. The first films of this style were *Shiri* (1999) and *JSA* (*Joint Security Area*, 2000). *Shiri* broke the local box-office record set by *Titanic* the year before, selling 2.43 million tickets. A year later, *JSA* set another record, with 5.89 million ticket sales. Considering the basic concept of the Korean-style blockbuster as telling specifically Korean stories with Hollywood language, it is no coincidence that both *Shiri* and *JSA* dealt with tragedies caused by the national division between South and North Korea since 1948. However, the two films differed in their approaches to adapting the Hollywood blockbuster style and their depiction of North Koreans. Directed by Kang Je-kyu, *Shiri* was a political thriller about a North Korean terrorist organization infiltrating South Korea during a jointly sponsored soccer match between South and North Korea teams in Seoul. At the center of this terrorist threat lies the tragic love story between a South Korean intelligence agent and a North Korean sniper disguised as a civilian. The style of the film is fairly conventional, following the model of Hollywood action thrillers like *The Rock* (1996), for example, with North Koreans as the antagonist.

Alternatively, *JSA*, which was directed by Park Chan-wook, was the first film to depict North Koreans in a sympathetic light. Since the national division, the

South Korean government held a harsh anticommunist stance; therefore, media depictions of North Koreans were always evil. However, *JSA*, which tells a story of a forbidden friendship between Korean soldiers within the demilitarized zone, depicted both sides as the victims of the ideological divide. The film was made possible by the thaw between South and North Korea, with South Korean president Kim Dae-jung and North Korean president Kim Jong-il having the first summit meeting in Pyongyang, North Korea, in June 2000. Thus the film was a product of the time, which is in line with the concept of the Korean-style blockbuster.

The Korean film industry's openness to and successful localization of the blockbuster to address local issues seems to be related to Korea's postcolonial situation, which is different from those of Latin America and Africa. Korea was colonized by Japan, not the West; therefore, it was Japanese culture that had been banned in Korea until the late 1980s. After the liberation from Japan in 1945, American culture rapidly replaced Japanese culture in Korea. The Americanization of the Korean culture soon took place, while all things Japanese were considered suspicious. Korean people had more access to American culture and values than to Japanese or even Chinese cultures, since China was a communist nation vilified by Korean governments. There had been no cultural exchange between Korea and China until 1992, when Korea established diplomatic relations with China. Thus Korea was less resistant to Western culture—in particular, American culture and Hollywood movies. They were not something to overcome but to emulate and adopt in order to draw audiences to local products. Whether Korean-style blockbusters remain a mere "colonial mimicry"[21] or are creating a "third space" is open for debate; however, it is safe to say that Bong Joon Ho's films represent the cultural hybridization that creates a third space in which new forms of cultural production and meaning are created and the identity of Koreanness is negotiated. They adopt the Hollywood language in order to resist mere mimicry and to localize issues for the Korean audience.

While Korean blockbusters led the resurgence of the local film industry's share of the domestic market to an unprecedented level (53.5 percent in 2003), the auteur-centered art films were making their waves in international film festivals. As was briefly mentioned previously, making auteur cinema was discussed among the new generation of filmmakers as another strategy to revive the failing Korean film industry. The central idea was that since it is almost impossible to compete with Hollywood in the commercial realm, Korean cinema should concentrate on producing auteur films to elevate their artistic quality and international reputation in the film festival circuit.[22]

The cultural influences that shaped Korean cinema were indeed a mixture of elements. The new generation of cinephile filmmakers grew up mostly watching Hollywood movies on TV; however, the French New Wave and its notion of the auteur were equally influential, if not more so, especially among the young film critics who were as much involved in the resurgence of Korean cinema as the young filmmakers were. During the 1970s and especially in the 1980s under the military regime, film culture in Korea was almost nonexistent. Theatrical releases of foreign films were limited, and most of the Korean films were either adaptations of literary classics or soft porn films, often referred to as "hostess films." Therefore, many young people interested in film went to screenings held in the French Cultural Center and the German Goethe Institute in the city of Seoul. French New Wave films shown at the French Cultural Center left a lasting impact on this new generation, making the French term *nouvelle vague* the talk of the town. Accordingly, in contrast to the Hollywood mode of production, the Korean film industry tends to give established directors full control over their work, although recently, more and more directors are hired by the production company.

Thus the notion of the Korean-style blockbuster and the emphasis on the director as the auteur are crucial in positioning Bong Joon Ho and his films within New Korean Cinema. He has a strong sense of himself as the auteur of his films, writing the screenplay and having the right of final cut for his films. While other filmmakers of New Korean Cinema—such as Hong Sang-soo, Kim Ki-duk, Park Chan-wook, Lee Chang-dong, and so on—make more auteur-oriented art films that appeal to more sophisticated film viewers and circulate in the international film festival circuit, Bong Joon Ho, together with Kim Jee-woon, make blockbuster genre films with a strong sense of authorship. Bong's third feature film, *The Host*, is a great example of the Korean-style blockbuster film in terms of both its production value and its huge box-office success. It sold over thirteen million tickets, smashing the all-time box-office record.

THE 386 GENERATION AND NEW CULTURAL SENSIBILITIES

Born on September 14, 1969, Bong Joon Ho belongs to the tail end of the 386 generation. This term was coined in the late 1990s to refer to the generation who was at the time in their thirties (3), had entered college in the 1980s (8), and was born in the 1960s (6). This generation left a distinct mark in contemporary Korean history with their crucial role in the 1980s democratization movement, which brought an end to the twenty-seven years of military dictatorship. And they are the first generation since the Korean War who has studied Marxism and Leninism through underground groups in college, aspiring to liberate workers and peasants from exploitation, even though all Marxist writings were banned during the military dictatorship.

Because of their unique historical experience of this political resistance, risking imprisonment and torture under the draconian military regime, the members of the 386 generation tend to share a strong sense of social justice and freedom as well as a keen interest in class issues. The 1980s antidictatorship struggle was the catalyst for the emergence of this new political and social generation, which was comparable to the May 1968 generation in France. As a "social generation"—to use Karl Mannheim's term—they were significantly influenced by a particular historical event in which they were actively involved during their youth, and in turn, they exerted influence on the political and cultural events that shape the future generations.[23] Cinema was no exception, as it was mostly 386 generation filmmakers such as Park Chan-wook, Kim Jee-woon, Im Sang-soo, and Bong Joon Ho who led the renaissance of Korean cinema in the late 1990s onward.

Bong entered Yonsei University in 1988, a year after the parliamentary democracy was achieved through the intense 1987 June Democratic Uprising. This meant that the student activism and political protests became less central to college life, although Bong participated in student demonstrations against the newly elected Roh Tae-woo administration, which, although elected by direct vote, still represented a continued military regime. Bong also had participated in the June 1987 uprising as a high school student. He was a socially conscious student, and in the summer of 1990, he was arrested for using a Molotov cocktail during a protest organized by the Korean Teachers and Education Workers Union.[24]

While less intense student protests continued during his college years, the 1988 Seoul Summer Olympics brought with it some revised cultural policies by the government. The overseas travel ban was lifted in 1989 (previously, only those who obtained government approval could travel outside Korea), and the publication ban on the works by writers and poets who voluntarily or involuntarily chose to stay in North Korea after the Korean War was lifted in 1988. And between 1998 and 2004, the Korean government gradually lifted the ban on the importation of Japanese popular culture.

Following the liberation from Japanese colonialism in August 1945, the Korean government restricted and regulated the import of Japanese pop culture in order to revive and protect the Korean language and culture, which had been nearly destroyed by Japan's harsh assimilation policy during the 1930s and 1940s. The ban on Japanese pop culture was also in consideration of the people's harsh feelings toward Japan. Japanese cinema and songs were banned from TV network broadcast until 1998, when the government took the first measure to open up the market. In 1998, the ban was lifted for manga and for films that won awards from prestigious international film festivals; in 1999, stage performances of Japanese songs were allowed, and the scope of films that could be released expanded; in 2000, Japanese video games, TV broadcasts of sports, documentaries, and news broadcasts were allowed, as was the importation of anime for theatrical showings; and finally in 2004, all restrictions were lifted on films and sales of CDs and cassette tapes of songs. The ban on Japanese popular culture is now a thing of the past in Korea.

Thus unlike the 386 generation, those born in the 1970s and 1980s were exposed to a more diverse and hybrid cultural experience. While the 386 generation is more influenced by the political movement of the 1980s, those born in the 1970s had a more culturally rich experience in the postdemocratic Korea. Indeed, the 1990s saw an explosion of popular culture both in terms of production and consumption. The 386 generation's energy and enthusiasm for political activism had now transferred to an enthusiasm for popular culture—in particular, for cinema. It opened a new era of "film mania." The weekly *Cine 21* became a must-read film magazine for film buffs, and the monthly *Kino* attracted more sophisticated film audiences with in-depth analyses and introductions of films and film history. International film festivals were launched starting with the Busan International Film Festival in 1996, followed by Bucheon International Fantastic Film Festival and Seoul International Women's Film Festival in 1997 and Jeonju International Film Festival in 2000. These festivals introduced films from around the world to Korean audiences and at the same time exposed previously little-known Korean films and filmmakers to the international festival circuit.

Bong Joon Ho's films have elements taken from what the 386 generation represented, such as their particular attention to the socially weak, and his critical stance toward authorities and the United States is evident in his films—in particular, *Memories of Murder* and *The Host*. His strong sense of social justice and political commitment can also be attributed to the characteristics of the 386 generation. However, at the same time, it is equally important to point out the ways in which Bong Joon Ho differs from them, especially in terms of cultural influences. Bong's cultural experience was closer to that of those born in the 1970s, who benefited from the cultural freedom resulting from the political changes of the late 1980s. Bong stands between the "political" generation and more "cultural generation," thus being in a position to meld the political with the cultural in his films.

One distinct factor that separates this later generation from the 386 generation is a love for Japanese subculture, especially manga and anime. In fact, those born in the 1970s form the first *otaku* generation in Korea.[25] It is well known through numerous interviews Bong gave that he is an avid fan of Japanese manga, and we can observe its influence in his films.[26] In particular, *Barking Dogs Never Bite* manifests comic-book-inspired fantasy scenes and characters with exaggerated actions.

FORMATIVE YEARS

From early on, Bong dreamed of becoming a film director. In his 2014 essay "Never Even Imagined of Doing Different Work," he writes that it was the only job he ever wanted.[27] From a young age, Bong watched almost all the films that were shown on TV. He says in an interview, "I saw Henri-Georges Clouzot's *The Wages of Fear* (1953) on TV when I was in elementary school. I was fascinated by its crazily intense tension. So I decided to become a filmmaker then."[28] Bong's experience of becoming a film buff is significant in that it reflects the similar trajectory of many young people in his generation who were "film maniacs" and led the nationwide cinema fervor of the 1990s into the new millennium.

Although he is the first one to work in film, Bong comes from an artistic family. His father was a professor of graphic design who had a library of foreign design books in his study at home. An introvert, Bong spent most of his time looking at these books. He also liked to draw comics. His mother was an elementary school teacher who retired to become a full-time mother when she had her first child.[29] His mother was the second daughter of Park Tae-won, one of the leading figures of modern Korean literature during the Japanese colonial period. One of his greatest novels, *Ch'ŏnbyŏnp'unggyŏng* (*Scenes from Ch'onggye Stream, 1936*), sketches a collage of the daily lives of seventy ordinary people living around the Ch'onggye Stream in Seoul. Park was a modernist in his formal experiments but a realist in capturing the daily lives of the people living in the period of transition from the rural to the urban. His works were banned in Korea until 1988 because he voluntarily chose North Korea during the Korean War. In the postwar period, writers and other artists who chose North Korea over South Korea became taboo.

Not only were the works of these writers banned, but the remaining families in South Korea were disadvantaged due to the guilt-by-association system. Park Tae-won lived as a prominent writer in North Korea, producing epic historical novels until his death in 1986. However, when I asked Bong about his maternal grandfather, he replied that he was not too aware of his presence in the north, nor did he read his works. The first time he remembers the family members talking about his grandfather was when the government lifted the ban on his work. He remembers that the adult members of the family discussed the royalties from the sales of his newly published works. Recently, when his uncle published a book about his grandfather, Bong wrote on the back cover, "People who major in literature will read this book because of their curiosity on the 'novelist Park Tae-won,' but for me, this is just a story about my maternal grandfather."[30] Bong is not directly influenced by his grandfather or his work; however, he is like his

FIGURE 1. Bong Joon Ho (*Cine 21*).

grandfather in his keen observation of the lives of everyday people. The difference is his grandfather was a writer, and Bong is a filmmaker.

In addition to drawing comics since childhood, when he entered middle school, Bong began collecting film magazines such as *Screen* and *Roadshow*. From these publications, he came to know Hitchcock and other directors. He studied film through reading the articles. And he watched films voraciously. It was during a time when an increasing number of young people became interested in films as more than just entertainment. Translations of film books began to be published. Louis Giannetti's *Understanding Movies* and Jack C. Ellis's *History of Film* published in 1988 were the first scholarly film books translated into Korean. The two books became kind of bibles for young film lovers, who were at the same time beginning to see a variety of movies thanks to the introduction of VHS home video.

It appears that everyone interested in cinema read these books, including Bong, who was able to read Giannetti's book even before it was available in bookstores thanks to his elder brother, who was one of the uncredited translators of the book. It was through his brother and his translation work that Bong Joon Ho learned for the first time such cinematic terms as *mise-en-scène*. He obsessively watched the films shown on TV, which included both Hollywood movies and European art films. AFKN (American Forces Korean Network) was a movie haven for the teenage Bong. He would watch movies on the channel by himself at midnight, when all other family members were in bed. The films he watched included B movies by John Carpenter and Brian De Palma as well as Hammer Film Productions' horror movies and blaxploitation films.[31] He did not understand the English dialogue, so he would create his own version of the narrative as he watched the films. Viewing films in a language he did not understand stimulated his imagination and visual storytelling. And he watched the same films again and again and analyzed the scenes on his own.

Bong decided to major in sociology rather than film production in college. Perhaps this also has to do with his good academic record, which allowed him to enter one of the top universities in the nation.[32] At the time, the top universities in Korea did not have film programs. But at the same time, he was afraid to apply to the theater and film program because he thought he had to have a special talent. And the fact that the best filmmakers of the time did not major in film reassured him to study sociology. He thought he would actively participate in a film club instead. As his aforementioned 2004 essay chronicles, he spent his college days more like a film studies major, since he devoted much of his time studying film outside of school. While he took two years off from college in order to perform his mandatory military service, he took a film studies course at a place called Film Space 1895, which ran a program called Twenty-Four-Hour Film School. Here, Bong took a course that taught David Bordwell and Kristin

Thompson's book *Film Art*. Film Space 1895 was formed and run by the new generation of film critics, including Lee Yong-kwan and Jeon Yang-joon.

Bong returned to college in 1993 and formed a film club, Yellow Door (*Noranmoon*),[33] with two other students. He spent more time watching films at the film club than studying sociology in the classroom. Having watched many third-world films in Yellow Door, Bong wrote his undergraduate sociology thesis on third-world cinema and political ideology. In fact, he was worried about graduating because he was so concentrated in film and filmmaking, he had neglected to study sociology. But fortunately for him, his proposal to write about third-world cinema in his thesis was approved. During the 1980s, it was common for college students to choose sociology for their major because of their interest in the social structure of Korean society; however, it was unusual for a college student to write a thesis on cinema.

Bong prepared himself well to pursue filmmaking during his college years. He describes his activities at Yellow Door as the "most important turning point in [his] whole life."[34] He shot his first short film, *White Man* (*Paeksaegin*, 1993), with the club members. Later, he submitted this short film to the Korean Academy of Film Arts (KAFA) and was accepted. KAFA is a one-year film production program run by the Korean Film Council. His thesis film, *Incoherence* (*Chirimyŏllyŏl*, 1994), received much attention from the Korean film community and opened the door for him. He also met his future wife at the film club.

Bong led the directing subcommittee of Yellow Door. The members would watch a film and then would analyze shots and sequence structures. For example, if the theme of the week was murder, they would analyze murder scenes from such films as *The Godfather* (1972) and *The Silence of the Lambs* (1991). In his essay, he also writes about his "hidden" debut film. It was made before his official first film, *White Man*, and was titled *Looking for Paradise*. It was a twenty-minute stop-motion animated short using a gorilla doll. He writes that at the time, his only dilemma was whether he wanted to make live-action films or animation in the future. But when he learned from his experience that three days' worth of work only resulted in ten seconds of animation, the choice became clear.

KAFA played a crucial role not only in Bong's career but also in the emergence of New Korean Cinema. Established in 1984 by the government-sponsored Korean Film Council as the cradle for training film professionals, KAFA had an important role in the early 1990s as a link between would-be filmmakers and the Chungmuro. Modeled after the American Film Institute (AFI), KAFA provided a one-year course for filmmaking. The tuition was free when Bong attended. KAFA graduates became the central force in modernizing the Korean film industry and innovating filming techniques. Not only directors but also many of the new generation of cinematographers were KAFA graduates. One of the leading cinematographers is Kim Hyung Koo who worked with Bong Joon Ho on

Memories of Murder and *The Host*. Upon graduating KAFA, Kim went to California to earn a master of fine arts in cinematography from AFI. Kim explains that what he learned from film schools was the concept of the DP (director of photography). Previously in the Korean film industry, the cinematographer was considered a technician; however, the notion of the DP allowed Kim to rethink the role of cinematographer, who has to consider not only the photography but also the lighting and other elements for visual expression. The role of the DP taught him to take a holistic approach to shooting a film.[35]

Until the mid-1990s, the Korean film industry relied on an apprentice system, and thus it was difficult to break into the field for those who did not have connections and those who did not study film production in college. KAFA opened the door for these people by providing a network as well as professional training. The shift from the apprenticeship system to film school education helped improve the technical expertise of the filmmakers. It also gave film school graduates "the opportunity to showcase their talent through short films."[36] For Bong also, it was his short films (*White Man* and *Incoherence*) that opened the door to enter the Korean film industry.

White Man is an eighteen-minute, 16 mm film he made during his Yellow Door film club years. The title comes from the word *white collar*, since the protagonist (his name is Hakrak in the script, although it is never said in the actual film) is a yuppie. The film has almost no dialogue, and the plot is conveyed through the news on the TV. Although the filmic techniques are less refined, the film already shows the seeds of the major traits that would characterize his later feature films: his eccentric sense of humor and imagination; his concern for the socially weak (in this case, a blue-collar worker); and his social commentary on injustice, hypocrisy, and apathy toward the marginalized.

After graduating from KAFA in 1995, Bong was idle for a while. But he had a fateful meeting with Park Chan-wook. Park, who was impressed by *White Man*, contacted Bong. They met, and Park suggested Bong write the screenplay for his second feature film. The project did not work out, but through Park, Bong made the acquaintance of other filmmakers who would later become major directors of New Korean Cinema, including Ryoo Seung-wan and Yim Pil-sung.

Meanwhile, his thesis film, *Incoherence*, received its first public screening in May 1993 at the Seoul Film Festival organized by *Cine 21*. It was then invited to the Vancouver International Film Festival. Most importantly, the film led him to meet Tcha Sung-jai, who would become the producer of his first feature film, *Barking Dogs Never Bite* (2000), as well as his follow-up, *Memories of Murder* (2003). Tcha was the leading figure of the new generation of film producers at the time and was looking for new talent. He had liked *Incoherence* and another KAFA thesis film *2001 Imagine* by Jang Joon-hwan, for which Bong Joon Ho was the cinematographer. *Incoherence* is a social satire that mocks intellectuals' hypocrisy, a theme that would consistently appear in his later films, and displays Bong's offbeat sense of humor and satire and his biting social critique of the establishment.

Before making his debut feature, Bong worked on three films as either a directing assistant or a screenwriter. The first film he joined as a crew member was an omnibus film, *7 Reasons Why Beer Is Better Than a Lover* (1996). Seven well-established directors participated in this comedy film, each making a fifteen-minute segment about beer. However, the film was a box-office flop and received harsh criticism for its dirty jokes and misogyny. It was even selected as the worst film of the year by female audiences. Bong confesses that he was thrilled to be on set for the first time but felt ashamed to be part of such a film.[37] He dreaded going to the set and did not go to the theater when it was released.

After *7 Reasons Why Beer Is Better Than a Lover*, Bong joined director Park Ki-yong's *Motel Cactus* (1997) as the first assistant director. The film was produced by Tcha Sung-jai, the first film they worked on together. Bong also wrote the screenplay for director Min Byung-chun's *Phantom, the Submarine* (1999), Tcha's next project. *Motel Cactus* is experimental in its narrative structure and style, consisting of four episodes of different couples having sex in the titular motel. It was shot by Christopher Doyle, a frequent collaborator of the Hong Kong filmmaker Wong Kar-wai. On the other hand, *Phantom, the Submarine* was a conventional genre film for which Bong was one of three writers given two core narrative elements to work with: "There should be a submarine, and Japan should be included in the story."[38] They were asked to write the script as a war genre. It was the first submarine film in Korea's history, and it dealt with mutiny within the submarine. The conflict was built around a plan by an ultranationalist lieutenant to attack Japan with nuclear weapons. The film was released in the same year as *Shiri* and embodied the idea of the Korean-style blockbuster; however, it did not succeed at the box office.

As merely a hired screenwriter, Bong did not have any creative freedom. However, this experience was beneficial to his own filmmaking. He learned that the scriptwriting stage was crucial and that much of the preparation is done before the actual shooting. The seed for meticulous preproduction Bong is known for was sown at this early stage of his career.

After working with Tcha for five years, Bong was given an opportunity to make his own feature. From 1995 to 2000, many important changes took place in the Korean film industry that paved the way for the rise of New Korean Cinema. Pusan (now Busan) International Film Festival was launched in 1996 as the first of its kind to be held in Korea, film magazines *Cine 21* and *Kino* were founded, and many films by first-time directors were released and made a big mark with their new approaches to filmmaking. They included Hong Sang-soo's *The Day a Pig Fell into the Well* (1996), Kim Ki-duk's *Crocodile* (1996), Yim Soon-rye's

Three Friends (1996), Hur Jin-ho's *Christmas in August* (1998), Kim Jee-woon's *A Quiet Family* (1998), E J-yong's *An Affair* (1998), and Jang Jin's *The Happenings* (1998). They were diverse films, but all shared the spirit of experiment and innovation. They were different from the conventional mainstream Chungmuro films and more modern in their approach.

It was in this wave of changes[39] that Bong made *Barking Dogs Never Bite*. It was also an unconventional film with offbeat black humor. It was misunderstood by film critics at the time of release and was a flop at the box office as well. It was criticized for its odd sense of humor and unappealing characters. It was an unexpected outcome, since Bong was well known and had critical success with his short films. *Incoherence* was praised enthusiastically by critics and filmmakers alike and was invited to many film festivals. Thus the anticipation for his first feature was very high, making its critical and commercial failure all the more acutely felt. However, at the end of the year, *Cine 21* ran an article about the films that were misunderstood, and *Barking Dogs Never Bite* was reassessed by critics as representing the new generation's distinctive imagination and sensibility. Nevertheless, the failure of his first film was a big blow to Bong, who had been facing a dilemma about what kind of films he should pursue: the mainstream Chungmuro movie or the low-budget independent film. However, his dilemma was solved when he accepted Tcha Sung-jai's offer to produce a second feature, *Memories of Murder*.

Barking Dogs Never Bite taught him an important lesson that he followed in subsequent films: the need to make more clearly definable genre films. One of the difficulties *Barking Dogs Never Bite* faced upon its release was its marketing. Since it could not be pinned down to one genre, marketing had problems promoting it. Bong realized that in order to be successful, the film needs to be based on a genre, although his films would still deviate from mainstream genre conventions. This incident also demonstrated that Bong was a filmmaker who wanted to meet a larger audience; he wanted to make films within the commercial realm. *Memories of Murder*, then, was a huge success both critically and commercially, thus elevating Bong to a position as one of the most prominent young filmmakers in Korea. *Memories of Murder* also established one of his signature elements—humor. For Bong, humor was an excellent tool to maintain a critical distance toward conventional genre films and to deconstruct genre conventions. And one of the ways to incorporate humor in his films was to have a socially weak loser character as the protagonist. These unconventional loser characters taking on the serious job of police investigators provided ample opportunities for humor. *Memories of Murder*, *The Host*, and *Mother* all share this trait.

The late 1990s to mid-2000s were euphoric for the new generation of filmmakers to realize their new ideas about film without the harsh censorship that destroyed the creative energy of previous generations. Furthermore, they were far luckier than the generation that followed them. It is no exaggeration to say that by the second decade of the twenty-first century, in which blockbuster film-making has become the norm, that a midbudget film like *Memories of Murder* would have less chance to be greenlighted. In this climate, it would be unlikely that a filmmaker whose debut feature was a box office flop—like *Barking Dogs Never Bite*—would ever be given a second chance at feature filmmaking. Addi-tionally, a genre film whose story ends in failure is a risky project for producers to undertake. Thus Bong Joon Ho belongs to a generation of filmmakers who was lucky to have emerged during this period in Korean film history.

Bong's films exemplify the ways in which hybridity makes a contribution to cultural creation. Although culture, especially film and popular culture, is inher-ently transnational and hybrid in its nature, in the case of Korea, the melding of different cultures was intensified by its geopolitical and historical situation. As previously discussed, unlike other postcolonial nations such as those in Latin America and Africa, Korea had less resistance to Western pop culture because it was colonized by Japan, not the West. Thus adopting the notion of blockbusters and genres from Hollywood had less resistance in terms of the politics of adapta-tion. During the brief period in the 1980s when anti-American sentiment rose in the wake of the Kwangju Massacre and subsequent antidictatorship protests, Korea was nevertheless more open to Hollywood and American popular culture than that of Japan. The rise of New Korean Cinema in the 2000s was, in large part, an adoption and reappropriation of Hollywood's system and style.

HYBRID CULTURAL REFERENCES

Bong Joon Ho's filmic approach can be described as a "melting pot" of diverse cultural and cinematic influences. Hollywood movies, European art films, Asian art films, Japanese films, and manga and anime styles all come together in his films. The critical realism of the 1960s golden age of Korean cinema is also felt in his critical stance toward and realistic depiction of the social *pujoris* of Korean society. In particular, Bong considers director Kim Ki-young's 1960 film *The Housemaid* as one of the films that inspired and influenced him. Kim stood out during the 1960s as a filmmaker who made eccentric and intense psychosex-ual melodramas when the dominant trend in Korean cinema was critical real-ism films such as *Stray Bullet* (1961) and *A Coachman* (1961), which showed the influence of Italian neorealism. His films were more expressionist in style, but they captured the changes Korean society was experiencing in the postwar period, especially *The Housemaid*, which focused on the story of a middle-class family slowly being destroyed by their housemaid, a femme fatale who seduces the master of the household. During that time, most middle-class households had a young housemaid who was sent by her poor parents in the rural area to serve the more well-to-do in the city. It is well documented that the women in the audience yelled at the housemaid character in Kim's film because the story felt so real. Kim based his story on a newspaper article that reported the murder of a toddler committed by a housemaid. His keen observations into the core of Korean society and the sharp social commentary woven into a commercial genre anticipate Bong Joon Ho's approach to filmmaking. Bong paid direct homage to Kim in *Parasite*, which also deals with class issues set in a two-story house.

It is noteworthy that his cultural influences are mostly from visual media such as films, manga, and cartoons rather than, for instance, literature. *Barking Dogs Never Bite* includes several scenes that manifest comic book sensibilities, while its Korean title, *P'ŭllandasŭŭi Kae* (*A Dog of Flanders*), is borrowed from a very popular TV cartoon series. The story of the film has nothing to do with that of the cartoon, since the cartoon is about the friendship between a poor boy and a dog, but there is a reference to the show in a karaoke scene in which female protagonist Hyun-nam sings the cartoon's theme song.

Snowpiercer is based on a French graphic novel. However, Bong mentions in many interviews that he was inspired by another popular TV cartoon series, *Galaxy Express 999*, which captured the imagination of Bong's generation when it ran on TV for a year beginning in January 1982. *Galaxy Express 999* is a Japanese cartoon series based on the manga of the same name, written and drawn by Leiji Matsumoto, but most Korean children watched it thinking it was a Korean cartoon. During this time, Japanese cartoons dominated children's TV programs, but they were dubbed in Korean and had no reference to their creators. Bong developed a fascination for trains through this series and thought that he would make a film about them one day.

He also drew inspiration for *Okja* from another TV cartoon series titled *Future Boy Conan* (the directorial debut of famed animator Miyazaki Hayao), a postapocalyptic science fiction story that ran on Korean network television from 1982 to 1983 and was rerun in 1994 and 1996.[40] *Future Boy Conan* is an adaptation of Alexander Key's novel *The Incredible Tide* (1970), which is set in a not-so-distant future when humankind is on the verge of extinction by the devastating war between two nations that are using ultramagnetic weapons. The protagonist, Conan, is an eleven-year-old boy who brings a new hope to humanity. In the beginning of the story, Conan meets a girl named Lana, whom he rescues from captivity, and thus begins their adventure. In the *Okja* press conference at Cannes in 2017, Bong explained that he wanted to make a "girl version of *Future Boy Conan*." The almost supernatural power and action Mija exhibits in the film to save Okja is inspired by the character of Conan and his exceptional physical ability.[41]

As these examples show, the influence of Japanese subculture looms large in Bong's creative sensibilities, and his debut in 2000 signals the appearance of a new generation of filmmakers for whom comic books and anime offer strong influences on their creative work. Yet Bong is equally if not more influenced by Hollywood films, especially those of the 1970s. As mentioned previously, Bong watched American films on AFKN. He would watch into the late night, even in his middle school and high school days. He was especially drawn to the films of the American New Wave period. This is befitting since the films of this period have narrative structures and strategies that subvert the classical genre conventions and contain social and political commentaries on American society. Thomas Elsaesser summarizes the 1970s American films as manifesting the "pathos of failure," where the heroes lack motives and the films' "liberal outlook, their unsentimental approach to American society makes them reject personal initiatives and purposive affirmation on the level of ideology, a rejection which has rendered problematic the dramaturgy and film-language developed by classical Hollywood within the context of a can-do culture."[42] This description very much describes Bong's approach to reappropriating Hollywood genres to the realities of Korean society.

Since childhood, Bong loved to draw comics. He expressed in numerous interviews that had he not become a filmmaker, he would have become a professional cartoonist, and he still holds that aspiration. In college, he drew editorial cartoons for the college newspaper as a part-time job. It is also well known that he draws very detailed storyboards for all of his films. Indeed, he is a very visual person who often conceives the idea for a new film with an image that pops into his head. These images percolate in his imagination for a long time before being realized in his film.

For example, the concept of *The Host* started when he looked out from his bedroom window and thought he saw a large creature hanging from a bridge over the Han River when he was in high school. Perhaps it was an illusion created by his obsession with the mystery of the Loch Ness Monster, at the time very much in the public imagination through newspaper articles, magazines, and other popular media. The idea for *Mother* also sprang from a memory from his high school days. He saw a group of middle-aged women enthusiastically dancing in a tour bus when it arrived at its destination. He was visiting one of the national parks at the time when he came across this scene, and he could not make any sense of it. But it left an indelible mark on his memory, and he would make a film to re-create that image one day. The film was also inspired by the TV actress Kim Hye-ja, whose remarkable acting in his film captured the obsessive love for her disabled son. Kim was well known nationally as the sacrificial and nurturing mother that she portrayed in *Chŏnwŏnilgi* (*Country Diaries*), one of Korea's longest-running TV dramas. It aired from October 1980 to December 2002, with a total of 1,088 episodes. Bong wanted to make a film that would show the hidden side of Kim's character and subvert her established image as a "national mom." *Snowpiercer* also took almost ten years from the day he first saw the graphic novel at his favorite comic book store. *Okja*, too, started as an image that appeared to him while he was driving through Seoul. It was an image of a giant pig whose face was cute but sad at the same time.

These images stay with him for several years before he begins writing the script. Until *Parasite*, which was released two years after *Okja*, it usually took Bong three or four years to release a new feature film; however, he also made short films in between years. Unlike most filmmakers for whom the short film is conceived as a stepping-stone to making a feature film debut, Bong continued to make short films occasionally. Since his first short film, he has made five more, including *Shaking Tokyo* (2008), which he shot in Japan. While *Incoherence*, his thesis film at the KAFA, demonstrates major traits that will later manifest in his feature films, many of his short films have unique features not seen in his longer works.

Among his later short films, *Influenza* (*Inpeulluenja*, 2004) and *Shaking Tokyo* (2008) merit special attention. Both films were made as part of an omnibus film and demonstrate Bong's consistent interest in and observation of the peculiarities of a society. *Influenza* is a thirty-minute film shot in digital funded by the Jeonju International Film Festival's Digital Project 2004 titled "Digital Short Films by Three Filmmakers." *Influenza* is a fake documentary that shows corners of Korean society through the lens of surveillance cameras. Bong used two digital cameras fixed at the same positions as CCTV cameras to record the fictional character Cho Hyun-rae in various places, including ATM booths, on the street, and in an underground parking lot. Bound by the camera's immobility and the lack of editing, the film consists of ten long takes dating from 2000 to 2004 that captures Cho as he tries to earn a living. It starts with Cho standing precariously on a bridge over the Han River, followed by him selling small merchandise on a metro train. Despite his honest efforts, he is often confronted by various acts of violence and eventually turns to violence himself. The idea of blurring documentary and fiction, the use of surveillance cameras, and the theme of violence as a kind of viral influenza all demonstrate Bong Joon Ho's probing eye into Korean society. The film redefines what everyday life means to an ordinary person and how violence is embedded within it. The film also positions the viewers into that of a voyeur, surveilling ordinary citizens and watching as they are continually assaulted and demeaned, a process in which the audience itself is implicated.

Shaking Tokyo is a short film Bong made in Japan with a Japanese cast and crew. It is an odd love story between a *hikikomori* (the Japanese word for an agoraphobic man) and a young delivery woman. Earthquakes strike when they come in contact. The film again testifies to Bong's keen observation of a society. Bong expresses his impression of Tokyo as a city of solitude through a uniquely Japanese character of *hikkikomori*. And the "shaking" in the title implies both the earthquake (Japan is also a land of earthquakes) and the shaking of the heart, which is the feeling of love. The film displays Bong's brilliant and original imagination and his sense of humor.

As seen in these films and others, what animates Bong's films is his interest in looking at the lives of ordinary people within a larger social system and a sympathy for his characters, who are often pitted against the authorities and neoliberal capitalist injustice. What distinguishes Bong's films is the social and political awareness of the problems that ordinary citizens experience in their daily lives. In that sense, Bong Joon Ho is one of the most political filmmakers in the postdemocratic Korean cinema. After the successful transition from an authoritarian regime to a democracy, the political fever of the 1980s turned into a cultural fever, especially the love for cinema in the 1990s and 2000s. The Korean New Wave of the late 1980s, which dealt overtly with social and political issues, gave way to the rise of New Korean Cinema in the late 1990s and 2000s, which focused more on commercial, genre-based entertainment films. While in the 1980s, making films of social realism was an expression of political resistance to the status quo, in postdemocratic Korea, making a Korean-style blockbuster was an act of resistance against the onslaught of big-budget Hollywood films. Bong Joon Ho, however, is the leading filmmaker of New Korean Cinema who maintains both a social and political awareness in his films while making commercial successes. Bong Joon Ho stands at the threshold between the two eras of the "political" and the "postpolitical."

2 · CINEMATIC "PERVERSIONS"
Tonal Shifts, Visual Gags, and Techniques of Defamiliarization

While the primary objective of this book is to provide a sociopolitical analysis of Bong Joon Ho's films by placing each film within the local and global context of the time of its production, this chapter focuses primarily on the cinematic qualities that are commonly found in his work. The social absurdities or *pujoris* that define the Koreanness in his films are conveyed not only through the story and the issues each film engages with but also through visual and narrative techniques carefully designed to heighten audiences' cinematic enjoyment as well as their perception of social realities. Bong is deft in mixing unexpected ingredients together—in particular, adding slapstick or moments of laughter in a more serious genre. Who could have imagined a monster movie in which the monster stumbles down the riverbank while chasing the terrified citizens? And a serial killer crime drama where the police chief slips and tumbles down into the rice paddy where the first victim was murdered?

One of the most distinctive features in Bong's films is the laughter that peppers the most serious and dark moments. *Memories of Murder, The Host,* and *Mother* all tell pitch-dark stories of serial rape-murders, monster attacks, and murder cover-ups, respectively. At the same time, however, they all manifest an odd or even twisted sense of humor that comes at the most unexpected times. Bong's films constantly defy audience expectations with various techniques of what I call *cinematic perversions,* which create gaps and cracks in the narrative's cause-effect chain. The swift and seamless blending of disparate elements is often motivated by his genre-bending impulses, which are, in turn, triggered by the desire to tell specifically Korean stories.

Bong's definition of himself as a "pervert" is useful in understanding both his filmic world and his approach to filmmaking, especially his reappropriation of Hollywood genres. In a 2013 TV interview, Bong called himself a "pervert," explaining that, to him, being a pervert means being creative.[1] Thus he does not view himself as "a person whose sexual behavior is considered not normal or acceptable" but as a person who "twist[s] the meaning or sense of" what is generally done or accepted.[2] As a self-conscious creator whose instinct is to provoke and challenge established rules and conventions, Bong meets this definition precisely.

As a "cinematic pervert," he is naturally inclined toward "defamiliarization," a notion developed by Russian formalist and literary critic Viktor Shklovsky to define what differentiates literature/art from ordinary language. He posits that artistic language works by making something familiar unfamiliar through the process of what he termed "defamiliarization." Making the familiar strange allows readers to see ordinary things in new ways.[3] This defamiliarization is a frequent trope in Bong's films: familiar genres are made unfamiliar by subverting established conventions, familiar spaces are made strange when turned into sites of horror and disaster, and well-known actors and actresses are cast against type to make them appear different and new. These defamiliarization techniques become not only aesthetic devices but also political tools that lay bare the social ills of contemporary Korean society.

Bong's use of the term *pervert* also indicates that he is playfully provocative. He takes pleasure in misdirecting the audience, and the extreme tonal shifts and genre bending contribute to these deceptions. The extreme tonal shifts are not just a fun ride but a means to embrace the absurdities and weirdness of the given situation. Thus they also function as defamiliarizing devices. This tendency to mix humor, drama, action, and political commentary reaches a new, more radical height in *Okja*, a sci-fi fantasy film that starts as a sweet tale of friendship between a girl and a superpig in an idyllic mountain village, then turns into an adrenaline-pumping action film, and finally switches to a biting indictment of the grim world of the meat industry and corporate greed.

However, Bong's most iconic perversion is his offbeat humor. It is so unique that French film journal *Cahiers du cinéma* borrowed the Korean word *piksari* to sum up his filmic world.[4] *Piksari* is a slang word that describes a voice that is out of tune or goes off-key while singing, especially at the climactic moment. The most memorable instance of *piksari* in Bong's films happens in the scene toward the end of *The Host* where the Park family confronts the monster on the riverbank. The kidnapped girl's uncle, a former student activist, grabs the last Molotov cocktail to throw at the monster. If he succeeds, it would be the final blow to the already battered monster. At this critical instant, the cocktail bottle slips from his hand and drops to the ground. In *Mother*, as the police attempt to re-create the murder of a young girl using a mannequin, the mannequin's head falls off in the tensest moment; in *Snowpiercer*, the leader of the revolt slips on a fish at a crucial moment when battling the train's security forces.

These moments of *piksari* are visual gags, but they are also visual cues in tune with Bong's filmic leitmotif. These comic moments, while relieving the tension that has been built up toward the climax, are effective in heightening the sense of absurdity of the situation presented on-screen. This "art of *piksari*" can be extended to include the tendency of his narratives not to arrive at the expected result—a "proper" ending with a clear resolution. Thus *piksari* is in itself a type of misrecognition, the core leitmotif of Bong Joon Ho's films.

As indicated previously, Bong Joon Ho's films are firmly rooted in Korean realities. His first four feature films and *Parasite* tell Korean stories with Korean characters in situations set in specifically Korean locations. The spaces, relationships between characters, dialogue and dialects, and symbols and iconic images all render a locality that is specific to Korea. Some scenes, such as the collective memorial altar in *The Host* and the dancing mothers in a tour bus in *Mother*, are scenes one would only see in Korean films. However, it is not only his stories, themes, and locations that are intrinsically Korean; the visual terms through which they are conveyed are also reminiscent of traditional Korean paintings.

Bong pays a great deal of attention to realistically portraying Korean landscapes and everyday spaces, which led Korean architect Hwang Tuchin to describe him as one of the representative artists of "Chin'gyŏng" (translated in English as real-view or true-view) landscapes in film.[5] This "real-view landscape painting" style emerged in the nineteenth-century Chosŏn dynasty (the last monarchy of Korea), when a group of painters, including Jung Sun, broke from following the Chinese tradition of idealistic painting and began to draw the real scenery of Chosŏn. The real-view landscape painting is a fitting metaphor for not only Bong's sense of realism but probably more so for his approach to filmmaking itself. He borrows Hollywood genres, but he does not simply follow their rules and conventions; instead, he modifies them or outright subverts them to tell specifically Korean stories in a realistic way. Even his fantasy film *The Host* has realistic settings and cinematography.

Cinematic perversions and real-view landscapes are two basic approaches that shape the aesthetics of Bong's films. Understanding these concepts and their significance in his work provides an insightful perspective for analyzing his unique approach to genre filmmaking. His films go against expectations in numerous ways, and this defiance, or subversion, is based on his urge to tell realistic stories. As Korean film critic Huh Moonyung aptly describes, Bong displays the ethics of a third-world artist in that he is self-conscious about refusing to "do it like Hollywood."[6] His films demonstrate how the genre conventions of the "first cinema"[7] may not be able to reflect postcolonial third-world realities. Christina Klein also points out the ambivalent relationship between Bong's films and Hollywood by quoting Bong's own words: "It's like you want to be influenced but you don't want to be overwhelmed."[8] He rejects the mere imitation of

Hollywood movies. Instead, he localizes them and, in the process, reinvents the genres.

How, then, does Bong's focus on Koreanness translate visually and formally? The first factor in this is his tendency to combine disparate elements, not only genre bending and tonal blending but also utilizing visual contrasts; the second is his use of realistic aesthetics and cinematic real-view landscapes; the last is his act of defamiliarizing everyday spaces. In terms of genre filmmaking, all of these qualities contribute to making Bong's films "familiar yet unfamiliar" to audiences accustomed to watching Hollywood genre movies. This technique of "making familiar things unfamiliar" is, in many ways, prompted by Korean realities. Thus except *Snowpiercer*, which is set on a fictional train, Korean social and cultural references abound in his films.

VISUALIZING THE KOREANNESS: TONAL SHIFTS AND VISUAL CONTRASTS

There are many instances where crucial information about the story, character, or setting is conveyed visually, with little or no dialogue. Bong is bold enough to use image and sound alone to communicate narrative information, thus allowing the viewers to make the connections themselves. One of the prime examples of these cinematic moments comes in *Memories of Murder*, when detective Seo Tae-yoon arrives at the spot where the schoolgirl has been mercilessly killed by the serial rapist. The heavy rain and the monochromatic tone heighten the gloomy mood of the scene; everyone is wearing black raincoats and holding black umbrellas. As Seo walks up the hill toward the victim's body, an inexperienced cop throws up after seeing the corpse, thus implying how gruesome it must be. A small Band-Aid on the body of the victim functions as the visual reminder of the personal attachment Seo has to the girl. Viewers remember that he had helped her put the Band-Aid on her back when he visited her school a few days before. When it is peeled from her body, Seo winces as if his own skin is being pulled, and he violates a basic rule of investigation by touching the body to pull down the shirt to cover her bare waist, an act that shows his affection for her. This is the pivotal moment where Seo, who believes in strictly following proper investigative procedures, transforms into as ineffective and irrational a detective as his rural counterparts.

Enraged, he walks down the hill and immediately goes to where Park Hyun-kyu, the third suspect, lives. Upon seeing him, Seo kicks Park in the chest; with a match-on-action cut, the scene transitions to a railway track in front of a large tunnel, where the climactic confrontation between Seo and the suspect unfolds. Seo firmly believes Park is the killer and is waiting for the DNA document to arrive and confirm it. The moral ambiguity that has been at the center of the film is reinforced powerfully in this scene, which has little dialogue. Detective Seo has become so irrational, he resorts to violence to force a confession from Park. The good (detective) versus evil (suspect) dichotomy is blurred here, as Park is sympathetically presented because of the way he is treated by Seo. However, when the DNA document arrives and shows that Park is not the killer, the tension collapses into anticlimax. The black monochromatic tone reflects the lack of emotional satisfaction and harmony; it is as if the film is mocking Seo for being too naive to have trusted scientific investigation, saying that he would have been able to capture the killer using his rational methods. However, both Seo and Detective Park Doo-man have failed because they are part of the corrupt institution. The DNA report, the document in which Seo had so much trust, is ripped irreparably as the train runs over it, a powerful image that conveys Seo's disillusionment and moral collapse.

What separates *Memories of Murder* from typical Hollywood crime movies is the basic question it raises about the nature of the system. Clint Eastwood's *Dirty Harry* movies are similar in this regard, but the character's lack of faith in the police in those movies does not expand to questioning a larger system or government or culture at large, as in *Memories of Murder*. A lack of faith in both government institutions and professionals features prominently in all of Bong's films. As exemplified by the scenes previously discussed, the cinematography in *Memories of Murder* is not slick or glossy; rather, it is devoid of color and strongly evokes the film noir style. Powerful images are used to convey the corruption and ineptitude of the police detectives. For example, when the first suspect, Baek Gwang-ho, is killed by the train, his blood splashed onto Detective Park Doo-man, who was desperately trying to save him.

After showing Baek being hit, the camera captures one of his sneakers, which the detective had bought for him, being thrown off the track. It is an image that informs us of his death and perhaps of the trust he had in the detective. The camera then shows us Detective Park's face and body splashed with Baek's blood and lingers on a close-up image of his bloody hand, the hand used to force a false confession out of Baek. The image implies Park's guilt in Baek's tragic ending; he is part of the institution that not only is unable to protect but also actively harms the socially weak. It is a symbolic image that reveals that the police are part of the larger system.

Although *Memories of Murder* is a crime drama, the narrative engine that moves it forward is not investigative procedures and progress; rather, it is the detectives' increasing frustration at their own incompetence and helplessness in trying to capture the killer. In Korea, one of the main publicity posters for the film carried the tagline "We so desperately wanted to catch you. Who are you?" ("Mi-ch'i-to-lok chap-ko sip'-ŏss-sŭp-ni-ta. Tang-sin-ŭn nu-ku-ip-ni-kka?"). Audiences are led to follow the detectives' reactions and responses to the institutional failures to support their efforts. First, the military government is not able to provide them with support on the day they planned to capture the killer, and second, the DNA test results from the United States betrayed their expectations. As they become increasingly exasperated to the point of madness, the color on-screen is also drained. The film takes their failure to a visual extreme by moving from the warm golden rice field of the opening scene to the monochromatic grayness of the tunnel sequence at the end. The light and color gradually drain away as the film progresses, reflecting the transformation of the characters themselves. Detective Park loses confidence in his instinctual fieldwork approach, while Detective Seo loses his cool and becomes violent, to the extent that he fires a gun at the third suspect. Indeed, the arc of the story lies in the gradual merging of the personalities of the two detectives, who at the beginning of the film were polar opposites.

As the focus of the film is the evolution or de-evolution of characters, the director presents wide shots that allow the actions of the actors to unfold without cutting, as in the long take of the crime scene of the first victim; these shots are often juxtaposed with close-up or extreme close-up shots of their faces, thus allowing the audience to follow their emotional arc. However, this juxtaposition of wide-angle shots and extreme close-ups is most prominently used in *Mother*. Unlike most American crime movies, which employ fast-paced plot progression coupled with constant action, *Mother* progresses at a slow, constant pace by focusing on the emotions and determination of the mother. It is a film that relies heavily on the performance of veteran actress Kim Hye-ja. The juxtapositions of wide-angle and close-up shots are effective in accentuating the intensity of her emotional toil and isolation, such as the scene in which the mother looks at Do-joon urinating near the bus stop and another scene in which she is in Jin-tae's house. Both are also examples of scenes that highlight the ways in which Bong Joon Ho uses images alone—rather than employing dialogue—to convey important narrative information.

The urination scene opens with an extreme close-up of the mother's hand carrying a bowl of brewed herbal medicine as she walks hurriedly to Do-joon, who had left home without finishing his lunch to meet his friend Jin-tae. "You shouldn't skip your medicine," she had told him. She arrives at the concrete wall on which Do-joon is urinating, approaches him, and looks down intently at his genitals as if to check his urinary health. As she places the bowl to his mouth and urges him to drink, this medium shot cuts to an off-center close-up of the back of Do-joon's head from above. The angle and the frame are carefully calculated to show both the mother's hand holding and tilting the bowl to Do-joon on the upper left and the urine flowing down below. It is as if the liquid herbal medicine he is being fed is coming straight out of his bladder. This is a captivating image that conveys the futility of the mother's extreme concern and

FIGURE 2. *Mother*. The mother checks on her son, who is urinating on the wall.

overprotection. Do-joon runs to the bus before finishing his medicine; after the bus has left, the mother is framed in the center of a wide shot against the gray concrete wall, heightening her isolation. She is small, alone in the shot, and the huge wall is cold and indifferent. Then in this static, wide shot, the mother walks toward the wall and tries to cover up her son's urine. Without any dialogue, the scene shows the nature of her relationship with her son and foretells her cover-up of her son's crime.

The scene where the mother spies on Jin-tae having sex with Mina also juxtaposes an extreme close-up of her eye and an extreme wide-angle shot of the landscape that surrounds Jin-tae's house. After Jin-tae and Mina fall asleep, the mother leaves the closet and tries to sneak out of the room. She had sneaked into the house in search of evidence to prove Jin-tae is the killer and had to hide in the closet when Jin-tae returned home with Mina. As she tiptoes toward the door, she accidentally spills a water bottle. Extreme close-ups of her face and feet and Jin-tae's fingertips as the spilled water closes in all contribute to intensifying the tension. She has to hide quickly as Jin-tae walks out of the house, and the wide-angle shot of her hiding down the hill is quickly juxtaposed with an extreme close-up of the head of a golf club that she has sneaked out of the house as the proof of Jin-tae's crime. The extreme close-up of her resolute profile conveys her emotional state, her determination combined with anxiety. These close-up shots are juxtaposed with extreme long shots of her walking alone toward the police station in which she is barely discernible as a small moving dot. As such, these juxtapositions heighten the intense emotional undertone of the scene.

In addition to these contrasts of angles, Bong uses horror tropes as visual aids in many of his films. These are useful not only in creating tension but also in playing with audience expectations. One example of this is the scene in *Memories of Murder* where a village woman is going out to take an umbrella to a family member on a rainy night. As she walks along the rice field, she stops suddenly because she hears somebody whistling. As she turns around to face the camera, her back is obstructed entirely by the open umbrella she is carrying. At this point, the audience would expect the killer to attack her from behind, but when she turns back, what is revealed instead is a concrete factory building, standing tall like a monster. The ominous presence of the factory represents the changes rural villages were experiencing nationwide in Korea in the 1980s. Just as the golf course in the village in *Mother* represents a space for outsiders—especially hypocritical intellectuals, arrogant and hostile to the village people—the factory building in *Memories of Murder* appears like a monster that harms the villagers. The modernity represents the demise of the village community. While the first two suspects are from the village and are familiar to the locals, the final suspect is an outsider, a factory worker; because he is not from the community, he becomes the object of greater suspicion. Urbanization—the industrialization of rural villages—replaces the sense of community with the fear of the unknown.

Crime, disaster, and social ills are all presented in the horror genre convention, as demonstrated in the basement scene involving the janitor in *Barking Dogs Never Bite*; the scene where the factory is presented in ominous lighting in *Memories of Murder*; the scene of the grandfather's death during his battle with the monster in *The Host*; and the scene in which the mother returns home and finds Jin-tae in Do-joon's room, and Jin-tae confronts her about her suspicions that he is the real murderer in *Mother*. These scenes all incorporate such horror movie conventions as low lighting and point-of-view shots. As will be elaborated in chapter 4, the "boiler Kim" scene in *Barking Dogs Never Bite* is a long sequence that does not move the narrative forward but instead contextualizes the apartment complex within Korea's dark history.

Images of water also contribute to creating an atmosphere of horror, with rain and rivers playing ominous roles in both *Memories of Murder* and *The Host*. For instance, the serial killer in *Memories of Murder* becomes active on rainy days; the film even uses a Korean song titled "Pitsogŭi Yŏin" (A woman in rain) to signal the killer hunting his next victim. The song begins when a woman hastily gathers up laundry from outside as the rain starts to fall. She is the character who later becomes a victim as she walks by a rice field on her way to bring an umbrella to a family member. The song continues as the scene changes to show schoolgirls in traditional dress waiting to wave Korean flags and welcome the president's motorcade as it passes by the village. (Mobilizing students and villagers to greet such motorcades was common practice during the military dictatorship of the 1980s.) The scene goes on to show detective Cho forcefully dragging away a female worker during an antigovernment protest. This is a significant moment because it shows the local police and law enforcement, including Detective Cho, busy suppressing political protests on the day the serial killer was expected to carry out his next rape-murder. Bong's direction implies that the dark shadows of the military dictatorship prevented the detectives from capturing the killer. Throughout these scenes, both the rain and the song stir up terror, aided by the violent suppression of civil disobedience.

Additionally, as previously elaborated, the body of the last victim, the school-girl whom Detective Seo had come to know and grow fond of, is found in the mountains in heavy rain. Thus in *Memories of Murder*, rain reminds the audience of the terror of the 1980s, when state violence was rampant, while heavy rain conjures up the traumatic history of the Kwangju Massacre in *The Host*. The Park family confronts the monster at night on the riverbank, where the grandfather meets his violent death in heavy rain. Additionally, it is from the dark waters of the Han River that the mutant monster first appears to terrorize the citizens of Seoul. In *Mother*, it is in pouring rain that the fateful first encounter between the mother and the junkman, who turns out to be the only witness to her son's crime, occurs.

While heavy rain often creates an ominous atmosphere, Bong's unique sense of combining disparate and even opposing elements plays a significant role in creating remarkable tension throughout his films. These combinations bring out the bizarre and the absurd while propelling the narrative forward, such as with the forced teamwork between the rural and urban detectives in *Memories of Murder*, the monster emerging from the peaceful Han River in *The Host*, and the loving mother and her monstrous murder in *Mother*. Bong's deftly choreographed tonal blending disperses the rules of the genre or combines them with elements of other genres to create unique and unpredictable outcomes. However, on closer examination, we can discern that each film foretells this outcome in its opening scene. Bong's films usually have a prologue before the opening credit sequence that establishes the location and the mood as well as a subtle hint to the ending. Coincidentally, most of the opening scenes involve the theme of "hiding," perhaps to allude to the idea that the truth is going to be hidden.

In *Memories of Murder*, the first victim's corpse is hidden in a ditch in an otherwise idyllic Korean landscape: a blue sky and a golden rice field ready to be harvested. In *The Host*, toxic material is secretly being poured into the Han River by the U.S. Army, and a few months later, a suicidal businessman sees something hidden in the river before jumping off the bridge. *Mother* begins with the mother dancing in the meadow and then hiding her hand in her jacket. These scenes portraying hidden things foreshadow the fact that the perpetrators (the killer, the U.S. Army, and the mother) are not going to be revealed and that crimes will remain unsolved. In line with this, as will be detailed in chapter 3, the boy in the beginning sequence of *Memories of Murder* alludes to Detective Park failing to capture the killer.

Thus these opening scenes symbolically set up the stories' themes or outcomes. The opening sequence of *Mother* does this particularly well by suggesting to us that the woman either is already or will become mad, as her facial expression and dance movements portray both soullessness and emotional pain. As the film title appears, she hides her hand in her jacket, symbolizing that she is going to hide something from us, whether a crime, a sin, or something else. In terms of hiding the truth, *Mother* is strongly in tune with Bong's previous films—*Barking Dogs Never Bite*, *Memories of Murder*, and *The Host*—in which the guilty parties essentially get away with their crimes. These films tell the stories of monsters—whether inhuman or human—and their violent acts. What makes these monstrous acts unique, especially in *Barking Dogs Never Bite* and *Mother* (and, to a certain extent, Detective Seo in *Memories of Murder*, who turns violent toward the end), is that they are driven by the increasingly dire socioeconomic circumstances of Korean society. The perpetrators are not ferocious in appearance; rather, they are visibly pitiful souls (the monster in *The Host*, for instance, is small in stature and looks somewhat lost), which makes their monstrousness come as an unexpected shock.

Bong also goes against general expectations in his choice of aspect ratios, particularly with *The Host* and *Mother*. For *Mother*, he used the cinemascope 2.35:1 aspect ratio, which is usually reserved for films of epic scale. Conversely, for *The Host*, a monster movie that is traditionally supposed to provide a greater number of spectacular moments, he chose the flat 1.85:1 aspect ratio. In using cinemascope for a film that focuses on the characters' intense emotions, especially those of the mother, Bong's choice of aspect ratio is reminiscent of Nicolas Ray's unusual but brilliant use of the widescreen format in films focused on characters' estrangement (e.g., *Bigger Than Life*, 1956) or Otto Preminger's 1958 film *Bonjour Tristesse*, which also focused on the characters' emotions. In these films, the cinemascope ratio accentuates the intensity of the feelings and the characters' emotional expressions. In *Mother*, the widescreen format poses a challenge, as there is little horizontal movement within the frame. However, Bong uses the framing to highlight the mother's isolation and loneliness. The close-ups and extreme close-ups of her face allow the audience to follow her emotions closely and intensely, while the empty spaces around her face effectively heighten the sense of anxiety and panic. Cinemascope was intentionally adopted to emphasize the isolation and loneliness of the mother and Do-joon, who have no one to rely on but themselves.

Further, Bong also released a black-and-white version of *Mother* five years later in 2014. This clearly differed from the original color version, especially in terms of focusing more attention on the characters and their expressions. Devoid of the color that could misdirect the viewer's attention, the black-and-white screen and subdued backdrop place the focus squarely on the intensity of the characters' emotions, as revealed by their facial expressions. The black-and-white scheme also adds to the anxiety, uncertainty, and shock in the film's mood, subsequently adding extra layers of horror and a ghostly quality to the experience. As a result, we can follow the mother's journey into madness more intensely. The film transforms from black and white into color at the exact moment when the mother inserts one of her acupuncture needles into her thigh on the tour bus, which she does as a desperate attempt to forget the murders both she and her son have committed, hoping to free herself from the burden of guilt. After the acupuncture, she stands up and joins the other mothers dancing on the bus. The black-and-white scene, which focused solely on her, suddenly becomes colorful, expanding the audience's attention to the other mothers. Now she has become one of many mothers who would perform the same (monstrous) act for their children.

FACES: CLOSE-UPS

Bong also uses close-ups to great effect. Close-ups—or even extreme close-ups—of faces are often used in climactic moments to emphasize the characters' emotional reactions and to heighten the tension that has been built up prior to that moment. *Memories of Murder* and *Mother* are both films in which the use of close-ups is especially prominent. Indeed, *Memories of Murder* opens and ends with an extreme close-up, beginning with a boy in the middle of a rice field and ending with Detective Park Doo-man's piercing look toward the audience. It is no exaggeration to say that the drama of the film and the emotional trajectory of the two protagonists are relayed through the frequent close-ups or extreme close-ups carefully placed at climactic moments. The best example of this is the confrontation between Detective Seo Tae-yoon and the third suspect, Park Hyun-kyu, in the railway tunnel toward the end of the film.

Enraged by both the cruel murder of the schoolgirl he had befriended and his conviction that Park Hyun-kyu is the killer, Seo points a gun at him in an attempt to force him to confess his crime. Long crane shots of their physical fight are juxtaposed with extreme close-ups of both their faces as they confront each other. The scene continues with Detective Park Doo-man running toward them with the DNA test results from America. Seo, whose investigation relied on his trust in documents and evidence, hastily opens the letter. The camera zooms in on his face as he reads it with an expression of disbelief, tears of despair running down his face. His expression says everything. A series of close-ups of the three characters heightens the gravity of the situation; Park Doo-man's face is emphasized as he looks at Park Hyun-kyu and confesses that he cannot read his face (he had boasted at the beginning of the film that he can recognize the criminal by just looking at faces), so he does not know whether he is the killer. The close-up of

Park Hyun-kyu's stony face is ambiguous. All Park Doo-man can do is ask an off-the-mark question—"Do you get up in the morning too?"—before adding in resignation, "Go. Just go, fucker." Their frustration and sheer anger at their inability to confirm Park Hyun-kyu as the killer, their disbelief and disappointment at the DNA results, and their final resignation that they must let Park Hyun-kyu go are all bathed in the pathos conveyed through their facial expressions. Close-ups and extreme close-ups are used effectively to capture the intensity of the moment.

In *Mother*, extreme close-ups are used sparingly to convey the sense of precariousness and insecurity that dominates the film. Since the film is shot in the cinemascope 2.35:1 ratio, extreme close-ups of faces cut off either the forehead or the jaw, thus focusing particularly on the expression conveyed by the eyes. The film is shot largely from the mother's point of view; however, the film relies on her facial expressions to convey subtle uncertainties. Since the film revolves around the mother's deception regarding her crime and the murder committed by her son, the mother's and Do-joon's eyes play crucial roles in conveying their emotional cores. Extreme long shots and extreme close-ups are combined effectively in the opening scene of the mother dancing. The long shot isolates her from her surroundings, accentuating her loneliness and the fact there is no one in whom she can confide. When she visits her son in prison, close-ups and extreme close-ups of their profiles and faces dominate the scene. In particular, immediately before Do-joon confronts his mother with his memory of her attempt to poison him, an extreme close-up of his hideous face, which is bruised and distorted after his fight with other inmates the previous day, builds tension between the two. The eyes of both the mother and the son are extremely compelling, and Bong uses extreme close-ups of those eyes as a major device in the storytelling.

As Béla Bálazs states, the close-up shot is what defines film as a specifically expressive form and "what makes film a specific language of its own."[9] When we see a face isolated in a close-up, he explains, "we lose our awareness of space, or of the immediate surroundings."[10] What we are left with are emotions and thoughts. The facial expressions are what Bálazs terms "visual performances" that do not need explanations, dialogue, or even specific spaces for context. Thus in *Mother*, which concentrates on following the inner agony of a mother, Bong uses close-ups and extreme close-ups as effective cinematic tools to lead the audiences' attention to only focus on the mother's emotions and feelings.

If a film relies heavily on close-ups and the facial expressions of its characters, then casting is crucial, since the success of such storytelling rests on the actors' performances. For *Memories of Murder* and *Mother*, Bong cast accomplished actors; Song Kang-ho in *Memories of Murder* and Kim Hye-ja in *Mother* are excellent examples of Bong's approach to casting. He stated in an interview, "However much we emphasize the CG, eventually what is most important is the actor's face, performance, and dialogue."[11] He usually writes scripts with actors already in mind. *Mother* is a fine example of this and of Bong's propensity to cast well-known actors against type. Kim Hye-ja is a household name in Korea as an icon of a good, wise, and sacrificial mother, earning her the nickname of "national mom." However, in *Mother*, she is cast as the obsessive mother who slowly turns into a murderess and liar. Bong turned the "national mom" into a monstrous mother. Her son, Do-joon, is played by Won Bin, who is enormously popular in Asia as a *Hallyu* (Korean Wave) star and is also cast against type. In the film, his handsome face becomes that of an intellectually disabled character who cannot remember things properly.

Actors and actresses bring their own personas to their films, and accordingly, audiences hold certain expectations about them. However, Bong seems to take great pleasure in drawing out a completely different side to these performers, thus defying audience expectations. Tilda Swinton in *Snowpiercer* is another example of this. While her androgynous image from Sally Potter's *Orlando* (1992) works well with the Mason character's gender ambiguity in the film, audiences are taken by surprise as her looks in *Snowpiercer* are so completely transformed that it is almost impossible to recognize her. The same is the case with Chris Evans, although to a lesser degree. He is well known for his role as Captain America, but in *Snowpiercer*, he is dressed in rags as the rebel leader of the tail section. Byun Hee-bong, who plays the janitor in *Barking Dogs Never Bite*, first chief inspector in *Memories of Murder*, and the kidnapped girl's grandfather in *The Host*, was a well-known character actor on Korean TV in the 1960s and 1970s. He mostly played villains, such as portraying a North Korean spy in an anticommunist TV series that was popular during the military dictatorship. In Bong's films, however, he represents the side of good, cast not as a criminal but instead as a victim of social *ills*. For instance, he sacrifices himself during the Park family's confrontation with the monster in *The Host*, making him a martyr reminiscent of the victims of the Kwangju Massacre.

"Lovable loser" characters are another important tool in defying genre conventions. Bong's critical stance toward the classical genre often manifests through unlikely humor that lies outside of the chosen genre's norms, and this humor often comes from such characters. For example, Detective Park Doo-man and his assistant Cho Yong-gu are as incompetent as they are funny. They adopt all sorts of ridiculous investigative methods based mostly on traditional superstitions, such as peering into the faces of suspects, going to a fortune-teller, and even using voodoo-like rituals at the crime scenes. Detective Park's investigation method, which is based on some logic, also provides a humorous moment: since the killer never left hair at the site, Park goes to public baths looking for men with no pubic hair. These measures are mocked in comparison to the more scientific methods used by Detective Seo. However, neither method turns out to be useful in finding the serial killer. The Park family in *The*

Host is also incompetent, albeit in a different way. However, it is natural that they are incompetent, since they are not professionals; rather, they are thrown into a situation where they have to rely on their instinct and knowledge to save the girl trapped in the monster's cave.

Both Byun Hee-bong and Song Kang-ho appear in four of Bong's films—Byun in *Barking Dogs Never Bite, Memories of Murder, The Host,* and *Okja;* Song in *Memories of Murder, The Host, Snowpiercer,* and *Parasite* (2019)—to offer moments of laughter and humor. Both are known for perfectly portraying typical Korean characters. In particular, Song Kang-ho's appearance and demeanor resonate with Korean audiences as a typical everyman. This ordinary Korean typicality shines brightly in *Memories of Murder,* where he represents the traditional, premodern style of investigation. Byun Hee-bong in *The Host* also represents the traditional Korean way of doing things as he pleads and bribes his way to secure the family's escape from quarantine and into the restricted area of the riverbank to find the monster. By contrast, the new generation, represented by his former student-activist son, constantly defies the authorities; however, he ends up making an absurd mistake at a crucial moment—the *piksari* moment of dropping the last Molotov cocktail.

REALIST AESTHETICS: CINEMATIC REAL-VIEW LANDSCAPES

Jeong Seon (pen name Kyomjae) was the leading figure of the real-view landscape painting movement in the eighteenth-century Chosŏn dynasty. He established his own style by moving away from the existing mainstream landscape painting that mimicked the Chinese style. However, according to Korean art scholar Kim Jin-kyoung, Kyomjae's paintings were not exact reproductions of real landscapes and instead differed significantly from the actual landscapes that he captured. His paintings clearly went through a reconstruction process involving omission, modification, exaggeration, and simplification to capture his own impression or understanding of the place. Kim describes Kyomjae's painting as landscapes "recorded by foot rather than the eye."[12] Kyomjae visited his chosen locations numerous times to observe the view; based on these observations, he reconstituted Korea's landscape as he understood it. Since he painted specifically Korean landscapes, the Chinese style of landscape painting was limiting, hence the real-view art. Korean architect Hwang Tuchin lists three basic elements of real-view art: first, the tedious observation of the object/landscape; second, the content based on such observation; and third, the transcendence of that object.[13] Thus the result is the artist's own interpretation of real scenery.

This description of Kyomjae's real-view landscape painting process is similar to the way in which Bong Joon Ho spends enormous amounts of time and effort searching for the right locations for his films. He prefers location shoots that position characters in real settings, with *Snowpiercer* his only film shot entirely on a movie set. *Memories of Murder* and *Mother*, both set in a rural village, were shot mainly on location. Indeed, *Memories of Murder* was shot entirely on location with the exception of interior scenes in the police station and the basement interrogation room. In *Mother*, the mother's house and the prison where the mother visits Do-joon were built on a set, while the deserted house where both A-jung and the junkman are killed was an open set built on location. *Memories of Murder* was shot in approximately fifty different locations and *Mother* in about thirty different locations. The production team was divided into several small groups who spent many months scouting locations nationwide. The *Memories of Murder* locations were concentrated in the southwestern part of Korea, and the *Mother* locations were scattered across the country. While the real story of *Memories of Murder* took place in a specific town—Hwasŏng—the film does not specify the name of the village. It could be any rural town in Korea, since the lack of faith in local institutions and the state and the distrust in the system that the film conveys are national issues. The locations for *Mother* were deliberately not based in any specific locality in order to direct attention solely to the relationship between the mother and her son and to their emotional struggles.

This process of finding locations was painstaking due to the rapid changes that landscapes and towns experience in Korea. During the audience Q&A at the Busan West Film Festival in November 2011, Bong explained that because Korea is a country in which new developments and constructions are abundant, things change so much within a couple of months that the biggest challenge after finding a location is to preserve it until the shooting date. For example, the tall, towerlike factory building in *Memories of Murder* was gray when they decided to shoot there; however, it had been freshly painted green by the time they were ready to film, forcing them to repaint it gray. In the case of *Memories of Murder*, for which re-creating a 1980s rural village was crucial, what looks like one location on-screen was usually shot in multiple locations. For instance, the railway tunnel scene at the end was shot in southeastern Kyŏngsang Province, the extreme close-up of Detective Seo was shot in Gyeonggi Province near Seoul, and the scene depicting Park Hyun-kyu's room immediately preceding the tunnel scene was shot in Chŏlla Province in southwestern Korea. Even portraying the roadside ditch where the body of the first victim was found involved shooting in multiple locations; this meant the production team had to carry the stone cover they made for the ditch from place to place.[14]

The situation was similar for the filming of *Mother*. Bong drew a picture of a rural village he envisioned for the story to take place, and eight location teams searched the whole nation for six months to find places to create this village on screen. They took more than forty thousand photos of possible locations.

Multiple locations were assembled to create the imagined but realistic rural village for the film. For *Okja*, since the idyllic mountain village where Mija lives hardly exists any longer, the location scouting team had to visit 1,080 places to find the right locale, and for the scenes of Mija playing with Okja at the waterfall, they had examined 750 different places.[15] The relationship between the location and the story is closely interdependent in terms of realizing Bong's cinematic real-view landscape.

While the notion of "real-view" landscapes is a good metaphor for the realist aesthetics of Bong's films, further verisimilitude is added to the narratives through his frequent use of long takes, news footage, and photos and his incorporation of real events and places. His films are, in short, fictionalized real views and real events. Bong is often inspired by newspaper articles and regularly incorporates them into his stories, a testament to his strong interest in the goings-on of Korean society. Indeed, Bong conducts a great deal of research during his writing stages. He spent six months researching the Hwasŏng serial murder case before writing the script for *Memories of Murder*.

To keep his films as close to reality as possible, Bong not only researches the material but also interviews real people. For *Memories of Murder*, he interviewed several people who were involved in the actual investigation of the serial murder case that inspired his film; in order to create Hyun-nam, the apartment management office's accountant character in *Barking Dogs Never Bite*, Bong interviewed high school graduate accountants; and for *The Host*, he sat down and drank with the owners of a snack stand on the banks of the Han River, the site of the monster attack,[16] which is how he found out that some of the snack stand owners were evictees during the late 1980s. Even trivial episodes, such as the absurd death of a drunken professor on a subway track in *Barking Dogs Never Bite* and the sexual exploitation of a minor in *Mother*, are borrowed from real incidents.

The Host was inspired by the "McFarland incident," which provided the idea that mutant fish could emerge from the Han River. The McFarland incident occurred in 2000, when the American mortician Albert McFarland forced his Korean assistant to pour 480 bottles of formaldehyde into a drain. In the prologue in the film, the U.S. Army sergeant orders his Korean assistant to pour the toxic material into the river, which is what causes the monster to be created; however, they are never pursued or punished in the film. The U.S. and Korean governments even get away with spreading the virus hoax. As in all of Bong's films, truths are not revealed within the diegesis; only the audience knows the truth. However, since the social *ills* are played out in these realistic settings and situations, the seriousness of the problems becomes more palpable. Although *The Host* is a fantasy monster movie, Bong also focuses on maintaining a realistic look. The monster is not an alien but a relatively small mutant fish whose existence seems rather plausible. The production team spent a great deal of time researching mutations in order to make a realistic-looking beast. As a result, it looks like a giant fish rather than a Godzilla-sized ferocious monster, and it was designed to perform realistic movements as well. The 1.85:1 aspect ratio was chosen over the cinemascope size in order to emphasize the monster moving within a closed space and to make the vertical spaces stand out.[17]

For *The Host*, several other real incidents were researched as well, such as major man-made disasters, including the 2003 Daegu subway fire and the 1995 Sampoong Department Store collapse, with a focus on how follow-up measures were carried out, how the collective funeral altars were set up, and how the government responded to the disasters, among other things. In particular, the comic-tragic scene of the collective memorial altars set up in a large gymnasium is one that only a Korean monster movie can have. There is an ironic and oddly amusing moment when the members of the Park family—the grandfather, father, aunt, and uncle of Hyun-seo, whom they think has died from the monster attack at this point of the narrative—gather together for the first time in a long time. The grandfather tells Hyun-seo's photo on the altar, "Thanks to you, we are all here," suggesting that they are a dysfunctional family. Thus the monster movie conventions are outright subverted when this maladjusted family—instead of scientists and government authorities—battle the monster in order to save their girl.

Further, when Bong was writing *The Host*, the SARS outbreak was a topic of great concern and interest. Bong's research focused less on the disease itself and more on the collective hysteria surrounding the outbreak.[18] Many of the scenes in the film were inspired by the hysteria of SARS; in fact, in the scene in which Park Gang-du is locked in a plastic biohazard body bag, Bong even used the same type of bags used during the SARS crisis to quarantine the infected. All the effort Bong puts in at the preproduction stage of his films helps create stories that resonate with Korean audiences on many levels.

Thus many of Bong's films are based on real events, as is the case with *Memories of Murder*, and if not, real news footage is inserted, thus combining these real-life stories with the fictional ones. In *Barking Dogs Never Bite*, the news footage of a female bank teller single-handedly catching a robber is actual footage recorded on a bank's surveillance camera. *Memories of Murder* shows actual news footage of the arrest of Detective Moon Gwidong, an infamous officer who tortured numerous prodemocracy activists and even carried out sexual torture on a female labor activist. This footage is shown in the scene in which detective Cho is drinking at a local pub after having been scolded by the police chief for using violence on suspects. The breaking news that everybody in the pub is watching on TV effectively equates Cho with the torturer. News scenes in *The Host* were actually shot in a real broadcast studio of a TV station in Seoul; the production team shot and edited the news sources, ran it on TV, and then shot that TV screen. These news scenes give information about how the government authorities and the United States are reacting to the monster attack—in other words, about the virus hoax they are spreading.

The long take is one of the techniques of cinematic realism, as argued by André Bazin. In Bong's films, long takes are not used as the central aesthetic principle, as they are in Hou Hsiao-hsien's films, for example. However, Bong does make significant use of long takes, especially when it is necessary to convey a sense of urgency and chaos. His most impressive use of this technique is the scene in *Memories of Murder* immediately following the prologue and the credit sequence. Detective Park Doo-man arrives at the crime scene of the second rape-murder victim. The crime scene response team has not yet arrived, and the rice field is full of onlookers, including children running around the corpse. A steady cam follows Park as he hastily tries to preserve the footprints, to no avail. Ignorant of what is going on in the field and oblivious to the call by Park to stop, a tractor driver runs over and crushes the footprint left on the dirt road. The chief of police arrives but stumbles down the ridge of the rice field, and the crime scene response team follows suit. The uninterrupted long take of the scene conveys the total disorder and chaos of the situation as well as law enforcement's utter incompetence in dealing with the murder case.

Another rather memorable sequence shows Detective Park Doo-man and Seo Tae-yoon meet for the first time. Again, misrecognition plays a role in creating an absurdly comic situation. Arriving from Seoul, Seo looks lost in the middle of the road. Upon seeing a young woman walking in front of him, he calls and says he wants to ask her something. However, she is terrified because she thinks he might be the town's serial killer. She runs away but slips and falls down the ridge of the rice field. Seo goes down to help her out, but she screams in terror. At that moment, Detective Park passes by, hears the scream, and comes to her rescue. Upon seeing Seo touching the woman (as he was trying to help her stand up), Detective Park drop-kicks him. This drop-kick was an improvised action by actor Song Kang-ho, but the camera follows these actors' unexpected movements in real time.[19] The spontaneity and "realness" of this action is preserved.

The misrecognition on the part of Detective Park here is shared by the audience, as the sequence in which Detective Seo appears for the first time is constructed in such a way that it tricks the audience into identifying him as a possible killer. The scene starts with a long shot of Seo walking on the path alongside the ditch where the first rape victim was discovered. A heavy mist and the eerie nondiegetic piano music create an ominous mood that suggests something might be about to happen. Seo emerges from this heavy mist and walks toward the camera. On the right, a scarecrow with a red-colored shirt draws our attention. On it is written, "If you don't turn yourself in, you will rot and die"; it is a reproduction of the actual scarecrow the police in Hwasŏng set up in the 1980s.

FIGURE 3. *Memories of Murder*. The arrival of Detective Seo from Seoul.

The sequence of the grandfather's death in *The Host* is shot in a documentary-like fashion, evoking the civilians' tragic deaths in the Kwangju Massacre of 1980. Prior to this scene, Hyun-seo's family members—the grandfather, father, uncle, and aunt—sit together inside the snack stand having supper. Suddenly, Hyun-seo appears behind her father and joins the table. Everybody is eager to feed her. This fantasy scene is a reflection of the thoughts that the family members must be sharing at that moment; while they are eating, they are thinking about Hyun-seo and how hungry she must be. They all want to feed her, and they perhaps feel a little guilty about their own appetites. Thus this scene represents the family members' most ardent dream of being reunited with Hyun-seo.

Blending fantasy scenes into realistic ones is common in Bong's film style, and he often exerts a manga sensibility by blurring the line between what is real and what is fantasy. This is most apparent in his first feature film, *Barking Dogs Never Bite*, in which the two chase scenes unfold in a manga-like fashion. When Hyun-nam, the female protagonist, witnesses the killing of a dog from the apartment building rooftop, she immediately runs to that building and gets in the elevator, where she puts on her yellow hood. From that moment on, the color yellow comes to symbolize the film's manga influence. The chase between Hyun-nam and Yoon-ju, the dog-killer protagonist of the film, unfolds in an unrealistic, exaggerated fashion. In the second chase scene, this time involving Hyun-nam and the homeless man on a rooftop, Hyun-nam is cheered on by people in yellow raincoats throwing confetti on the rooftop of the apartment building on the other side. This playful moment provides relief from the high tension built up by the confrontation between Hyun-nam and the homeless man. In these scenes, the images are edited in a cartoon-like way, with the frames connected in comic strip format.

Despite these occasional fantasy moments, Bong's films are realistic in terms of both the stories, which are oftentimes based on real events, and the style, which can be summed up as the aesthetics of real-view landscape. This notion of real-view landscape can also describe his approach to genre filmmaking in that he rejects Hollywood conventions and instead reinvents them in order to accommodate local stories. However, what is truly unique about his filmmaking is that he defamiliarizes real, everyday spaces to lay bare hidden secrets and ills.

THE DEFAMILIARIZATION OF EVERYDAY SPACES

One of the most conspicuous characteristics of Bong Joon Ho's filmmaking is his ability to make familiar spaces unfamiliar, where the spaces taken for granted in our daily lives suddenly assume a different meaning. The basement of an ordinary apartment building, a peaceful rural village, a golden rice field, the Han River, and even a train—all these spaces become the sites of man-made disasters. Space in Bong's films gives the social ills in Korean society their geopolitical significance, and individuals' stories play out within a larger sociopolitical context. Thus uniquely local stories are told in specifically Korean spaces. When he brings Hollywood genres into this Korean space, they clash with Korean chaos and absurdities and eventually collapse, since they cannot contain the specifically Korean stories. From these clashes and the eventual collapse of the structure of the genre, a slice of Korean society is then revealed. His films are about uncovering the dark truth hidden beneath the seemingly peaceful and normal surface. Oftentimes, this revelation is achieved by taking a closer, deeper look at what lurks within these everyday spaces. Thus in his films, familiar, everyday spaces are made unfamiliar, becoming sites of terror, disaster, and deception. Ultimately, the truth that is presented to the audience does not necessarily triumph within the diegesis. Instead, the truth remains hidden unlike in Hollywood films.

Cinema itself is an art of manipulating space and time; however, in Bong's films, space in particular plays a hugely significant role in the narrative construction. It is no exaggeration to say that space acts as a character in his films; space is not simply a vehicle for containing the story but instead serves an important dramatic function. A story needs to take place in a particular space because it fulfills the drama's structural requirement. Why is it from the Han River that a mutant fish appears and wreaks havoc? Why is the apartment complex from which dogs go missing at the edge of Seoul? Why do professors come to play golf in the small rural village? As Han Mira argues, Bong's films "capture particular places in the real world and picture the topography of sociocultural situations around them, calling up the temporality of modern and contemporary times in Korean society."[20] The narrative spaces in Bong's films acquire a specific locality; abstract space becomes a concrete place that carries sociocultural significance. It is these locally specific spaces that narrate the stories of failure.

Bong's acute sense of spatial construction and mise-en-scène seems to stem from his practice of drawing the storyboard himself. Except for *The Host*, which relies heavily on computer graphics, Bong was the storyboard artist for his films. In the Korean film industry, it is common to hire storyboard artists to draw each shot in order to save time and money during the shooting. Storyboarding is an important part of the creative process of visualization; it is, as Steve D'Katz defines it, "the most useful tool the filmmaker has for visualizing his ideas and the one most directly related to his responsibilities."[21] So it is crucial for story-board artists to understand cinematic mechanisms such as the different effects of framing, camera positions, and angles.[22] This means that storyboarding the film himself gives Bong a greater sense of the space, which in turn contributes to the visualization of the concept and story he has also developed. Bong is an avid reader of comic books, an amateur illustrator of comics, and a cinephile, and he truly is the main visual architect of his films.

In Bong's films, including his shorts, space functions as a silent charac-ter. It may not have any dialogue, but it certainly displays a personality of its own—and oftentimes, a quite unexpected one. Bong's spatial choice is similar to his tendency to cast against type. Space sheds its perceived image and reveals its unknown or hidden side and is also often given a rich historical background to add character depth. For example, the origin of the apartment complex in *Bark-ing Dogs Never Bite* is narrated by the janitor in a long sequence in the basement. We learn it was built during the late 1980s as part of the Korean government's effort to beautify the city for the Seoul Olympics. At the same time, it was also a site of embezzlement, murder, and cover-ups. Thus the space adds a valuable layer to this story of moral corruption. The Han River, with its numerous bridges that light up beautifully at night, is a popular object of tourist photographs and boasts of the economic miracle Korea has achieved. However, in *The Host*, it lays bare a completely different character; under the command of the United States, it becomes a contaminated body of water that breeds a monster that preys on small businessmen. The banks of the Han River are a popular site for leisure activities for Seoulites and are often featured on TV shows and news stories; however, a closer look reveals they are also a location where people commit sui-cide, as the water is dark and opaque, and the current is rough. Despite its histor-ical significance, the Han River is just a familiar everyday space to most people. In *The Host*, however, it is transformed into an unfamiliar space from which a monster appears.

Like the Han River, the spaces Bong prefers are those that look ordinary but at the same time emanate tension and disruption beneath the surface. In *Memories of Murder*, an ordinary and peaceful rural village of the 1980s is revealed as a space of fear and crime. Usually, closed spaces, vertical spaces, and dark basements are the sites of horror, spaces that people do not pay much attention to in their daily lives. Corruption and crime are carried out behind the scenes in these overlooked, dark spaces. For example, we see the sewage works of the Han River where the monster collects the bodies of its victims or the basement of the apartment complex in which dogs are cooked and a boiler repairman is secretly buried. Similar to the scene portraying the grandfather's tragic death, the bodies piling up in the sewage works provide a strong allusion to the Kwangju Massacre. In *Memories of Murder*, the body of the first victim is found in the narrow, dark sewage drain of the rice paddies. The interrogation room in which the police threaten violence against innocent suspects is also a vertical place in the basement. The basements in Bong's films are spaces filled with secrets.

The train in *Snowpiercer* is another clear example of the type of closed, narrow spaces featured in Bong's films. This claustrophobic space with no exits is the site of a class struggle between the have-nots (in the tail section) and the haves (in the front section). The closed space in this film can be interpreted as a metaphor for a social structure or social order that is so fixed, there seems to be no way out except by destroying the system and starting anew. In fact, the conflict between different classes in Korean society is also reflected in different spaces. In *Barking Dogs Never Bite*, this division is visualized through the different spaces they occupy—the light but mundane apartments (although the killing of the dog takes place here) and the dark, secretive basement. This contrast is particularly significant in *Parasite*, as the social classes are represented by the space they live in: a sunlit two-story mansion, a half-lit semibasement house, and a dark basement.

The spaces and places in Bong's films are also realistic. The stories unfold in realistic settings, and the audiences are familiar with the spaces and environments in which the characters live. Even in *Memories of Murder*, which required much production design work given that the story is set in the 1980s, the spaces appear natural. In Bong's films, the production design team's work goes almost unnoticed, as the spaces are very much based on real spaces and sets are seldom used. These real spaces often carry symbolic meanings. The apartment complex in *Barking Dogs Never Bite* is near the Kŏyŏ subway station. The name of the village is revealed on a signpost in the subway scene in the beginning. This village is located at the edge of Seoul, which indicates that the apartment complex is situated in a neighborhood that is home to lower-middle-class residents. It is a place of the marginalized. *The Host* was shot on location at the Han River and its banks, an area that symbolizes the postwar economic miracle; however, it is also a place where the monster appears, symbolizing the dire consequences of compressed economic growth. In a symbolic reading of the film, the Han River is where the Kwangju Massacre—the most traumatic event in contemporary Korean history—is carried out.

Compared to the spaces and places of Bong's previous films, the rural setting of *Mother* is devoid of specificities both in spatial and temporal terms. The directorial intention seems to be to concentrate on the mother character and her relationship with her son. This vague sense of place also suggests the mother's story pertains to all mothers in Korea or even around the world. Meanwhile, the locale is where the transition from rural to urban, from traditional to modern, takes place. For example, the undeveloped meadow in which the mother dances is juxtaposed with the golf course where professors from the city come to play. Thus the urban is represented as the corrupt force from outside. The transition from rural to urban, from premodern to modern in postwar Korea is the chronotope of Bong Joon Ho's films, and it is reflected in the visuals of the locations. While the golf course represents the transition in *Mother*, the factory building plays the same function in *Memories of Murder*. It is portrayed as having an ominous force, one that produced the most likely killer. The third suspect, Park Hyun-kyu, has an urban look. In this way, the rural/urban juxtaposition functions similarly to the friction between victims/marginalized and perpetrators/dominant.

In *Okja*, this juxtaposition expands its scope to a global scale.[23] In the film, Mija crosses the Pacific Ocean from Korea to New York to rescue Okja from the grips of the Mirando Corporation. The film begins in an idyllic countryside mountain in Korea where Mija lives with her grandfather and Okja. This green mountain forest, a clean and peaceful environment, is where the friendship between Okja and Mija is beautifully portrayed. The forest full of trees and the sound of a rushing stream re-creates an ideal image of a Korean landscape (as does the image of a golden rice field at the beginning of *Memories of Murder*). It is an almost premodern landscape, although the existence of a superpig tells us the seed of global capitalism is already sowed here. This peaceful and harmonious life with nature begins to shatter when the filming team from the Mirando Corporation arrives to record how their superpig has grown in the last ten years. Headquartered in New York, the Mirando Corporation represents the neoliberal corporatism of the multinational giant companies. Eventually, Mija flies to New York, which is a forest of concrete buildings where the Animal Liberation Front members are beaten savagely by the police. This scene reminds American viewers of the 2011 Occupy Wall Street movement, a resistance organized against the expansion of global capitalism. Mija is now at the heart of the financial center of capitalism. Thus her countryside home in Korea, which portrays a nostalgia for the nature-friendly, premodern environment free from capitalist greed, is effectively juxtaposed with the chaos of postmodern New York. It is in New York that Mija learns about the workings of the multinational corporation and for the first time in her life engages in a capitalist deal, exchanging Okja with the gold pig her grandfather had given her in compensation for Okja's departure from their home. Between Mija's home and New York lies the city of Seoul, which is already implicated in global capitalism. The Mirando Corporation has a branch office there.

It is ironic that Okja, the genetically modified animal produced for food consumption, is successfully bred in the traditional rural setting free of contamination or environmental pollution. It is as if to indicate that once peaceful and beautiful rural areas are being penetrated by the ills of neoliberal global capitalism. In that sense, *Okja* is a warmer or prettier version of *The Host*, with which it shares a similar concept. They both rely heavily on computer graphics and visual effects for the creation of the giant mutant or genetically modified animal; however, the locations and settings of each film are realistic.

Thus the spaces in Bong's films are those in which the social *pujoris* or contradictions are manifested. They are spaces that bear a traumatic history, as in the basement in *Barking Dogs Never Bite* and the sewage works in *The Host*. *Memories of Murder* constructs spaces of 1980s Korea in which people are terrorized. The village where the rape-murders continue to occur becomes a symbolic representation of the past. The Han River in *The Host* also functions as an allegory of the modern history of Korea. In this sense, the spaces in Bong's films are geopolitical spaces that lay bare Korea's postcolonial present.

What distinguishes Bong Joon Ho's films is their Koreanness, not only in terms of their stories but also in terms of their visual imagery. The spaces, relationships between characters, dialogue and dialects, and symbols and iconic images in the films all render a locality that is specific to Korea. Some scenes, such as the collective memorial altar set in a large gymnasium in *The Host* and the dancing mothers in a tour bus in *Mother*, are scenes one would not see in any other films but Korean ones. The most absurd and grotesque incidents that are in many ways the consequences of Korea's rapid economic development take place in the most ordinary spaces. Bong's brilliant articulation of turning familiar, everyday spaces into unfamiliar ones corresponds to the films' narratives, which are focused on social *pujoris*. Strange things occur in spaces that we walk around every day, and social *pujoris* are part of daily life in Korea.

3 · SOCIAL *PUJORIS* AND THE "NARRATIVES OF FAILURE"

Transnational Genre and Local Politics in *Memories of Murder* and *The Host*

Although Bong Joon Ho works within Hollywood genres, he draws more inspiration from Korean society than from genre conventions. For Bong, what is important is not making a specific genre film but rather making a film that is specifically Korean. Since his first feature film, *Barking Dogs Never Bite* (2000), and even in his earlier short films, Bong has consistently grappled with contemporary Korean society. Further, all of Bong's films, except the sci-fi film *Snowpiercer* (2013) set in the near future, present stories with a high degree of verisimilitude.[1] Even *The Host* (2006), a monster movie, is inspired by a real event, and its characters and settings are realistic. Bong's genre films tell stories that are specifically Korean, with very Korean characters whom one would expect to bump into in everyday life. And it is these Korean elements—the peculiarities that are specific to Korea—that create the cinematic conditions or situations in which genre conventions are bound to be twisted or subverted. In particular, *Memories of Murder* (2003) and *The Host* are excellent examples of how local Korean politics serve as important subtexts that cause gaps and cracks in the narrative that traditional generic conventions are unable to contain.

Memories of Murder is a crime thriller based on an actual unsolved serial-killer case in Korea. Set in 1986, the film follows two rural detectives and a special detective from the capital city of Seoul as they desperately try to capture the serial killer who has turned an otherwise quiet rural town into chaos and fear. The rural detective Park Doo-man and the city detective Seo Tae-yoon are incompatible, since their investigative approaches are polar opposites. Park is intuitive, even relying on superstitious methods, while Seo thinks more scientifically and trusts documents. The oppressive political climate of the time adds to their frustration as the military regime is busy fending off massive protests for democracy. The best chance of capturing the killer in action slips away as the local police are denied support from the government. As the story unfolds, the incompetence of the local police is shown to be the inevitable result of the oppression by the military regime as well as the pervasive corruption of the authorities.

The Host is a monster movie set in the city of Seoul. The Park family, who runs a snack stand on the bank of the Han River, is swept into a maelstrom when their teenage girl, Hyun-seo, is snatched away by the monster that emerged from the river. Hyun-seo's father, the dim-witted Gang-du, is quarantined, as the authorities believe he is infected by the virus derived from the monster. However, while in the hospital, Gang-du receives a call from Hyun-seo, whom everybody assumed was dead. From that moment, Gang-du and the rest of the Park family, consisting of Hyun-seo's grandfather, uncle, and aunt, decide to find and save their girl from the monster themselves. Instead of chasing the monster, the government authorities are busy chasing the Park family while trying to cover up their false claim of the virus. The U.S. Army and government are portrayed as responsible for creating the mutant fish by dumping toxic material into the Han River and collaborating in the virus hoax cover-up.

Both films were immensely successful at the Korean box office and earned critical acclaim and, with respect to The Host, international success. Memories of Murder was the highest-grossing film of 2003, while The Host broke Korea's all-time box-office record three years later. Memories of Murder ranked seventh in the Korean Film Archive's "100 Greatest Korean Films" in 2014, the only film of the new millennium to be named in the top-ten list. Premiering at the Cannes Film Festival in 2006, The Host was an international breakout film for Bong. The French film journal Cahiers du cinéma ranked The Host fourth in its list of best films for the 2000–2009 decade.[2] In the United States, The Host also received critical acclaim, with a 92 percent "fresh" rating on Rotten Tomatoes.[3] The fact that these narratives of failure struck it big with Korean audiences attests to two things: first, the films' high commercial value and, second, their ability to capture and express the collective sentiment of Koreans. In fact, in both films, Bong borrows commercial genres only to subvert their conventions to channel the distrust, injustice, and cynicism that Koreans share.

Bong's most prominent subversion of genre conventions is the denial of a happy ending. Both Memories of Murder and The Host represent what I call narratives of failure, and it is because these stories end in failure that the films constitute biting critiques of Korea's political power structure. Both films are about the inability and/or unwillingness of Korean authorities to protect ordinary citizens. In this sense, these films are political allegories disguised as popular genre films: *Memories of Murder* is a crime thriller, and *The Host* is a monster movie. Both films, however, negate their respective genres from the outset. In both films, it is Korean social and political realities that make a successful resolution impossible.

This chapter analyzes the ways in which the two films challenge and subvert Hollywood genre conventions and how these subversions are prompted by the narrative of failure, which in turn reflects the social realities of Korea and the collective sentiment of its people. In particular, this chapter focuses on how the decade of the 1980s, a crucial period in Korea's democratic movement, is represented in each of these films. These two films touch upon the theme of historical trauma as represented and symbolized by disasters: a serial rapist and killer in *Memories of Murder* and a monster attack in *The Host*. The 1980s serve as a crucial link between the two films: *Memories of Murder* is set in the 1980s, and *The Host* comments on the legacy of the 1980s from the perspective of the present. *The Host* can even be considered a sequel to *Memories of Murder* in that it shows the continuing incompetence of government authorities twenty years later. The difference between the two periods—the 1980s and the 2000s—lies in the fact that in *Memories of Murder*, it is the oppressive military regime that prevents a successful investigation, but in *The Host*, it is Korea's neocolonial and postcolonial conditions and the aftermath of neoliberal economic policies that harm ordinary citizens.

THE 1980S AND THE NARRATIVE OF FAILURE

My concept of the *narrative of failure* is informed by Namhee Lee's study of the 1980s Korean democratic movement, *The Making of Minjung*. Lee states, "Korea's trajectory of decolonization resulted in a sense of the failure of Korean history."[4] The notion of the narrative of failure reflects Korea's inability to resolve issues crucial to establishing a fair and just society since its independence from Japanese colonial rule in 1945. Among other things, two major issues are particularly important in postcolonial Korea in terms of restoring social justice: first, the liquidation of the remnants of Japanese colonialism, especially pro-Japanese collaborators, and second, bringing justice to the perpetrators of the bloody suppression of the prodemocratic Kwangju Uprising in May 1980, which cost hundreds of lives and left thousands wounded or missing.[5]

For most of the first half of the twentieth century, Korea was under Japanese colonial rule. Annexed by Japan in 1910, Korea was liberated in 1945 when Japan lost World War II to the Allied Forces. After the defeat of Japan, Korea underwent a three-year occupation by the Allied Forces to rebuild the country, with the United States occupying the southern half of the Korean peninsula and the USSR the northern half. U.S. administrators who did not understand

Korea, its history, or its immediate situation rehired those who had collaborated with Japanese colonial authorities.[6] Thus unlike what occurred in France, for example, where Nazi collaborators were quickly tried and executed, most Japanese collaborators in Korea retained their privileged positions in the postwar political and social system. Alternatively, the Act on the Honorable Treatment of Persons of Distinguished Service to Independence, a Korean law honoring the activists of the independence movement under Japanese rule, was not established until December 1994, almost half a century later. This unfair treatment—collaborators and their families became powerful and the families of the patriotic fighters marginalized and forgotten—left a deep sense of injustice in the public mind, which continues to foster a widespread cynicism and defeatism among Korean citizens.

The repressive military dictatorships of the postwar period also contributed to this negativity. Korea came under military dictatorship in 1961 when General Park Chung-hee took power through a coup d'état. His anticommunist, authoritarian government lasted for eighteen years until his assassination in October 1979. Although a brief hope of democracy arose after his death, it was soon crushed when another military general, Chun Doo-hwan, carried out a coup in December 1979. In response, massive civil protests for democracy erupted nationwide in May 1980—in particular, in the city of Kwangju. Chun Doo-hwan moved ruthlessly against the protestors. The military closed the city borders and sent in paratroopers to put down the protests. The protestors attempted to defend themselves by forming a civil militia, but they were no match for the military forces pitted against them. The unprecedented massacre lasted for ten days, from May 18 to May 27, 1980. This bloody suppression of the Kwangju Uprising ended all immediate hope for a Korean democracy. Chun Doo-hwan became the next president through a rubber-stamp election by the nation's electoral college in August 1980, and his presidency lasted until 1988.

The massacre, also referred to as the "5/18 Democratic Movement" was a turning point in contemporary Korean history and is the key to understanding current Korean society. In his book *Social Science of May*, Korean sociologist Choi Jeong-woon writes, "Post-1980s Korean society can never be understood without understanding May 18 and its myth. It is an event that restarted not only Korean history but also the personal histories of all of us."[7] This incident was harrowing not only for the massive loss of life but also for the government's traumatic pitting of Korean against Korean and the tremendous guilt that resulted from this enforced murder disguised as a military operation. Most of the paratroopers who carried out the massacre were young men serving their mandatory military service, not professional career soldiers. At the time of the massacre, in fact, there were rumors that the paratroopers were drugged to carry out the atrocities. Many paratroopers were reported to have suffered psychological trauma from having used their military weapons to kill civilians. Lee Chang-dong's 1999 film, *Peppermint Candy* (*Pak'asat'ang*), one of the first films to depict the trauma of the Kwangju Massacre, features a protagonist who was sent to Kwangju while he was serving his mandatory military service. He is severely traumatized by his participation in the massacre and eventually commits suicide.

Although a failure, the Kwangju Uprising had a tremendous impact on Korea's subsequent social movement for democracy. Specifically, the democratic movement changed from a struggle led by students and intellectuals to a *minjung* (people's) movement that mobilized laborers, peasants, and the urban poor as the new agents of social revolution. The revitalization and radicalization of social and political movements against the new military regime eventually led to the 1987 June Democratic Uprising, which finally brought about political democracy. And as I elaborated upon in the previous chapter, the 386 generation played a pivotal role in bringing about democracy. It is fair to say that Korea has a long history of resistance in the twentieth century: in the first half, against the Japanese, and in the latter half, against military dictatorships. Intellectuals and students were at the forefront of these movements.

Another important change resulting from the uprising was the rise of strong anti-Americanism previously unheard of in Korea. From the end of World War II through the Cold War era, there was virtually no anti-American sentiment manifested among the Korean public. However, after the Kwangju Massacre, the attitude toward the United States changed, particularly among the leaders and activists of the democratic movement. They had considered the United States their supporter in the fight for democracy; however, it turned out to be otherwise. The Korean Army's Twentieth Division was sent from the DMZ (demilitarized zone) to suppress the Kwangju Uprising, and this mobilization could have occurred only with the consent of the U.S. commander. Disappointed and feeling betrayed, political activists adjusted their direction and distanced themselves from the United States.

This anti-American sentiment grew stronger during the 2000s as the result of several incidents that exposed the public to the unequal relationship between Korea and the United States. For example, in June 2002, a U.S. military vehicle fatally struck two middle school girls. When a U.S. military court found the soldiers not guilty and sent them back to the United States, widespread anti-American anger broke out against the SOFA (State of Force Agreement), which stipulates that U.S. military personnel stationed in Korea are under the jurisdiction of U.S. military courts and thus immune from Korean justice. Again in 2003, public protest erupted when the Bush administration asked the Korean government to send troops to Iraq and the government complied. To many Koreans, these events revealed Korea's subservient relationship with the United States.

Among the three periods of crucial importance in terms of historical rectification—the Japanese colonial period (1910–1945), the Korean War period (1950–1953), and the military dictatorship period (1961–1987)—the 1980s occupies a particular importance in *Memories of Murder* and *The Host*. The dark and oppressive atmosphere of the decade looms large in *Memories of Murder*, and iconic images of the 1980s are abundant in *The Host*. *Memories of Murder* is set during the Chun Doo-hwan presidency. While *Memories of Murder* is a fictional reconstruction of a certain period in the 1980s and is based on the hunt for an actual serial killer, *The Host* is a political satire of the current state of affairs in Korean society whose origin can be traced back to the 1980s. Thus *The Host*, in effect, depicts the legacies of the 1980s, seen from the perspective of the year 2006.

How are the 1980s represented or interpreted in *Memories of Murder* and *The Host*? First, as one of the representative filmmakers of the 386 generation, Bong reflects in these two films a strong social consciousness and perspective in his attention to the plight of ordinary people (*minjung*) and to Korean social injustice. One legacy of the failed Kwangju Uprising was the rise of film and video activism and particularly *minjung* cinema, which called for the realistic depiction of the lives of the lower classes. Bong Joon Ho's attention to the marginalized and often disabled hints at this *minjung* consciousness: *minjung* as the oppressed who nonetheless have the potential to rise up against the system. This *minjung* consciousness underlies much of Bong's work: in his films, the socially weak are often the victims of disasters. In *Memories of Murder*, the murdered women are not the only victims; the wrongfully accused suspects are also victims of police violence and of the social atmosphere that allows such violence. In *The Host*, it is the dysfunctional family members who are the victims of the monster attack, unable to save Hyun-seo even though they are the ones to kill the monster.

Second, in both films, Bong engages in a metaphorical and political critique of the role the United States has played in Korean local politics. In *Memories of Murder*, the sense of betrayal Detective Seo Tae-yoon feels about the DNA test results conducted in the United States and clearing the detective's final suspect of the murders can be read as a metaphor for the sense of betrayal Koreans felt toward the United States in the 1980s. In *The Host*, it is the American mortician in the U.S. military base in Seoul who orders his Korean assistant to dump a large amount of toxic material into the drain that leads to the Han River, bringing about the birth of a giant mutant fish. Thus the monster is the product of this allegorical depiction of Korea's subservient relationship to the United States. Later in the film, the United States also tries to hide the truth about an alleged virus and uses a chemical agent to fight the monster despite a massive demonstration by the Korean people against its usage. Thus a sense of betrayal and subsequent distrust toward the United States, a direct result of the 1980s, can be seen in both *Memories of Murder* and *The Host*.

GENRE SUBVERSIONS AND NARRATIVE TECHNIQUES

Memories of Murder and *The Host* demonstrate how certain genre conventions collapse when confronted with Korean realities such as local stories, situations, and characters. As the result of his localizing Hollywood genres, the idiosyncratic characteristics of Bong's films emerge: the mixing of genres; dual narrative structures; the combination of disparate elements, especially the distinctive mixture of comic and horror; an attention to the socially weak; and the use of realist aesthetics. All these techniques are deftly woven together to heighten the sense of irony and absurdity that shapes contemporary Korean life.

First, Bong skillfully combines different generic components into a single film. *Memories of Murder* and *The Host* are both mixed genre films. *Memories of Murder* contains elements of the crime film, buddy movie, mystery thriller, horror movie, and silent comedy, while *The Host* mixes the monster movie, political satire, family drama, and slapstick comedy.

Second, *Memories of Murder* and *The Host* each take a narrative turn as the film progresses, resulting in a dual narrative structure. What might first appear to be a typical genre story turns out to be a more complex, carefully calculated narrative that leads the audience to gain a larger perspective on Korean society and an understanding of the political nature of crises and disasters. In short, the narrative dictated by the chosen genre is just a tool Bong uses in the game he plays with audience expectations. *Memories of Murder* starts out to be a story about capturing a serial killer; however, as the film progresses, the story turns into one about the oppressive Korean political situation in the 1980s. Likewise, *The Host* starts out as a typical monster movie; it then soon becomes clear that the film is not about the creature but about family. The monster is not the villain in the film; the real villain is the Korean government's response to the disaster (the monster attack) and its treatment of the monster's victims. In both cases, the dual narratives serve to reveal the political nature of the tragedies individuals suffer.

One of the unique narrative strategies in Bong's filmsis his unexpected combination of disparate elements to achieve wild tonal shifts—in particular, his use of startling moments of comic relief. Bong uses comedy not to relieve the tension of a particular situation but to accentuate the sense of irony or even tragedy. The audience is led to laugh at the most unlikely and surprising moments. This odd combination of comedy, horror, and drama that runs through his films—especially *Memories of Murder* and *The Host*—is extremely effective in representing the peculiarities and absurdities of Korean society. A sudden burst of laughter amid horrific moments leaves an emotional, lingering pang of sadness.

The prime examples are the collective mourning scenes in *The Host*. In a scene that follows a terrifying monster attack, while families gather in a gymnasium to mourn their losses, a man in a yellow hazmat suit walks in with an air of authority but then suddenly slips and falls, causing an unexpected laugh. Similarly, in *Memories of Murder*, the chief of police arrives at the murder scene and slips off the ridge of the rice field, giving the audience a moment of laughter. These moments are typical of Bong's films, in which most of the laughs come at the expense of authorities and thus satirically criticize their bumbling incompetence. At the same time, however, the overhead shot in *The Host* that captures the four members of the family crying hysterically and rolling around on the floor is one of the funniest moments in the film, but in this case, the sudden laughter pierces the audience with a deep sense of the tragedy the family is experiencing.

In addition, Bong's consistent attention to the socially weak, whom he describes as "lovable losers,"[8] contributes to the sense of injustice his films convey because these loser characters are the ones most likely to be victimized by social ills. The plight of the weak is one of the major themes—perhaps the most crucial one—in Bong's films. More specifically, Bong's emphasis on socially weak characters results in unpredictable outcomes because these characters are forced to carry out impossible tasks. For instance, it is not the scientists, the police, or the military who fight the monster in *The Host* but the victim's family. In these specifically unpredictable narratives, arising from the characters' lack of social support and protection, Bong's films ultimately make strong political commentaries on the social injustices and corruption that are so widespread in Korean society today.

Finally, Bong's films are notable for their realism. In part, such realism is effectively built into the Korean film industry. Specifically, Korean films must be realistic to be commercially viable in the domestic market. Hollywood sci-fi and fantasy films fare well in Korea, but domestic sci-fi films and monster movies have been conceived and produced as children's movies until recently and thus have not been taken seriously. Furthermore, Korean cinema has a long tradition of social realism or critical realism, as many films of the 1960s golden age of Korean cinema and those of the 1980s Korean New Wave were realist films that dealt with social problems and issues of the time. Among the domestic all-time top one hundred box office movies in 2013, only four films belong to the sci-fi/fantasy genre: *The Host* (2006, sixth), *Snowpiercer* (2013, eighth), *D-War* (2007, twelfth), and *A Werewolf Boy* (2012, nineteenth), all films made in the twenty-first century.[9] The fact that major producers and investors declined to be involved in the production of *The Host* when Bong announced his plan to make a monster movie also testifies to the Korean film industry's negative view of monster movies and sci-fi films.[10] Bong's combination of a fantastic genre with realism is both a way to appeal to the majority of Korean audiences and an effective way to weave the director's social or political commentary into a commercial film.

While remaining squarely in the realm of commercial entertainment, his work probes the social problems and historical issues of Korean society in a politically and socially conscious way. *Memories of Murder* and *The Host* make it possible to understand local phenomena within the context of Korean society's structures as a whole. *Memories of Murder* contextualizes the ways in which seemingly apolitical crimes are in fact closely related to politics, and *The Host* provides an understanding of national disasters within Korea's postcolonial conditions, mapping Korea's relation to the social and economic organization of global politics. In sum, in Bong's films, local politics intervene in the narrative to produce Korean variations of Hollywood genres; the result is films that question the Korean status quo and trace the causes of Korean social problems to deeper structural issues.

MEMORIES OF MURDER: REPRESSION UNDER MILITARY REGIMES

Memories of Murder is based on a series of actual rapes and murders that occurred in Hwasŏng, Kyŏnggi Province between 1986 and 1991. In what was known as the "Hwasŏng serial murders," a serial killer took the lives of ten women between the ages of fourteen and seventy-one. Who committed the crime and why remained unknown at the time of production. In 2003, when *Memories of Murder* was released, the fifteen-year statute of limitations on murder had lapsed, and the case—which had once shaken the entire nation—was disappearing from the collective memory. The commercial and critical success of the film not only brought Bong fame as one of the most promising directors in Korea but also ignited a new interest in the Hwasŏng murders. A petition to extend the statute of limitations was signed by many supporters, and on December 21, 2007, the statute for murder cases was extended to twenty-five years. *Memories of Murder* not only brought back the forgotten past but also reinvestigated and revived it.

The screenplay is loosely based on a stage play titled *Come to See Me* (*Nal porŏ wayo*), first performed in February 1996. Written and directed by Kim Kwang-lim, the play focused on the investigation of the case by four detectives and their increasing frustration at not being able to find the killer. In adapting the play, however, Bong focused more on the question of why the investigation failed rather than on how the investigation was conducted by the detectives. Most significantly, his film departs from the play by interweaving the oppressive climate of the 1980s into the detectives' story.

In fact, it was during his research that Bong realized that the 1980s should not serve simply as the background of the story but should become the film's main character. While reading newspapers of the time, Bong noticed that articles on the Hwasŏng murders often appeared on the same page as articles on the 1986 Seoul Asian Games, the police tortures of political dissidents, the 1988 Seoul Summer Olympics, and other major incidents of the time. These juxtapositions allowed him to put the serial murder case into a broader political and historical context. In particular, when he discovered that a thirteen-year-old girl was murdered on the fifteenth day of the month (November 15, 1990), the day of Korea's monthly civil defense and blackout drill, he knew for certain that the story must be about the era of the 1980s.[11] At that time, the military regime used the monthly drill to constantly remind citizens that they were living under a threat of war with North Korea. Given this state of impending war, any unrest in the form of protests and demonstrations was unacceptable. Alan Moore and Eddie Campbell's comic book *From Hell*, which is about Jack the Ripper, also gave Bong the idea that the detectives' failure had to do with the crudeness of the era.[12] At the suggestion of fellow filmmaker Park Chan-wook, who had also been interested in adapting the play, Bong once contemplated a fictional ending in which the crime is solved and the murderer caught; however, he ultimately decided against it.[13]

Although from the outset, viewers know the detectives are going to fail to solve the murders,[14] the film maintains a dramatic tension that grips the audience until the end. The film focuses not on the killing spree or on the murderer, whose face is never shown, but on the two detectives desperately trying to find the killer. The two detectives, Park Doo-man and Seo Tae-yoon, begin the film as polar opposites in every way; intriguingly, they become more and more similar as the film progresses. Specifically, Detective Seo, the elite officer sent from Seoul who had been opposed to Park's use of violence against suspects, resorts to violence himself out of despair and frustration at not being able to prove the final suspect is the killer. Ultimately, the film becomes a story of a society built on violence: not only the violence committed on female victims but the detectives' violence perpetrated on suspects and state violence executed on civil disobedience. These three different levels of violence are intricately interwoven into the story of the failed investigation. Thus the dark era of the 1980s military dictatorship, an era in which everyone was complicit in violence, becomes the very subject of the film.

Indeed, the film is imbued with national angst from the start. *Memories of Murder* begins with a prologue that presents a seemingly idyllic image of a Korean countryside: a golden rice field ready to be harvested under a clear blue sky, boys running around capturing grasshoppers. A golden rice field is a traditional image of peace and prosperity in Korea. However, hidden under this perfect image of a

FIGURE 4. *Memories of Murder.* Detective Park looking at the first victim.

national landscape lies the corpse of a rape and murder victim, the first of many to come. This victim serves as an ominous sign of a looming crisis that is further foreshadowed by the image of grasshoppers. As a common pest in rice fields, these grasshoppers serve as a symbol of social ills threatening the peace of the nation. In fact, the opening shot is a close-up of a boy in the middle of the rice field. After capturing a grasshopper from a rice stalk, the boy stands up and sees a tractor approaching. Detective Park Doo-man is sitting on the rear end of the tractor. The camera cuts from him to a close-up of a glass bottle, half full of captured grasshoppers, that the boy hides behind his back. Park gets off the tractor, approaches the ditch, and discovers the body of the first victim in the drainage. We also see a grasshopper sitting on her body. A title shows the date: October 23, 1986.[15] The boy follows Park and mimics his words and actions. Park looks at the boy with a puzzled expression; the boy makes a face at him; Park looks back at him blankly. And then the title sequence starts.

This prologue sets up the film, in an allegorical way, as a story of a nation in crisis or in harm's way. The fact that the boy hides his bottle of captured pests from Detective Park foretells that Park is going to fail to capture the killer. In addition, the film takes place in an anonymous village. Even though the film is a dramatized retelling of the Hwasŏng serial murder case and was marketed as such, the town in the film is not named, hinting that it could be any rural village in Korea—anybody can fall victim, because the real threat is, as the story will tell, the oppressive military regime. As Christina Klein states, the film reveals the "deep crime" of a pervasive wrongdoing by the military regime under the "surface crime" of the killer. Referring to a central convention of the American crime film in which the "process of investigating the surface crime often reveals a deep crime," Klein concludes that the distinctly Korean deep crimes revealed in *Memories of Murder* include "the corruption and abuse of police power, the casual disregard of civil rights, and the government-stimulated fear of North Korea as a means to keep the civilian population in check."[16]

However, unlike in most American crime films, the revelation of the deep crime in *Memories of Murder* does not help solve the surface crime. The deep crime—that is, the military regime and its systemic repression—is beyond any individual's power to rectify. Furthermore, the law enforcement that is supposed to solve the surface crime is, in fact, part of the deep crime. Even though Detectives Park and Seo desperately try to capture the killer, their effort is ultimately thwarted by the establishment. On the night Park and Seo are certain the killer is going to attack another victim, they contact the regional headquarters to request two squadrons of riot police to cover the potential area of the impending crime. However, this request is denied because all available police are mobilized to suppress massive political protests in a nearby city. And indeed the next morning, the body of another victim is found. The agenda of the repressive regime has cost the detectives the chance to catch the killer. Furthermore, Detective Park and his partner Detective Cho Yong-gu often resort to violence and threats to drive suspects into submission. They do not hesitate to fabricate evidence in order to close the case.

If the defining concept of the state is, as Max Weber expounds, "the legitimate use of physical force within a given territory,"[17] *Memories of Murder* shows that the state uses that monopoly on violence to defend itself from its own citizens. The film ultimately questions the legitimacy of a military regime that came to power by using its military force to suppress protests for democracy in Kwangju. In fact, the period of the Hwasŏng serial murders coincides with the time when state violence was at its peak in Korea. The torture of political activists was rampant. One of the most notorious cases was that of Park Jong-chul, a university student who was tortured to death in 1987. His death fueled the June Democratic Uprising in 1987, the ultimate turning point in Korea's progress toward democracy. Another notorious case was the sexual torture of female activist Kwon In-sook by Detective Moon Kwi-dong in an investigation room at the Bucheon Police Agency in Kyŏnggi Province in June 1986. During this time period, the late opposition leader Kim Geun-tae was also tortured, which left him disabled for life. In Bong's film, political tensions and signs of unrest are everywhere. The scenes of demonstrations and riot police are shot in documentary style, and at one point, we see Detective Cho Yong-gu brutally dragging a protester away. Thus the police brutality against suspects in the serial murders overlaps with the state's violence. Beneath the story of a serial murder, the film

vividly re-creates a Korean rural town whose police engage in the same infuriat-
ing injustices and brutal violence that is simultaneously plaguing the nation as a
whole.

It is this portrayal of the detectives where *Memories of Murder* deviates most
from Hollywood crime movies. The two detectives are the protagonists who
desperately try to solve the serial murder case; however, they are not the same
kind of "good guys" as those of American crime films. Detectives Park and Cho
are portrayed as part of the corrupt system; for instance, they have no qualms
about beating suspects to force false confessions. In capturing the ambivalent
nature of the detectives' work and methods, the film effectively shows the extent
to which violence permeates everyday life. This is demonstrated most tellingly in
the detectives' interrogation of the first suspect, the intellectually disabled Baek
Gwang-ho. In one scene, Detective Park, Detective Cho, and Baek are eating
noodles together while watching the popular TV series *Susabanjang* (Inspector
chief). The three share a friendly camaraderie, and all appear to be enthusiastic
fans of the TV program. In the blink of an eye, however, the mood changes. A
woman officer brings Park photos she has developed, including a photo Park has
falsified of Baek's footprint at the crime scene, and Park immediately threatens
Baek with the photo.

In addition to this instantaneous invasion of intimidation and violence into
moments of "ordinary" leisure of TV viewing, *Memories of Murder* contains
Bong's characteristic comedy. After Baek is proven innocent (despite the evidence fabricated against him), the detective team has dinner at the restaurant
owned by Baek's father. Park has brought Baek new sneakers to make up for his
false accusations. But the sneaker's brand is NICE—a fake Nike! At another
point in the film, the desperate Park investigates a local public bath to find
a man with no pubic hair. He came to a supposition that the killer must have
congenital atrichia, since he never left any pubic hair at the crime scenes. These
weirdly comic moments, interwoven into the film's grim situation, reflect Bong's
unique sensibility; behind all this comedy lurks a genuine sense of despair. These
run-of-the-mill, even comedic moments of everyday corruption, violence, and
absurdity suggest that Korean society at the time was complicit in authoritarian
violations of basic human rights.

In portraying the serial murder case and the 1980s era as realistically as possible,[18] the film uses the realist aesthetic of long takes, TV news footage, and
various documents to give this retelling of the case a documentary feel. The
160-second take of the crime scene at the beginning of the film effectively conveys the urgency and chaos of the situation and at the same time sets the film
apart from Hollywood crime movies. A typical Hollywood film would show
a street in an urban district where yellow tape surrounds the crime scene and
lights flash on parked police cars. Police officers would be busy trying to preserve

all forensic evidence; detectives would arrive and start investigating the scene. In contrast, the initial crime scene of *Memories of Murder* is an open rice field in a rural town. Kids run around the victim's body; Detective Park desperately tries to keep forensic evidence intact but fails miserably when a tractor runs over and smudges a clear footprint. The police chief arrives but stumbles down the slope. It is total chaos compared to the typical cool competence seen in a Hollywood crime film.

Making a crime thriller with a realistic setting in Korea inevitably deconstructs the genre's conventions. When making *Memories of Murder*, Bong Joon Ho thought it would be interesting to "have rough rural feel clash with the very American genre of thriller."[19] He described the film as a "rural thriller" in which Korea's most popular TV rural family drama, *Chŏnwŏnilgi* (Country diaries), meets the Hollywood thriller *Se7en* (1995). To depict Korean realities, however, Bong must reorganize and effectively re-create the genre, as *Memories of Murder* demonstrates. Further, the difference between Hollywood's treatment of the police in murder mysteries or detective films and the Korean treatment of them in similar genres is crucial to understanding Bong's social commentary in *Memories of Murder*. Through the detectives' corrupt, brutal, and ultimately ineffective methods and the film's depiction of three socially weak characters as wrongfully accused suspects, Bong communicates a general distrust of and lack of confidence in the police and the political system at large.

In addition, Bong inserts TV news footage and newspaper coverage of actual contemporaneous events into the dramatized story to heighten the film's realism. For example, in one scene, Detective Cho Yong-gu sits in a restaurant, drinking to drown his anger and frustration after the chief forbids him from using violence against suspects. On the restaurant TV, actual news footage of the arrest of the notorious detective who sexually tortured a female political activist is playing. People in the restaurant are watching the news, and when a group of college students condemns the torturer, Cho shatters the TV set with a kick and picks a fight with them. The film thus clearly relates Detective Cho to the torturer of political dissidents. Likewise, many painful memories and images of the 1980s are embedded in the film. To Korean audiences, the middle school girl in traditional Korean dress waving the national flag to greet President Chun Doo-hwan, protesters clashing with riot police, defense drills, and blackouts are all familiar images of the 1980s.

Bong also uses certain objects and iconic images of the 1980s to add political layers to particular scenes. For example, in one of the police office scenes, a photo of Lee Soon-ja, the notorious first lady at the time, is seen between the two detectives, who are looking at each other with their heads resting on their desks. They are feeling frustrated and incompetent because they have no clue as to who the killer is, and the photo of Lee in the middle of the frame tacitly suggests that their limbo is connected to the regime's corruption. Also, as Joseph Jonghyun Jeon has elaborated, the film's use of close-ups of various fictional documents—newspapers, FBI documents, and so on—links the diegetic action of the characters to structures of power. Jeon states that "dates in the film are constantly provided with regularity, not only extradiegetically on the screen but also consistently in diegetic form via the news media, particularly in print."[20] Thus while the documents are fictional, audiences are reminded of real calendrical time.

The film deftly mixes horror, tension, and humor in Bong's signature style of commingling seemingly incompatible elements. Much of the humor comes at the expense of the detectives, especially the local detectives Park and Cho, whose method of investigation is appalling and comical at the same time. The ineffectualness of this rural detective team is contrasted with the more scientific investigative approach taken by the elite Detective Seo. While Park relies on his own instincts and consults a fortune-teller, Detective Seo relies on documents and evidence and comes up with the theory that the murders happen on rainy days to women wearing red clothes. The rivalry between the two detectives escalates as Seo effectively proves that the suspects Park charges are in fact innocent. However, Seo's own approach is nullified when the middle school girl is murdered neither on a rainy day nor while wearing red clothes but instead on the day of the blackout drill. When Seo meets the third suspect, a defiant factory worker, he is confident he has found the killer, and he expects the FBI's DNA test results to prove he is correct. However, when the FBI's results show that the DNA does not match, Seo loses control and becomes violent toward the suspect. The fact that Bong changed the location where the DNA test is conducted from Japan—where the DNA test in the actual case was performed—to the United States suggests that Bong intended to highlight U.S. involvement in Korean local politics.

The irony of the story reaches its peak near the end of the film, when it turns out that the first suspect the detectives interrogated, the intellectually disabled Baek Gwang-ho, is not the killer but, in fact, a witness to the crime—which is why he was able to describe the killing method so accurately when detectives first questioned him. If the detectives had known this, they would have solved the case early on and prevented the later murders. The detectives were so intent on capturing the killer, however, that they "made" Baek the killer by fabricating evidence. This is a comment on how public authorities worked in 1980s Korea—they were more concerned with achieving goals on paper than achieving actual success in the real world. This lost opportunity to have solved the crime by interpreting Baek's account correctly adds a sense of tragedy to the story, and this sense of regret is heightened when the last victim in the film, the sweet middle school girl, is brutally killed during the monthly defense drill.

One important technique that *Memories of Murder* employs to re-create the sense of anxiety that imbued the 1980s is the killer's point-of-view shots, which Bong borrows from slasher films. The film never shows the killer's face, since he is never caught or identified. However, via his gaze, he is very much present in the film. Although his face remains indiscernible, the killer appears on-screen on three occasions: when he attacks a woman holding an umbrella as she is going to greet her family member on a rainy day; when he hesitates over which prey to follow (Detective Park's girlfriend or the middle school girl) as he looks down at the road from the hill; and when he prepares to kill the girl on the mountain slope. These slasher-film point-of-view shots are effective in painting the 1980s as the age of horror.

The Korean title of the film, *Sarinŭi ch'uŏk*, also reflects the point of view of the killer. *Sarinŭi* means "of murder," and a better translation of *ch'uŏk* is, in fact, "nostalgic recollection" rather than "memory." The Korean word for "memories" is *kiŏk*. Thus *Nostalgia for Murders* would be a closer translation of the Korean title, implying that the killer is looking back at his past crimes with a certain fondness or wistfulness. Thus the film could be interpreted as the story of the Hwasŏng serial murder case retold by the killer himself. In fact, Bong Joon Ho told me in an interview that when the film was released, he had imagined the killer sitting in the audience.

If *Memories of Murder* is an allegory of Korean society's complicity in the violence toward the socially weak and its distrust of authority, the film suggests that neither these social attitudes nor the horror and anxiety of the 1980s ended with the demise of the military regime, as the film's epilogue demonstrates. It is 2003, and Park is now a family man who runs a small business. He revisits the scene of the first crime, the ditch by the golden rice field. His point-of-view shots, especially the one that looks into the ditch, convey an ecrie feeling, as if we are again sharing the killer's point of view. As Park looks into the drainage, an elementary school girl approaches him and asks what he is doing. When she says she saw another man looking into the ditch a few days earlier, he asks if she saw the man's face, and she replies that he looked "just ordinary." The film ends with Park peering at the audience with a piercing yet uneasy look. The killer still haunts the present.

THE HOST: MAN-MADE DISASTERS AND THE SPECTER OF KWANGJU

On the surface, *The Host* is a monster movie; in its Korean context, perhaps it makes more sense to read it as a disaster film. Specifically, it is a film about what it is like to be a victim of a man-made catastrophe. The film is an allegory of Korea's corrupt and incompetent authorities, who breed disasters and fail to help the victims. The film was partly inspired by an incident that took place in 2000 at the U.S. military base in Seoul in which an American mortician ordered a Korean assistant to dump a large amount of formaldehyde down a drain that fed into the Han River. Known as the "McFarland incident,"[21] it inspired *The Host*'s prologue, which leads to the birth of a giant mutant fish, entirely consistent with monster movie conventions. However, the similarity to a conventional monster movie ends there. Unlike most monster or creature movies—such as *Alien* (1979), for example, where the audience has to wait until the end to see the monster in its entirety—*The Host* reveals the monster in broad daylight only thirteen minutes in. Even in Japanese *kaiju* films, it usually takes longer than thirteen minutes for the audience to see the beast, after much tension has been built around it. In *The Host*, the appearance of the monster is sudden, and from the minute it appears and attacks people on the riverbank, the film is less about the monster and more about the family whose teenage daughter has been kidnapped by it. As we will see, Bong has borrowed the popular monster movie genre to produce a biting critique of social injustice in Korean society and the inability of Korean government authorities to protect ordinary citizens.

Hollywood blockbuster monster movies usually feature destructive creatures who wreak havoc on a city and the heroes who save the city from the monsters. In the Japanese monster movie *Gojira* (1954), government officials, scientists, and law enforcement authorities form an emergency headquarters and collaborate to contain and destroy the monster. In her essay about 1950s American science fiction films, titled "The Imagination of Disaster," Susan Sontag lists the five phases of the monster-movie narrative as (1) the arrival of the thing (a monster, a spaceship, etc.) witnessed by the hero, usually a young scientist; (2) the confirmation of the hero's report by a great act of destruction that is witnessed by many and that alerts the police to the situation; (3) conferences between scientists and the military leading to the declaration of a national emergency and international cooperation; (4) further atrocities, including one that puts the hero's girlfriend in grave danger; and (5) more conferences leading to the development of the ultimate weapon and the final repulsion/destruction of the monster or invaders, followed by the leading couple's embrace.[22]

The Host, however, does not follow this typical narrative progression. Instead, the film depicts, on one hand, a family who has lost its teenage daughter to the monster and, on the other hand, highly incompetent government officials who are unwilling to help the family find her. In the monster attack at the beginning of the film, Park Gang-du, our unlikely hero, and his daughter, Hyun-seo, are running away from the monster when Park loses his grip on Hyun-seo's hand. He watches, horrified, as the creature snatches her up and carries her across the river. At first, he assumes she is dead. However, while he is quarantined in a hospital—the result of authorities' ostensible concern that the monster is carrying a mysterious virus—Park gets a call from Hyun-seo. He tries to tell the authorities that his daughter is alive, but nobody is willing to listen, as they firmly believe Hyun-seo is dead. In their desperate effort to find and save her, four family members—Hyun-seo's grandfather, Hee-bong; her uncle, Nam-il; her aunt, Nam-joo; and her slow-witted father, Gang-du—manage to escape from the hospital. The film focuses on their struggle to locate Hyun-seo and to kill the monster. Authorities, in fact, make no effort to help the family; rather, they put them on a wanted list and chase them. In the end, the monster is killed by the hapless family, and in one of the greatest departures from the typical monster movie narrative, Hyun-seo does not survive.

Susan Sontag argues that the core of good science fiction films, including monster movies, lies in the "aesthetics of destruction," since "science fiction films are not about science but about disasters."[23] In *The Host*, the "aesthetics of destruction" is displayed only briefly in the monster attack that occurs at the beginning of the film. Nonetheless, the monster represents the "disasters" Korean people have historically had to endure, which are quite often, if not always, man-made. Therefore, the film does follow the generic convention of the monster attack serving as an allegory for a real-world disaster. Although the computer-generated monster on-screen identifies the story as a "fantasy," the rest of the film's settings and characters are realistic. Even the monster's size is smaller than that of the typical movie monster, making Bong's monster seem more probable. It looks like a giant mutant fish one could believe would emerge from the Han River as the result of toxic contamination.[24]

FIGURE 5. *The Host*. Gang-du and his daughter, Hyun-seo, running away from the monster.

Moreover, the monster's destructive reach is contained. The monster does not run rampant through downtown Seoul, trampling pedestrians and toppling skyscrapers. Rather, it is confined to the riverbank and sewer system. It is not ferocious; it even stumbles clumsily down the riverbank during its attack. Ultimately, the monster does not look invincible, which makes us believe authorities could have captured and destroyed it had they tried. Instead, to legitimize the false claim of the "monster virus," the U.S. government and World Health Organization (WHO) decide to use an experimental biocide, Agent Yellow, to treat the Han River. A massive demonstration is held against the use of Agent Yellow, and it is during this protest the Park family faces down the monster and kills it.

The Host is Bong's most satirical look at Korean society. The film boasts his signature tonal blending/genre bending at its finest and his "art of *piksari*" at its best. It mixes the horror of a monster attack with slapstick comedy; it is a monster movie in which law enforcement, scientists, and other government authorities are more bent on chasing the victim's family than the monster; and it is an outbreak narrative in which the viral threat is a government and international hoax. The result of this genre bending in *The Host* is a weird twist on the monster movie in which the dysfunctional family of the monster's victim has no way to save her except to track down the monster themselves.

This ostensibly unlikely story is not that implausible, however, in view of the ways in which victims of major disasters have been treated by Korean authorities. Indeed, as mentioned in the introduction, social media discussions of the Sewol ferry disaster in 2014 drew parallels between it and *The Host*, contending that *The Host* predicted the government's neglect and unfair treatment of the families of the victims of that horrific disaster. As is the case in Bong's other films, the dual narrative structure of *The Host*—the monster story turning into a story of a family's struggle—serves to reveal the political nature of disasters that fall upon individuals. Man-made disasters, allegorized as the monster attack in the film, are, in fact, not "natural" or "accidental" but systemic failures bred by authorities' corruption and incompetence. Many of these man-made disasters occurred in Korea in the 1990s and early 2000s, such as the 1994 collapse of the Seongsu Bridge, one of the main bridges over the Han River, and the 1995 collapse of the luxurious Sampoong Department Store. The latter, which killed 502 people and injured 937, was the deadliest peacetime disaster in Korean history.

These disasters resulted from institutional failures to comply with or enforce safety rules and regulations, and the losses they caused were often compounded by the lack of an effective response. In addition, in the aftermath, victims' families were often neglected. Subsequent investigations often revealed or raised suspicions of governmental cover-ups of incompetence, negligence, or misconduct. A peculiarity of these disasters, however, is that victims tend to blame themselves rather than the true authors of such catastrophes, a tendency that Bong explicitly deplores. One such disaster to which Bong specifically refers in *The Host* occurred on February 18, 2003, when an arsonist set fire to a subway train in Daegu. A total of 192 passengers were killed, and 151 were injured. A later inquiry, revealing the errors and use of inadequate emergency equipment that authorities attempted to cover up, established that many of these casualties could have been avoided. Nonetheless, many of the victims' parents blamed themselves for their own devastating losses. They lamented that if they had been rich enough to buy their children cars, their children would not have taken the subway that day.[25] Bong makes a covert comment on the Daegu subway disaster in the collective funeral scene in *The Host*. One of the funeral wreaths standing in the gymnasium is from the "Daegu Subway Disaster Victims' Families Committee," drawing a clear parallel between the monster attack in the film and actual man-made disasters in Korea.

In this context, then, *The Host* is quite realistic in having unlikely heroes—the victim's family—go after the monster rather than scientists, the police, or the military. It is, in fact, appropriately Korean that Hyun-seo's dim-witted father and the three other family members take on the task of finding and saving her. And it is this very Korean situation that is the source of the story's unpredictable progression and wild tonal blending. Unexpected moments of slapstick comedy in the midst of serious situations accentuate the absurdities of Korean life. As noted, often it is authorities' incompetence that receives slapstick treatment; comedy occurs at the expense of the incompetent police, military, doctors, and scientists (both Korean and American).

As the progressive political scientist Choi Jang-jip argues, Korean culture and society have failed to democratize despite formal democratization in 1987. He states, "One of the major characteristics that Korea demonstrates after democratization is the issue of 'ineffective government.'"[26] He finds one cause of such an ineffective government to be what he defines as the "neoliberal democracy" instituted in the late 1990s.

After the Korean War (1950–1953), which devastated the whole nation, Korea was one of the poorest nations in the world; however, through state-led planned economic development, Korea achieved an economic growth on a par with the most advanced capitalist nations by the mid-1990s. Koreans' average annual incomes rose from $80 ($650 adjusted) in 1960 to over $10,000 in the mid-1990s.[27] This robust economic growth and prosperity were known as the Miracle on the Han River. However, in the late 1990s, because of the government's failure to manage properly the foreign exchange market at the onset of the Asian financial crisis in 1997, Korea experienced a severe economic downturn and was hit by a financial crisis that had devastating effects on its society and economic structure in the twenty-first century. This became known as the "IMF financial crisis" because, to prevent a total economic collapse, Korea had to ask for a bailout from the International Monetary Fund (IMF). In return, the government agreed to adopt such neoliberal economic policies as deregulation, a market-driven economy, procorporate policies, a flexible labor market making layoffs and part-time jobs easier for employers, and the privatization of state assets and public corporations. These measures benefitted large conglomerates at the expense of laborers and small businesses, and they resulted in massive layoffs and extensive unemployment.

Choi Jang-jip contends that because Korea's democratic government hastily adopted these neoliberal policies in response to the IMF financial crisis, it failed to bring either economic democracy or de facto democracy to Korean society.[28] Features of authoritarian governance persisted. This reality is conveyed in *The Host* in its portrayal of authorities' ineptitude and arrogance demonstrating that even though Korea has achieved democracy, ordinary people still suffer under authoritarian culture and corruption. The families of the victims of the monster attack were not given a detailed explanation of what was going on. They were just ordered to follow instructions while the Park family was able to sneak into the prohibited area of the riverbank by bribing the staff at the security checkpoint.

In particular, one of the devastating effects of the IMF financial crisis is what the media terms "IMF suicides." On February 17, 2007, *Dong-a Ilbo*, one of Korea's major newspapers, ran an article on the topic of "anomic suicide."[29] This article reports that the number of suicides increased from 5,856 in 1996 to 12,047 in 2005, making Korea the nation with the highest suicide rate among the member countries, all developed nations, of the OECD (Organization for Economic Co-operation and Development). The article interprets this increase in suicide as stemming not from personal problems but from social ills, especially the effects of the post-IMF reconstruction and the 2003 recession. Significantly, the article states that since 2003, small business owners have the highest suicide rate. Hence we see a small business man committing suicide in the beginning of *The Host*.

The Host is an excellent example of Bong's appropriation of a Hollywood genre as a tool for political commentary about Korea's twenty-first-century struggle with social injustices and economic inequality. In particular, *The Host* reveals various social problems caused by the neoliberal economic policies that in recent years have intensified the economic divide between the "haves" and the "have-nots." One of Bong's most pointed commentaries occurs even before we reach the narrative proper.

The Host begins with three prologues. The first, taking place in 2000, is the scene in the mortuary of the Eighth U.S. Army base, in which toxic materials are poured into the river by order of a U.S. officer. A superimposition visually depicts this toxic material being absorbed into the river. The second prologue, occurring in 2002, depicts two fishermen discovering a mutant fish in the river but failing to capture it. The third prologue is set in October 2006 and depicts an IMF suicide. A man in a business suit—a small business owner—stands precariously on the bridge spanning the Han River. Two men—a friend and an employee—run toward him, calling to him. The man says, "There is something dark in the water," and then asks them, "You really didn't see it?" When his friend replies, "What the hell are you talking about?" the man exclaims, "Morons to the end!" and throws himself into the river. The movie's title, *Gweomul* (Monster), then appears on-screen at the spot in the frame where the man hit the water. A monster is in the river, and a small businessman is its first prey. This prologue suggests that the monster symbolizes the economic disaster that neoliberal measures have brought upon Korea and that continues to plague the country today.

Indeed, this suicide communicates the core message of the film: the plight of ordinary citizens or the powerless in post-IMF Korean society. In this context, the Han River carries a strong allegorical meaning. As the phrase "Miracle on the Han River" demonstrates, the Han River is a powerful symbol of Korea's economic recovery after the devastation of the Korean War; it is conventionally seen as a beacon of modernity, industrial growth, and prosperity. However, the film turns this site of prosperity and pride into a site of disaster in which a monster is bred. In *Memories of Murder*, the golden rice field, a traditional image of prosperity, is tainted by the serial murders; in *The Host*, the Han River, once a symbol of national pride, becomes the source of a destructive monster. Thus *The Host* shows the continuation of the failure of the government to protect its citizens even in the postdemocratic era.

Further, while *Memories of Murder* depicts the 1980s military regime as the enabler of the murder crisis, *The Host* points to Korea's subservient relationship to the United States as the breeder of the monster. The American soldier, Sergeant Donald, who fights the monster but who dies from shock after the monster tears off his arm, represents the presence of American forces in Korea. As an individual, he is portrayed as a selfless man who is eager to fight the monster on the riverbank; as an American soldier, however, he becomes a government tool for spreading fear because his death is initially reported as having been caused by the mysterious (and actually nonexistent) virus. Despite Donald's individual act of sacrifice, the United States is depicted as the world power siding with and supporting the Korean government in hiding the falsity of the deadly virus. This is reminiscent of the U.S. support of the military regime during the Kwangju Massacre in May 1980.

Indeed, the 1980s plays a significant role in the film. If *Memories of Murder* is a story of a national crisis in the 1980s, *The Host* is that story taken up twenty years later. The most important connection to the 1980s is the monster itself. As noted earlier, Bong's films invite many different readings, and the monster has been interpreted as symbolizing many things, ranging from North Korea, to neoliberalism, to the Korean government. One interpretation, however, is that the monster attack is an allegory for the Kwangju Massacre and that the monster symbolizes the paratroopers sent to Kwangju to suppress the massive protests for democracy. Some Korean bloggers wrote that the attack scene reminded them of the massacre.[30] For example, one blogger wrote, "The U.S., the comprador government, the army, these three collaborating to surround a region, and the civilians isolated from the rest of the people, getting armed and battling to their death. . . . What does this remind you of? The region by the Han River completely surrounded by soldiers. It is the repetition of the same situation as the history of Kwangju in Korea, the city that the Army sieged with the consent of the U.S. on May 18, 1980."[31] As the biggest trauma in contemporary Korean history, the massacre left a deep wound that has not yet healed. As noted previously, the sense of betrayal and anti-American sentiment evident in the film grew out of this traumatic experience.

The monster attack compares to the massacre in several ways: the United States is involved in the birth of the monster (the United States endorsed the release of the army from the DMZ, thus supporting the massacre); the monster is confined to the Han River area and never goes out into the city as in most monster movies (the military isolated the city of Kwangju by shutting down the city border); the monster attacks people in broad daylight (paratroopers killed civilians in daylight); the Park family fights the monster with a rifle (Kwangju citizens formed a civil militia and fought back with rifles); the collective funeral is held in a gymnasium (photos of the victims were displayed in Kwangju municipal gymnasium); the monster attack is not reported in the media (the massacre was never covered by news media at the time, and the media was silent about the incident for many years afterward); the authorities accuse the Park family of carrying a deadly virus and put them on a wanted list (Kwangju protesters were accused of being communists and put on a wanted list after the protest was suppressed); and the monster is fought by former student activists and *minjung* (the Kwangju protesters killed and wounded some paratroopers during the massacre).

The fact that the monster is not as menacing as the giant creatures in conventional monster movies supports the interpretation of the monster as an allegory for the paratroopers. The scene in which Hyun-seo's grandfather, Hee-bong, dies is reminiscent of the civil militia's fight and the tragic civilian deaths that occurred during the massacre. After successfully escaping from the hospital and obtaining maps and rifles from black marketeers, the Park family sneaks into their snack stand home in the prohibited riverbank area and waits for the monster. The monster appears and attacks, and the family responds by shooting at it. When they are down to the last bullet in Gang-du's rifle, Hee-bong volunteers to approach the monster with the rifle to ensure the last shot is effective. However, Gang-du has miscalculated the number of bullets he had left; the rifle is actually empty. The monster grabs Hee-bong and hurls him to his death in front of his children. Gang-du runs to his dead father and cries, "Dad! Wake up, Dad! The soldiers are coming!" Unable to leave his father's body, Gang-du is caught by the biological warfare special forces that have been chasing the family. Both Hee-bong's violent death and Gang-du's desperate grief call up in the collective imagination images of hundreds, if not thousands, of similar violent deaths and the resulting chaos and grief caused by the paratroopers' victimization of the protesters in Kwangju.

In addition to its symbolic depiction of the Kwangju massacre, *The Host* explicitly depicts present-day ramifications of the 1980s oppressive regime. Specifically, the Park family, conceived as victims of the forceful evictions that took place in 1986 and 1987, represents how the suffering of the urban poor, the *minjung*, in the 1980s has continued into the twenty-first century. Sanggye-dong, a neighborhood in northern Seoul, is infamous as the site of brutal evictions associated with the 1988 Seoul Summer Olympic Games. Having succeeded in winning its bid to host the Olympics in 1981, Korea's military government decided to beautify Seoul for the event by eliminating unsightly slums and redeveloping poor neighborhoods into high-rise condominium complexes for the middle class. Occupants of these areas refused to be evicted, however, and battled city authorities for almost two years, only to lose their fight in the end. To compensate them for the loss of their homes, the government offered evictees the right to operate snack stands on the banks of the Han River. Learning of this arrangement while interviewing the actual snack stand owners, Bong included a dialogue in which Hee-bong talks about Gang-du growing up in Sanggye-dong in the original script but not in the final draft.[32]

Thus in its symbolic representation of the Kwangju massacre and implication of Olympics-related dislocations, *The Host* links the 1980s to the present from the perspective of the poor. Particularly with respect to the latter, the film demonstrates that in the intervening years, the *minjung*'s plight has continued and arguably has worsened, despite Korea's having been a political democracy for decades.

Further, an ambivalent attitude toward the 386 generation and the legacy of its role in the democratization movement, as described in chapter 1, is represented in the film by the character of Nam-il, the former student activist who is Hyun-seo's uncle. He is a "slacker" who criticizes his father for his attempts to get ahead (or get by) through bribes and subservience to authority. He still has a defiant and critical attitude, especially toward authorities. He complains that the government has not given him a job although he devoted his youth to the democratic movement. When the Park family is hunted by authorities, Nam-il seeks help from his college friend, also a former student activist, who is now working for a telecommunication corporation. This friend assures Nam-il that he can track down Hyun-seo's location by tracing the signal from her cell phone. This is a ruse, however, to lure him into a building where law enforcement officers wait to arrest him; the friend has betrayed Nam-il for the reward money to pay off his credit card debt. Nonetheless, Nam-il, who is nicknamed "the escape genius" because he was so good at evading detectives in his activist days, manages to escape from the building and avoid arrest.

This scene shows the two different paths the 386 generation took after democracy was achieved: either they became unemployed complainers who refused to conform or they completely bought into the system. Indeed, the 386 generation was the generation that both successfully brought democracy to Korea in the 1980s and headed the "IT (information technology) revolution" in the 2000s that led Korea to become the forerunner of global communication technology. Therefore, it is no coincidence that Nam-il's friend is an employee of a telecommunication company. Many student activists joined the civil government as lawmakers and government officials after 1993; however, they failed to bring about the fundamental changes necessary to establish a true democracy before losing general and presidential elections to the conservative party in 2008. Hence the 386 generation is viewed as both achieving and failing Korea's democratic movement—as both heroes and traitorous or ineffectual flunkies.

As such, Nam-il is the character who gives us the best *piksari* moment in the film as previously described; however, it is also the scene that demonstrates the solidarity among the activists and the people. Using his former activist skill of making Molotov cocktails, Nam-il prepares to kill the monster by setting it on fire. On his way to the riverbank, he meets a homeless man who joins him in the fight. The homeless man douses the monster with oil, and Nam-il throws several Molotov cocktails but fails to hit his target. At that critical moment, it is Nam-joo, his sister, who comes to the rescue. As a member of the national archery team, she always missed the target in critical moments because of her nervousness; however, this time she hits the monster with a flaming arrow and sets it on fire. Gang-du then delivers the fatal blow by stabbing the creature with an iron rod. Despite Nam-il's comedic bungling, however, this sequence is reminiscent of the *minjung* struggle of the 1980s. The monster is killed by the allied effort of a student activist (Nam-il), a woman (Nam-joo), and a homeless *minjung*. Further, Gang-du still wears his white hospital gown, so that, carrying the iron rod, he resembles a peasant fighter carrying a bamboo spear, an iconic image of a resistance fighter against the Japanese invasion in the late nineteenth century.

The original Korean title of the film, *Gweomul*, became a sort of catchword in Korea in the early 2000s. The definition of *Gweomul* is (1) a weird, strange, or grotesque creature and (2) an analogy for a bizarre and horrible person.[33]

Human monsters proliferate in contemporary Korean cinema. For example, in *Oldboy* (2003), the protagonist, who has been in captivity for fifteen years, says, "I have already become a monster." In Hong Sang-soo's *Turning Gate* (2002), the protagonist says, "If we can't be human, at least let's not become monsters." In *Turning Gate*, which mocks hypocrisy and snobbish intellectuals, the word *monster* symbolizes a person who is willing to sell out and comply with the corrupt system. Because the English title of Bong's film is *The Host*, most commentators have interpreted its main theme to be anti-America. The film does turn a critical eye toward the United States; however, as the Korean title indicates, its most biting critique and satire are directed toward Korean authorities and Korea's subservient relationship to the United States. Even with respect to the United States' influence in Korea, the weight of this critique is directed toward Korean authorities, as the film condemns Korea for its inability or unwillingness to resist U.S. pressure and demands. Ultimately, then, the Korean title reflects the cynicism and despair that pervade a society that has produced multiple monsters. In the film, the word *monster* actually has multiple meanings. The U.S. Army, the Korean government, the authorities, and the doctors are all monsters. In *Memories of Murder*, the two detectives cannot capture the serial killer in the 1980s, but in the 2000s, authorities in *The Host* do not even try to help. The difference between "cannot" and "do not" is enormous and reflects the change for the worse during the post-IMF period: empathy, compassion for the poor, and any sense of justice or fairness no longer exist.

In these ways, *The Host* provides a sharp yet subtle commentary on the historical and political complexities underlying present-day Korean society. Although set in 2006, the film includes characters and images that remind the audience of the 1980s, suggesting that the country's present state of affairs is closely related to that era. In sum, beneath its entertaining "monster movie" surface, the film is a biting assessment and critique of Korea's ambivalent legacy of the 1980s.

As *Memories of Murder* and *The Host* demonstrate, the difference between Hollywood genre films and Bong's localized versions are rooted in different historical experiences. Having lived through a harsh colonial period, a civil war, the division of the nation, and the separation of families in the first half of the twentieth century, the country then suffered a succession of draconian military regimes and the ill effects of neoliberal economic policies in the second half and into the twenty-first century. Koreans have become discontented with, if not hopeless about, their current circumstances; they are also deeply distrustful of the government and authority. Both films demonstrate and justify this discontent, distrust, and despondency by showing the extent to which corruption pervades all levels of Korea's political power structure.

Bong's films have certain aspects that remind us of Fredric Jameson's concept of "cognitive mapping," which makes it possible to understand local phenomena within the larger context of social structures. Jameson conceives cognitive mapping as a tool for perceiving an individual's relation to an entire social system; he states that its function is "to enable a situational representation on the part of the individual subject to that vaster and properly unrepresentable totality which is the ensemble of society's structures as a whole."[34] *Memories of Murder* offers insight into the political nature of the Hwasŏng serial murder case by linking it to the repressive military regime of the 1980s, while *The Host,* by showing that the monster was created by unavoidable pressure from the United States, contextualizes the disaster of the monster attack and the plight of the Park family within Korea's postcolonial and neocolonial situation. Both films create cognitive maps that situate local disasters and the sufferings of the individuals within the larger context of national and global politics.

While Bong's use of genre makes the films universal and internationally comprehensible, his subject matter makes them specifically Korean. Both *Memories of Murder* and *The Host* exemplify Bong's central theme of the incompetence or inadequacy of Korean authorities in protecting or caring for individuals, families, and the public. Bong compellingly expresses the intersection of politics and everyday life; in these two films, he puts a magnifying glass to Korean society to analyze what lies beneath horrible crimes and disasters. It is telling that in *The Host,* Hyun-seo, the monster's captive in the sewer, tells her fellow captive, a little boy, "I will go out and get a doctor, the police, and the military. Stay put and wait." These are her last words. She is not, in fact, able to escape to get help, and no help comes her way. No one saves her, but she is the one who protects and saves the little boy at the end.

4 · MONSTERS WITHIN

Moral Ambiguity and Anomie in
Barking Dogs Never Bite and *Mother*

Barking Dogs Never Bite (2000) and *Mother* (2009) both end with the main character in a troubled trance. In *Barking Dogs Never Bite*, Yoon-ju, who has bribed his way into a full-time teaching position, looks out a window during class as the curtains are drawn for a slideshow. As the room goes completely dark, he is shown in close-up, a dazed look on his face as he lowers his eyes in resignation. *Mother* starts with the mother walking into a meadow and breaking into a dance, again with a dazed, unfocused look on her face. As the story unfolds, we learn that she had violently killed a junkman who was the only witness to her son's crime immediately before this prologue. The film had opened *in media res*. In short, both characters try to cope with their overwhelming sense of guilt and shame by shutting down their consciences.

These scenes of troubled trances echo the hypnotic state, a notion Korean sociologist Chang Kyung-sup suggests is one of the consequences of what he terms the "compressed modernity" resulting from Korea's rapid postwar economic growth, "the most drastic and compressed process of national development in human history."[1] The concept of "compressed modernity" is widely accepted as the key component in Korea's historical experience of the twentieth century.[2] Chang explains that "the sheer tempo and amount of unprecedented economic and social transformation so amazed people as to create a hypnotic state, in which various serious problems and costs accruing to such transformations did not immediately irritate their senses."[3] While compressed modernity made the Miracle on the Han River possible, it also engendered dire consequences politically, socially, and most of all, morally. The economic growth, led by Korea's authoritarian state, was achieved at the cost of virtually everything else and, in particular, the concern for basic human rights of working people, safety measures, the concern for others, and moral principles.

It is no coincidence that both *Barking Dogs Never Bite* and *Mother* share these moments of troubled trances with their resonance of the hypnotic state. Both films represent the numbing effects and deep psychological impact of compressed modernity on individuals' daily lives. Unlike *Memories of Murder* and *The Host*, which reveal the state's systemic wrongdoings, *Barking Dogs Never Bite* and *Mother* focus on the lives of individuals who face moral dilemmas. Therefore, larger social issues are less foregrounded than in *Memories of Murder* and *The Host*. However, what the characters go through in *Barking Dogs Never Bite* and *Mother* is deeply connected to the social ills created by Korea's compressed modernity. The absurdities and social corruption that surround the lives of these characters and drive them to make moral compromises are the consequences of the overwhelming speed of change. Thus these personal stories can be read as allegories of what Korean society has become over the last half century.

While *Barking Dogs Never Bite* and *Mother* focus on the protagonists' moral dilemmas, Bong Joon Ho remains nonjudgmental of their actions. Throughout both films, the camera maintains an objective distance, leaving it to the audience to ponder and judge the main characters' immoral acts. Both films portray characters who are drawn into emotionally overwhelming situations and then, out of despair and desperation, slowly turn into human monsters. The difficulties and the moral crises they go through in trying to solve their problems expose how Korean society has lost its sense of social morality and justice. Is it acceptable to commit a moral crime if it is a customary practice? Can moral corruption be excused if committed in the name of motherly love? Bong raises these questions to provoke the audience to reflect upon the issue of social morality, as both films portray guilt, despair, and the psychological wounds most Koreans can easily identify with.

Furthermore, both films delve deeper into the issue of social morality by depicting a society in which the socially weak exploit the weaker. Attention to the socially weak is one of the mainstays in Bong Joon Ho's films; however, in these two films, the socially weak protagonists are portrayed differently from those of *The Host*, for instance, who are depicted as victims of an unfair and incompetent social system. Yoon-ju and the mother are no simple victims. Rather, in their daily struggle to get by, they become perpetrators of crime and moral corruption: Yoon-ju kills a dog and engages in bribery; the mother is a liar and a murderer. Despite the torments of their consciences, they ultimately decide to hide the truth for their own benefit. This is in stark contrast to Hyun-seo and Gang-du in *The Host*, who, respectively, protect and adopt the little orphan boy kidnapped by the monster. We see no such concern for the weaker in *Barking Dogs Never Bite* and *Mother*.

This apathy or even animosity toward the weaker is one of the consequences of compressed modernity, which was further exacerbated by a proliferation of neoliberal policies mandated by the IMF bailout measures in 1997. A flexible labor market drastically reduced job stability, various deregulatory policies deepened economic inequality, and privatization of government and public institutions drove Korean society into a "profit-oriented" frenzy. Korean political scientist Choi Chang-ryol states, "Today's Korean society can be summed up as a society in which 'a war of all against all' is carried out; everyone is out solely for himself or herself."[4] Korean society has become a Darwinian jungle in which only the fittest can survive, a state illustrated compellingly in both *Barking Dogs Never Bite* and *Mother*.

This chapter discusses Bong's exploration of these moral questions within the context of Korean society—especially its historical experience of compressed modernity—in *Barking Dogs Never Bite* and *Mother*. It focuses on the moral anomie this compressed modernity has brought to Korean society at large. As Alvin Toffler argues, an acceleration of change has "personal and psychological, as well as sociological, consequences."[5] On the surface, the moral dilemmas faced by the protagonists in these two films seem to be due to their individual actions and choices. However, as the stories unfold, the marks of an immoral society emerge in the anomie that results from Korea's failure to establish social justice even after achieving political democracy. The main characters' moral ambiguities reflect uniquely Korean social absurdities (*pujoris*) and moral blindness. Bong uses Korean realities to investigate the extent to which moral confusion and alienation dominate Korean society and the lives of the individuals within it.

COMPRESSED MODERNITY AND MORAL ANOMIE

Things have changed so quickly in South Korea, and we have become rich so fast that people don't know what to do. Even at my level, which, of course, isn't the highest level at all—we're just average—when I think about it, I really don't know how I should live. Should I just focus on my family? Or should I do something for society? Nothing is clear. (Mi-yôn's mother, November 2, 1995)[6]

This quote from a woman living in Seoul effectively sums up the dizzying pace of change that ordinary Korean citizens experienced in postwar Korea. The coexistence of traditional and contemporary values—in particular, the opposing values of feudal Confucianism and capitalist materialism—causes moral confusion and vertigo. This "contemporaneity of the uncontemporary," a term used by German philosopher Ernst Bloch to explain the coexistence of nonsimultaneous elements in a society, has caused the loss of a moral compass.[7] The desire for material gain and the protection of their own personal welfare has become individuals' and families' only concern, eliminating any broader regard for others.

This noncontemporaneity has resulted in a clash between, on one hand, the traditional emphasis on modesty and on the collective and, on the other hand, what Cho Hae-joang has summed up as the contemporary pursuit of the "3Ms" (money, market, me).[8] Cho suggests that compressed modernity has brought about a busy lifestyle that has "diminished people's capacity for thinking or self-reflection."[9] The rapid economic and social changes required people to make changes in their daily lives not only in material terms but also, perhaps more importantly, in ethical terms. Furthermore, the change from a strong sense of community and extended families to a modern focus on the nuclear family has contributed to today's selfish familism, a concentration on one's family alone that disregards social morals.

In the latter part of the twentieth century, moral anomie became pervasive in Korean society, and as the Korean sociologist Chang Won-ho claims, that society morphed into one "in which people who abide by the rules feel dejected." The arbitrary application of rules became Korea's most serious societal problem.[10] In the rapid process of compressed modernity, many laws were adopted from the West that did not quite apply to or reflect Korean realities. The results were gaps and ambiguities in the laws themselves but, perhaps more significantly, laxity in enforcing those laws. Further, the tendency for the application of law to be lenient toward the rich and the powerful bred a general distrust of the system; this, in turn, spawned moral laxity.

Compressed modernity also hurt the establishment of true democracy in Korea. The nation achieved parliamentary democracy in 1987 after decades of political struggle; however, the sense of achievement was quickly replaced by indignation and disappointment because a gap between parliamentary democracy and actual democracy was soon evident. This gap has only widened since the late 1980s. Chang Kyung-sup lists the consequences of Korea's unique compressed modernity as patriarchal political authoritarianism, despotic and monopolistic business practices of *chaebols* (Korean-style, family-run mega-corporations), abuse and exclusion of labor, neglect of basic welfare rights, and ideological self-negation.

Chang cites "collapse" as the key word for understanding the Korean peninsula of the 1990s. As noted previously, the decade ended with the IMF financial crisis that followed the IMF's emergency bailout of the Korean economy in 1997. One result of the IMF financial crisis was the collapse of a good deal of the nation's infrastructure and transportation systems. However, the impact of the crisis extended beyond buildings and bridges; it also brought about immoral business practices and political collusion so rampant that the resulting political, economic, social, and moral problems "seriously affected people's everyday lives."[11] Specifically, under the influence of this compressed growth, corruption and illegal acts were accepted as customary and even normal, eventually leading to a "winner-take-all society."[12] Korean political critic Kang Junman argues that because Korea's "condensed economic growth" was achieved through military-like strategies of top-down orders and directions, "there was no room for 'ethics' or 'autonomy' or 'social responsibility' to settle in."[13] This resulted in a "vulgar elite group" who has no sense of noblesse oblige, the moral obligation of the "haves" to help the "have-nots" through donations and charity work. Kang adds that the condensed economic growth also fostered in Korea a risk-taking culture that has, for instance, dismissed the need for safety measures to the extent that Korea has become a "brutal society." Significantly, this "risk-taking culture" encompasses not only physical but "legal and moral risks" as well.[14]

Chang Kyung-sup also contends that this rapid material growth resulted in "no less fundamental and unique transformations in South Koreans' cultural assets, ideologies and institutions." Because no indigenous social revolution has uprooted archaic cultural and institutional traditions, "there is a co-existence of traditional, modern, and postmodern trends, on the one hand, and of indigenous, foreign, and global elements, on the other." Clashes between these two forces result in institutional and cultural inconsistencies that have become "a very integral part of South Koreans' everyday modern life."[15] Furthermore, as Korean historian Ahn Byung-wook states, "After the financial crisis of 1997, owing to the proliferation of new liberalized policies, capital power and influence controlled nearly every corner of society," making Korea the "prey of capitalism."[16] Accordingly, the rapid changes Korea experienced in the twentieth century have created a confusion in values. Korea is one of the rare postcolonial societies to achieve both economic growth and democracy, but this rapid modernization was accompanied by the social problems of corruption, high suicide rates,[17] economic inequality, sexual crimes, and moral anomie.

WORLD OF *PUJORI*: SOCIAL INJUSTICE AND CORRUPTION

The Korean word *pujori* is crucial in understanding Bong Joon Ho's filmic world. Indeed, Bong characterizes contemporary Koreanness as *pujori*.[18] This characterization is a stark departure from that embraced by older generations of Korean filmmakers, such as the world-renowned veteran director Im Kwon-Taek, who defines *Koreanness* in terms of the unique beauty of Korea's premodern, traditional art and culture.[19] In order to appreciate the Koreanness of Bong's films, then, we feel the need to understand *pujori*.

The closest English translation of *pujori* is "absurd" or "absurdity." However, the English word does not accurately capture its whole sense. The Korean

National Institute of the Korean Language's *P'yojun'gugŏdaesajŏn* (Standard Korean dictionary) defines *pujori* as (1) going against what is right or an event of that sort, (2) a euphemism for a fraudulent act, or (3) the existential term for the meaninglessness of life.[20] On the other hand, the *Merriam-Webster Collegiate Dictionary* defines *absurd* as "ridiculously unreasonable, unsound, or incongruous."[21] The English word does not include the concept of corruption, which is the unique aspect of *pujori* that Bong deals with in his films. This sense of *pujori* is, in fact, the root cause of the absurdities of everyday life that Bong's films so adeptly depict.

Consequently, I use *pujori* to indicate corruption and other social ills and use the English word *absurd* or *absurdity* to express the nonsensical, irrational, and ridiculous. *Pujori* breeds moral blindness, which, in turn, allows unthinkable and unreasonable things to happen. In Korea, social *pujoris* benefit the rich and the powerful. Thus the world of *pujori*, as Bong conceives it, is a system rigged against the powerless.

Bong's first four films, set in Korea, reveal the structural violence and social *pujoris* that lie beneath the various crimes and disasters that are the films' content. Each of Bong's films reveals the systemic results of this social *pujori*: detectives who accuse and torture innocent civilians (*Memories of Murder*), doctors who attempt to extract brain cell samples from a purported victim of a virus they know does not exist (*The Host*), and a mother who lets an innocent boy be arrested for a murder she knows her son committed (*Mother*). These actions and choices are all examples of *pujoris* or absurdities. These films show that social *pujoris* breed human monsters and that their monstrous acts bring horror to the daily lives of ordinary people.

While a real monster wreaks havoc in *The Host*, "monsters with a human face" roam the world of *Barking Dogs Never Bite* and *Mother*. These human monsters are testimonies that immorality and monstrous qualities have become necessary means for survival and success. Whereas *Memories of Murder* and *The Host* leave the audience with an eerie feeling that the threat is still on the loose (the serial killer and the possibility of another river monster, respectively), *Barking Dogs Never Bite* and *Mother* leave the viewer perplexed. In these films, the audience is led to sympathize with the protagonists, who are socially marginalized, but then, in dealing with their troubles, they commit immoral acts, leaving audiences' allegiances torn.

Furthermore, Bong's refusal to judge these protagonists' actions heightens the sense of irony or tragedy. The camera maintains a distance that puts the audience in the position of a detached observer, and the films' open-endedness gives viewers space in which to reflect on the characters' actions. Neither film condemns the characters; rather, the films portray them as simultaneously *both* victims *and* perpetrators. Both *Barking Dogs Never Bite* and *Mother* show their protagonists being driven by circumstance into moral corruption. Indeed, in all of Bong's films, monsters have a tragic quality in that we see they are brought into being by social circumstances or *pujoris*. For instance, even in *The Host*, the monster is a man-made mutation that is smaller than other cinematic monsters and, at times, even clumsy. In some ways, its ferocious attack seems to stem from its sense of confusion and loss.

Thus while Bong's characters commit monstrous acts, the audience still roots for them precisely because of the moral ambiguity of their situations and choices. The line between good and evil is blurred. This, in turn, highlights the extent to which moral anomie and confusion have become "normal" in Korean society, and this is the uniquely Korean *pujori* that Bong represents in his films. Instead of judging the immoral actions of his ordinary characters, Bong sees them as becoming monsterized against their will. In his films, monsters are caused, in large part, by the chain reactions of pervasive *pujoris*. These circumstances thus infuse a tragic irony into the characters' situations and create the bewilderment audiences experience.

This sense of bewilderment is furthered in *Barking Dogs Never Bite* and *Mother* by the fact that these films are firmly rooted in the realities of the present day. They are not about the military dictatorship of the past, as in *Memories of Murder*, nor are they political allegories, as in *The Host*. Instead of critiquing the systemic failure of authorities to protect ordinary citizens, the films focus on the lived experience of ordinary citizens and explore the ways in which the deep structure of social *pujoris* impacts everyday lives. Thus compared to *Memories of Murder* and *The Host*, Bong's critique of the social system in *Barking Dogs Never Bite* and *Mother* is subtler; systemic problems and public corruption are embedded in the characters' lived environment.

Corruption among public officials, for instance, is a long-standing social ill that is shared by most postcolonial nations. According to research conducted by the Korea Development Institute, as of 2010, Korea ranked fourth among twenty-one developed nations—behind only Greece, Italy, and Portugal—in the rate of corruption among its public servants.[22] Corruption among politicians, public officials, and public servants is so pervasive that most Koreans accept it as "normal." This "typical Korean attitude," as Bong calls the general acceptance of social *pujoris* and the sense of resignation, is what he is driven to capture in his films.

Because of the pervasiveness of corruption and social injustice in Korea, it is no exaggeration to say that a desperate hunger for social justice has shaped not only the postdemocratic Korean society but also the psychology of its people. This hunger was manifested in the surprise best-selling 2010 book *Justice: What's the Right Thing to Do?* by Harvard University professor Michael Sandel. More than a million copies of the Korean translation have been sold—and this in the social sciences and humanities publishing market, in which sales of five thousand copies is considered a hit.²³

Furthermore, as *Barking Dogs Never Bite* and *Mother* demonstrate, Korea has no safety net for the socially weak. To survive and achieve a decent living, people often have to make moral compromises or actually exploit those who are even weaker. Korean historian Park Noja suggests state-led economic growth and neoliberalism in the twenty-first century have promoted intense competition among individuals and given rise to a culture in which "everyone is out for himself." He states, "Crushing the other for my personal desire has become like a national policy," adding that indifference to others' deaths has become the "social atmosphere in Korea," making it "a model nation of neoliberalism."²⁴ As Korean society has become one of the most advanced of neoliberal capitalist societies, it has been overtaken by economic polarization, profit-oriented corporate value, materialism, and selfish familism.

BARKING DOGS NEVER BITE: "BUT NOBODY FOLLOWS THE RULE"

Barking Dogs Never Bite is full of absurdities Korean audiences can identify with; in fact, its central plot is triggered by just such an absurd happenstance. To root this somewhat surreal film in concrete reality, Bong Joon Ho borrowed from an actual subway incident to give the film its ridiculous start. As it begins, we learn that Yoon-ju has been denied the full-time university faculty position he has applied for because he was not a "good lobbyist." However, the position becomes available again because of the sudden, absurd death of the successful applicant, Kung-min. After a brown-nosing night of drinking with the alcohol-loving dean, Kung-min is killed when his head is crushed by a subway train as he bends over the tracks to vomit. Kung-min was not a drinker; however, he got drunk because he felt obligated to keep pace with the dean, a heavy drinker. Then to save money, he went to the subway station instead of taking a taxi home, making his death even more pathetic.

Yoon-ju's friend Jun-pyo urges him to reapply for the position, arguing that this will be Yoon-ju's last chance to become a professor. Consequently, Yoon-ju contemplates bribing the dean with $10,000 to secure the position, even though he has previously rejected the idea of bribery. But how is he going to raise the money? And will he actually give in to temptation this time? In the meanwhile, with the prospect of not having a job hanging over him, Yoon-ju becomes irritated by the sound of a barking dog within his apartment complex. Out of frustration, he kidnaps the dog to get rid of it; however, he fails to drop the dog from the rooftop of the high-rise apartment building. He hides the dog in the basement of the apartment building, and the dog is eventually killed by the janitor, who

FIGURE 6. *Barking Dogs Never Bite*. Yoon-ju trying to kill the barking dog.

makes a dog soup out of it. Then it turns out that Yoon-ju has misrecognized the dog, and the actual barking dog is still around. He succeeds in both kidnapping and killing the second dog. Thus he has committed two dognaps, killing one of them.

These two missing-dog incidents spur the interaction between Yoon-ju and Hyun-nam, the female protagonist, and the absurd events around the apartment complex, including the comic-book-like chase scenes between Yoon-ju and Hyun-nam and between Hyun-nam and the homeless man living in the basement. Hyun-nam is a young woman who works as a clerk in the management office of the apartment complex, and feeling the sense of duty to find the dog killer, she goes out of her way to investigate the missing-dog incidents.

Yoon-ju's moral and financial dilemma constitutes the core conflict in the film, and it opens up a space in which the *pujori* in higher education—the pervasive bribery and pandering in the hiring process—is revealed and critiqued. In fact, corruption in higher education and among public officials is one of the most recognized social and political problems in Korea. In 2010, *pujoris* in the teaching profession became a national scandal when part-time lecturer Sŏ Chŏngmin committed suicide, leaving a five-page note exposing dire working conditions, part-time instructors ghostwriting for full-time professors' journal articles, and corruption in the faculty hiring process.[25] Bribery and donations to the universities to achieve professional advancement are open secrets in higher education. Therefore, the story of Yoon-ju in *Barking Dogs Never Bite* is a very familiar one to Korean viewers. The film deftly interweaves the consequences of compressed modernity into a story of "missing dogs," and absurdities such as Kung-min's death are abundant. The ingenuity of the film lies in how it reveals the deeper structure of *pujoris*: the corruption, materialism, and moral anomie that shape contemporary Korean society and frustrate many Korean citizens.

The film is set in a lower-middle-class apartment complex in Seoul.[26] In fact, most of the story takes place within this high-rise complex, whose mundane, everyday spaces provide a realistic setting for the moral and emotional struggles of ordinary citizens facing absurdities. Bong's use of a high-rise apartment complex as the film's setting effectively conveys contemporary urban living in Korea because this is the most prevalent type of housing in most cities. Indeed, the high-rise apartment complex is one of the symbols of South Korea's rapid modernization and urbanization. Korea is an extremely urban-centered nation, with a quarter of its population concentrated in the capital city of Seoul. Urbanization, especially the construction boom of high-rise apartments, peaked during the 1980s, and the film specifically comments on how many of those high-rises were shoddily constructed, built with cheap materials as a result of builders embezzling much of the construction funds.

Yoon-ju's apartment complex is one of those quick builds, and its background story is told by the janitor in a six-minute monologue presented as a horror/ghost story. This mini-interlude is inserted thirty minutes into the film as the chief janitor visits the building janitor, who is cooking the first missing dog. When the two janitors sit down to talk, the light bulb suddenly goes out. The chief turns on his flashlight and places it on the floor, creating the kind of low-level lighting used in horror films to create eerie, ghost-like visages. According to the janitor, the apartment was built in 1988 during the construction boom the government undertook as part of its urban beautification in preparation for Seoul's hosting of the Summer Olympics.[27] The janitor says that during that time, "everything was built slapdash." A man known as Boiler Kim was called in to fix the failing heating system, only to conclude that the real problem was that the builders had used cheap materials, pocketing the money thus saved from the construction budget. His accusations caused a fistfight, during which Boiler Kim was killed. The builders hid his body in a wall and cemented it over. The janitor tells the chief that the humming sound in the basement is from the ghost of Boiler Kim.

This mini-interlude has nothing to do with film's narrative progression; however, it is one of the most significant scenes in the film in that it reveals the social *pujoris* behind the construction of the apartment complex. It is a horror story that serves several purposes. First, it provides not only the apartment building's historical background but a concrete example of the elevation of monetary gain over safety, resulting from compressed modernity. Second, by means of the murder and the secret burial of the truth bearer, it illustrates the distrust and social injustice that pervade Korean society. Third, it calls forth the audience's collective memory of the 1980s. Finally, it captivates the audience with the kind of ghost storytelling they grew up with. In effect, Boiler Kim's story is a direct commentary on the 1980s, during which Korea achieved parliamentary democracy but social *pujoris* intensified.

Indeed, as Bong's first feature film, *Barking Dogs Never Bite* demonstrates the seeds of characteristic elements of his films—his deftness in tonal blending, his concern for realism—and his reflection of the 1980s as the most crucial period in contemporary Korean history: the period of harsh military dictatorship, the Kwangju massacre, the intense *minjung* movement for democracy, and the 1988 Seoul Olympics. It is no coincidence, for instance, that Boiler Kim was brought in from the southwestern region of Korea, near Kwangju. The "Boiler Kim" sequence in *Barking Dogs Never Bite* demonstrates how the specter of the massacre haunts contemporary Korean society. Many truths have been buried over the course of Korea's history; however, they continue—like Boiler Kim—to murmur in the dark.

In *Barking Dogs Never Bite*, Bong has created a microcosm of the clash of modern and traditional values in Korean society. The dog is a perfect vehicle to weave these clashes into a comedy full of absurdities and ironies. Indeed, the film can be summarized as the story of a dog hater being forced into becoming a reluctant dog owner by his wife, who has financed his bid to become a professor. She herself was coerced to retire from her job because of her pregnancy. She gives most of her retirement money to Yoon-ju to help him achieve his dream, and with a little bit of leftover money, she has bought herself a dog. She puts Yoon-ju in charge of taking care of the dog; however, in an ironic twist, he loses the dog and becomes the victim of a third missing-dog incident within the apartment complex.

The dog also carries different meanings to the film's two protagonists. For Yoon-ju, the unemployed PhD stuck at home all day doing housework while his pregnant wife goes to work (until she is driven to retire toward the end of her pregnancy), the barking dog is a reminder of his own emasculation and incompetence. It annoys him so much that, to put an end to it, he drops the dog from the apartment rooftop. For Hyun-nam, on the other hand, "missing dogs" provide the opportunity to be a hero and become famous on TV. Consequently, when she witnesses a man dropping a dog from the rooftop, she is determined to find the culprit and expose him. As Yoon-ju deals with both the moral and financial implications of his dilemma, Hyun-nam dreams of becoming famous through a brave and righteous act. Supporting characters—the janitor, the homeless man who makes the basement his home, the old lady who is the owner of the second missing dog—are all connected to each other through the dogs.

The dog provides a key element in portraying a society in which absurd comedies happen because "nobody follows the rules." The apartment complex and its inhabitants are a microcosm of a society without firm principles or a moral compass. All the hoopla surrounding the missing dogs happens because the dog owners break the homeowners association's rule that bans pets. The dialogue between Yoon-ju and the janitor captures the characters' cynicism toward a society that lacks principles:

YOON-JU: Dogs aren't allowed here, right?
JANITOR: Yeah, that's right, but nobody follows the rule.
YOON-JU: Nobody in the country follows the rules.
JANITOR: Ever since the liberation [from Japan].

With this dialogue, Bong has seamlessly inserted social commentary into the film's narrative. Korean audiences are familiar with this sort of cynical talk about Korean society, and thus it adds to the film's realistic picture of the everyday.

The dog also serves to distinguish between the residents and nonresidents/ employees of the apartment complex. For the residents, dogs are companions. The girl refuses to go to school unless her dog is found; the old woman whose dog is killed dies from shock; and for Yoon-ju's wife, the dog is self-compensation for her retirement from work. To nonresidents, however, dogs are nutritious food, as for the janitor and the homeless man, or a means for achieving fame and recognition, as Hyun-nam dreams. The contrast between the haves (albeit lower middle class) and the have-nots within the apartment complex corresponds to the clash between the traditional and modern. In the past, when Korea was one of the poorest nations in the world after the end of the Korean War (1950–1953), dog meat was a good source of protein, but as Korea became more affluent, the number of pet dogs substantially increased, and many consider the dog as their companion animal, as in the case of the old lady in the film. The contrast between the residents and nonresidents or haves and have-nots is also conveyed visually through the different spaces the characters occupy. The janitor and the homeless man spend much of their time in the basement, utilizing abandoned furniture and other items to create a living space for cooking, exercising, and sleeping. (The janitor, having tacked a world clock on the wall, evokes the concept of the unrecognized effect of globalization on their lives.)

Yoon-ju is a resident, but he is somewhat an in-between character. He is the only resident who visits the basement, but for him, the basement is a threatening space. Initially, he goes to the basement to hide the first dog, which he failed to kill, and when he goes back to retrieve the dog, he is forced to hide in a closet when the janitor is alerted by the noise Yoon-ju accidentally makes. The janitor approaches the closet, holding a knife stained with the dog's blood. However, Yoon-ju is saved from being discovered when the chief janitor arrives, and they begin talking about "Boiler Kim." Yoon-ju runs frantically to escape from the basement and return to the safety of his home. This is a playful moment in which Bong uses horror-film conventions to drive home the fact that Yoon-ju does not—or does not want to—belong there. Indeed, it is no doubt that fear of becoming a nonresident "basement dweller" that finally propels him to engage in bribery.

Misrecognition plays a vital role in heightening the irony and sense of the absurd in this film. The first dog Yoon-ju kidnaps but fails to kill is, in fact, not the barking dog that has been tormenting him. When Yoon-ju kidnaps this dog, which belongs to a little girl, he takes it to the roof but cannot bring himself to throw it to its death. Ironically, he is interrupted by the old lady, whose dog (unbeknown to Yoon-ju) is the real barker—whom Yoon-ju *will* eventually kill. The old lady's intervention stops Yoon-ju's first attempt at canine homicide. After locking the reprieved dog in the basement, Yoon-ju discovers his mistake when he hears the barking again. When he double-checks the little girl's "missing-dog" flyer, he sees that it reads, "Can't bark due to throat operation."[28] Thus the little girl loses her dog—consumed by the janitor—for no reason.

Yoon-ju then schemes to kidnap the real barker, the old lady's dog, and finally "succeeds" in throwing it off the apartment roof. Hyun-nam, trying out new binoculars from the roof of another building, witnesses Yoon-Ju killing the old lady's dog and goes after him, running frantically to the opposite apartment roof. Hyun-nam is neither talented nor versatile, but she is full of righteousness. Although she fails to catch Yoon-ju in her first attempt, she vows to do so after the old lady dies from shock at learning of her dog's murder. While Yoon-ju is dealing with his moral and financial dilemma, Hyun-nam dreams of breaking out of her tedious life by becoming a hero like the real-life female bank teller who received national media attention by single-handedly capturing an armed robber. In fact, Bong uses actual news footage of the bank teller in the scene in which Hyun-nam and her friend watch the news. For Hyun-nam, then, capturing the dog killer is a quest for self-realization. However, when the police catch the homeless man wrongfully accused of the dog killing and the story of the missing dogs is aired on the news, Hyun-nam's interview is cut out. Her dream ends up being nothing but a fantasy.

The circumstances surrounding the two missing dogs get more complicated when, out of the blue, Yoon-ju's wife brings home a dog. In an ironic twist, Yoon-ju, the dog killer, has been forced to become a dog owner, and because his wife works outside the home, he becomes the dog's caretaker. The dog's name is Soon-ja, the same as Korea's notorious first lady of the 1980s—another instance of inciting the collective memory of the 1980s. While walking her in the park, Yoon-ju loses Soon-ja when he is distracted by spotting a lottery ticket and contemplating its implicit potential of solving all his problems.

Thus Yoon-ju's own dog becomes the third missing dog. Yoon-ju's wife accuses him of abandoning the dog on purpose and then tells him that although she bought the dog with her severance money, she had planned to give him the rest to bribe his way into a professorship. Guilt-ridden, Yoon-ju must find Soon-ja. As he posts "missing-dog" posters around the neighborhood, he and Hyun-nam meet for the first time. Not realizing that Yoon-ju is the rooftop dog killer she is hunting, Hyun-nam is eager to help him. As Yoon-ju and Hyun-nam make copies of the flyer in a convenience store, their faces are lit from below by the copy machine. Tension develops as the two discuss Hyun-nam's efforts to find the man from the roof. When Yoon-ju asks if Hyun-nam saw the man's face, however, she reveals that she saw him only from the back.

In a final ironic twist, it is the now-dead old lady who triggers the resolution of the missing-dogs narrative. Hyun-nam inherits dried radishes from the old lady. She goes up to the rooftop to retrieve them and comes across the homeless man preparing to roast Soon-ja. In another comic chase scene, Hyum-nam, dressed in a yellow hooded T-shirt, goes after him. A group of people in yellow coats suddenly appear on the roof of the opposite building and cheer her on, throwing confetti. Eventually, Hyun-nam succeeds in capturing the homeless man, who is arrested and accused of kidnapping all three dogs. The truth is never revealed, and the real perpetrators (the janitor and Yoon-ju) get away. Yoon-ju pays the bribe and becomes a professor. Hyun-nam, however, is fired from her job for being out of the office too much during her quest to find the dog killer. The only character who was trying to help others (albeit for personal motives) is penalized for her efforts, suggesting the degree to which social injustice and apathy are rampant in Korean society today. To act for others is, in effect, to risk what is in your own best interests.

Alternatively, in becoming a dog owner and a professor, Yoon-ju has effectively been accepted into the system. He is no longer an outsider. The irony of this outcome is that he was helped by Hyun-nam, whose ultimate goal was to capture him, the dog killer. Yoon-ju tries to reveal to her that he is the dog killer she had been hunting. After Yoon-ju has delivered the bribe, he gets drunk to try to forget what he has done. Hyun-nam discovers him passed out on the street; she herself has also been drinking because she has been fired. The two begin to remove the "missing-dog" flyers they had posted together. Hyun-nam tells Yoon-ju of her layoff. Guilt-ridden, Yoon-ju tries half-heartedly to confess that he is actually the dog killer by running in front of her so she will recognize the dog killer she chased, but she never suspects him, thinking of him always and only as the victim of a dognapper. He tries again and again but ultimately gives up the effort. Here he is being a half coward; now that he is a professor, he has too much to lose to confess outright. Instead, he resigns himself to his moral guilt. The film ends as he looks out the classroom window at a green forest, only to have a black curtain close out the view, trapping him in the darkness of the classroom. In contrast, we last see Hyun-nam hiking into an open wood with a friend. Yoon-ju's life is secure but dark; Hyun-nam's future is insecure but wide open. Intellectuals are morally corrupt, while Hyun-nam faces uncertainty, but with hope.

Barking Dogs Never Bite is a critique of social *pujoris* that heavily influence ordinary lives in Korea. The apartment complex functions as a miniature version of Korean society in which only the residents who break the rules have pets. Stability and wealth are often built upon immoral acts, and thus they are insecure. Corruption is pervasive even among ordinary citizens. To climb the ladder, you must become part of the corrupt system. Hyun-nam, who went out of her way to find the truth and was penalized for doing so, ultimately fails in her effort, being too trusting to recognize the perpetrator even when he was right in front of her.

The film also shows how, in Korea today, everything is about money. Money is at the core of Yoon-ju's moral dilemma. Bong condemns one of the most respected jobs for being tainted with corruption. Even after bribing their way into faculty positions, junior professors still need to pander to those in power. In *Barking Dogs Never Bite*, the need for this pandering is viciously satirized with Kung-min's ridiculous death, in which he is stripped of all dignity. When Yoon-ju attends his college reunion, one of his former classmates describes a newspaper report that ranked men with humanities PhDs as forty-ninth in popularity as bridegrooms, with doctors and lawyers as first and second; in this report, people are explicitly converted into monetary values or commodities.

The film mixes different genre elements to create a tonal blend ranging from horror to social drama to fantasy to comic satire; however, the characters and their everyday life, as well as the situations they face, are "real." Bong heightens this "reality" with his use of real locations, news footage, and real news items, all of which lend a verisimilitude to his depiction of contemporary Korean life. The film starts as a farce about missing dogs but soon turns into a biting critique, with comic edges, of the effect of contemporary Korean society on the emotional and moral struggles of its citizens.

Barking Dogs Never Bite is a character-driven story, but Bong's comment on his characters is also a comment on Korean society. His critique, in fact, is a well-designed by-product of his characters' personal struggles for success. Bong brings a comic sensibility to the film; however, the stories are firmly based on everyday reality and reveal the hypocrisy of the middle class. Specifically, the film is the story of Yoon-ju's and Hyun-nam's dreams and struggles for success. One achieves his dream, while the other does not, but who has really succeeded? Achieving the dream brings not satisfaction but instead a sense of guilt. Hence Yoon-ju's troubled trance at the end of the film. Bong has created a truly offbeat and darkly humorous work that depicts the ways in which the consequences of "compressed modernity" affect the daily lives of Korean people.

"DON'T YOU HAVE A MOTHER?": THE MONSTROUS MATERNAL IN MOTHER

Mother tells the story of an ordinary woman desperately trying to prove her son innocent of a murder charge. The twenty-eight-year-old, mentally disabled Do-joon has difficulty remembering things and, like a child, is totally dependent on her. The mother knows her son to be incapable of killing even a waterbug, and thus, when the police are indifferent to her pleas that they reinvestigate the crime, she sets out to find the truth herself. As in *The Host*, an unlikely hero(ine) is forced to deal with a seemingly impossible situation because of the incompetence and indifference of law enforcement. *Mother* also resembles *Memories of Murder* in that it is a murder mystery set in a rural village; however, here the investigator is a simple mother who, unlike the detectives in *Memories of Murder*, is successful in identifying the killer; however, the truth she has discovered must be buried.

She learns the truth from an old junkman whom she initially believed to be the real killer; however, it turns out that he is the only witness to her son's crime. Shocked and enraged, she reacts violently and kills the man. Then to protect her son, she chooses to hide the truth of her son's actions and her own deed as well. Thus the film throws the virtue of motherhood into question, asking, in effect, Can these monstrous acts of murder and deception be justified when committed in the name of motherly devotion? In this film, motherhood is a metonym for moral corruption and anomie in contemporary Korean society: one of the dire consequences of the compressed modernity. *Mother* is an exemplary film that shows how life in the democratized but neoliberal capitalist Korea has driven the socially weak to the brink of madness and moral collapse.

By replacing a seasoned detective with a poverty-stricken, middle-aged woman, the film subverts genre conventions from the outset. The tragic irony, however, is that the mother's success in solving the mystery leads her to commit a horrendous murder herself, leaving the audience pondering what to make of this character. While *Memories of Murder* borrows from the crime thriller to reveal the state violence of the 1980s, *Mother* adopts and subverts the genre to explore and question traditional demands and expectations of motherhood. The mother's determination to prove her son's innocence is at the heart of the story; however, the film also draws our attention to the social *pujoris* that undergird her violent outburst. The animal-like, instinctual rage that fuels the murder she commits is all the more unsettling because the audience has been led to sympathize with her and the hard life she has led with her son. When Do-joon was five years old, she was so desperate that she attempted to poison him in a joint suicide attempt. Indeed, the film makes it clear that money has been a pressing issue throughout the family's life.

Moreover, money is at the center of all the unfortunate events in this rural village. The mother's investigation not only confirms her son's guilt but also uncovers a dark, disturbing, and debased activity that had secretly been ongoing in the village: Moon A-jung, the high school girl whom Do-joon has killed, was an orphan looking after her grandmother, who was suffering from dementia. To eke out a living—and sometimes literally for food—the teenager has been prostituting herself. This story of sordid sexual exploitation was inspired by real occurrences. Bong explains that "there were many similar incidents to the events surrounding Moon A-jung. One of them is that in a rural village, male villagers were regularly sexually exploiting a handicapped girl. There was one case that became a scandal because men were saying that you just needed 1,000 Korean won [approximately $1]. The girl later revealed, and it turned out to be true, that fifty men were involved. . . . There are many similar incidents. I have all the materials, and I based the Moon A-jung story on these incidents."[29]

The mother, played by "national mom" Kim Hye-ja, is established as a sympathetic character, even as the role is simultaneously distorted and undermined by the film, which takes motherly love to an obsessive level. The film accentuates the loneliness of the mother, who is deprived of any public support. Images of the mother's loneliness and isolation are frequent throughout the film. For example, in a scene in which the mother wipes Do-joon's urine off the street, she is captured in a long shot, alone against the backdrop of a cold, empty concrete wall. When she meets a lawyer in a bar, she sits alone, while the lawyer is surrounded by his former high school classmates and one of his cohorts of the national bar exam, indicating that he enjoys two of the strongest social networks in Korea. The cinemascope format that Bong uses in Mother also accentuates her loneliness and insecurity in the many extreme close-ups of her face.

However, unlike the Park family in The Host, the mother is depicted not as a simple victim but also as part of the social pujoris of corruption and deceit. This depiction arises not only from her morally reprehensible actions but also from her livelihood. She runs a small medical herb store that sells fake Korean products (substituting cheaper Chinese herbs instead), and she practices acupuncture without a license. The film suggests, however, that these are her only options for making ends meet; the implication is that this is a society in which you must be corrupt to survive. Further, her acupuncture skills are presented as one of the few means available to her to control the psychic toll of her existence. She has treated Do-joon with acupuncture to prevent him from remembering her joint-suicide attempt, but at the end of the film, she treats herself to erase her own bad memories, albeit temporarily. The memory of the murders she and her son have committed lie dormant, ready to haunt her at any time.

The moral ambiguity that forms and drives the mother character (she is never given a name, thus reinforcing her status as a mother and nothing but) makes her realistic and compelling. As K. Maja Krakowiak and Mary Beth Oliver have determined, morally ambiguous characters are "perceived by the audience as more realistic" and can cause the audience to feel "uncertainty and . . . ambivalence."[30] This feeling of uncertainty is matched by the uncertainty in the characters' lives. The mother experiences a series of events that keeps her on edge in her efforts to keep Do-joon safe. After the prologue of the mother's trance-like dance in the field, the film begins with her chopping herbs in her shop while keeping an eye on her son through the shop window. Startled when he is struck by a hit-and-run driver, she cuts her fingers. Later on, when Do-joon is arrested for A-jung's murder and taken away in a police car, the vehicle is hit by a truck. These jarring accidents both symbolize the rough road this mother and son have traveled together and foretell the hardships that lie ahead for them; they also illustrate the strain of the constant vigilance the mother has maintained throughout her son's life to try to protect him from harm.

The moral ambiguity existing within the mother is well expressed in a telling scene in which she first encounters the junkman. She suspects that Do-joon's friend Jin-tae is A-jung's killer, and she has smuggled a golf club out of his house because it is smeared with what appears to be blood. This apparent bloodstain, however, is soon proven to be lipstick, frustrating the mother's effort to prove her son's innocence. Distraught, she walks home in the pouring rain and passes the junkman and his cart of used goods. She pulls out an umbrella from the rear of the cart. Although he hasn't seen her do this, she approaches him and offers him two creased banknotes as payment. The junkman looks down at the notes and takes only one of them. This brief and seemingly trivial moment demonstrates the moral conscience of both characters. She offers him a generous sum for the junk umbrella; he does not take more than it is worth.

When their paths cross again, the circumstances of their meeting, as well as the audience's expectations, are completely overturned in a sudden twist of the narrative. Do-joon's unstable memory has cleared to the extent—by following his mother's "rubbing the temple" treatment—that he remembers seeing an old man at the site of the murder. It was the junkman. Convinced that the junkman is the killer, the mother visits him, pretending to be a volunteer acupuncturist. However, to her horror, he turns out to be not the killer but the only witness to the crime, which he confirms that Do-joon has in fact committed. Not knowing she is the murderer's mother, the junkman vows to report Do-joon to the police. Exploding into a violent rage, the maddened mother kills him. During the act of killing, she says, "You are not even worthy of my son's toenail."

The junkman, who lives at the fringe of society, is not free from corruption either. The mother's investigation reveals the sexual exploitation of A-jung within the village and that the junkman has been one of the men sexually exploiting her. Do-joon and the mother were able to identify him because he was included in the photos in A-jung's cell phone that the mother was able to obtain. A-jung had taken photos of the men who slept with her with her "pervert phone," which allowed her to take pictures without the clicking sound. The old junkman is guilty of sexually exploiting a minor; the mother is now a murderer. The moral conscience the two characters shared in their first encounter is now completely overturned.

In *Mother*, the murderers (Do-joon and the mother) and their victims (A-jung and the junkman), all of whom belong to the lowest of Korea's social strata, are telling evidence that there is no social safety net for the poor. Nobody cares about them, and nobody wants to find out the truth about their deaths. Detectives rely on obvious (albeit false) evidence to identify A-jung's killer, since they are also overworked. They are more interested in solving the case on record rather than in finding out the truth. And there seems to be no investigation into the death of the junkman and the fire that destroyed the house in which he died. The mother had dropped her acupuncture box while in the junkman's house, and it survived the fire. It remains undisturbed at the crime scene until Do-joon discovers and retrieves it toward the end of the film. Obviously, no one cared what had happened.

As in Bong's previous films, genre conventions are subverted in *Mother* by uniquely Korean *pujoris*, which include law enforcement's incompetence in protecting ordinary citizens. Then the depiction of police interrogation techniques reveals little change between the 1980s of military dictatorship portrayed in *Memories of Murder* and the postdemocratic 2000s in *Mother*. Admittedly, the level of violence is different: in *Memories of Murder*, suspects are kicked and tortured into false confessions, while in *Mother*, actual violence is restrained, but suspects are coerced into confessing by implicit threats. For instance, during Do-joon's interrogation, a detective demonstrates his skills at sepak takraw—a kind of kick volleyball—in order to coerce Do-joon into talking.

This interrogation scene is presented in a comical way to heighten the sense that law enforcement in Korea is absurd. The detective tells Do-joon to take off his pants and then reassures him, "This is not police torture, since I am taking my pants off too." He then asks Do-joon if he has heard of sepak takraw, which is popular in Southeast Asia but a minor sport in Korea. When Do-joon says he has not, he scolds him by calling him a fucker who only likes mainstream sports. He asks Do-joon to bite the apple and then, in a sepak takraw motion, kicks half of the apple out of Do-joon's mouth. He boasts about the power of sepak takraw and goes on to show Do-joon the movements.

This scene serves several purposes: first, it demonstrates that now the police are aware that they should not use violence on suspects but have found an indirect way to threaten them into a false confession; second, it makes a comment about how minor or unpopular things are being dismissed as trivial and how theses dismissals frustrate the people involved; and lastly, it effectively mocks the incompetent law enforcement. In addition, compared to those exhibited in *Memories of Murder*, the investigative methods in *Mother* are more scientific. The crime scene is properly preserved, and detectives invoke the American TV series *CSI* when referring to their scientific approach to crimes. Nonetheless, in both films, detectives are still incompetent and fail in finding the truth. The difference is, perhaps for the worse, that in *Memories of Murder*, the detectives are aware of their failure; however, in *Mother*, the detectives are completely unaware that they have arrested the wrong person. The incompetence and distrust of law enforcement in both films are the same.

The harsh realities of modern Korean society, steeped in the neoliberal capitalist policies that have intensified the gap between the haves and have-nots, surround these abandoned characters. *Mother* depicts how the social *pujoris* that are particular to Korea are now part of everyday life and how they drive the socially weak to the fringe of society. At the center of the film lies the moral corruption and anomie at the core of Korean society. Specifically, Bong exposes this moral anomie by setting up a narrative tension between motherhood and social morality. In traditional Confucian culture, the most important function of the family is the succession of the patrilineal bloodline. Thus a woman's place in society is legitimized only through bearing and raising sons. This Confucian patriarchal ideology results in a particularly close relationship between mother and son in the traditional Korean family.[31] Moreover, the "absence of the father" has been constant in modern Korean society because its tumultuous history has been a series of wars—the anti-Japanese independence struggle, the Japanese colonial draft of Koreans for World War II, the Korean War, the troops dispatched to the Vietnam War, and decades of anti-military-dictatorship struggles. In Confucian ideology, a woman is supposed to follow and obey three men in her life: her father, her husband, and her son. Thus upon the death of a husband, the son becomes a sort of substitute husband for his mother to depend on because Confucian ideology did not allow widows to remarry. This close relationship between widows and sons is still strong in Korean family culture, even though the ban on widows' remarriage has long been a thing of the past.

In his book titled *The Birth of a Man*, Korean political scientist Chŏn Inkwŏn uses his own experience to examine the formation of Korean male identity. Even though his father was not absent, he writes, "In a way, the relationship between my mother and myself was similar to that between a flirtatious married woman and her lover. . . . Because my father was not doing his role properly, my mother flirted with me. . . . The relationship between my mother and myself is not what I wanted but reflects my mother's will. Anyway, until the late 1960s, it was common that a mother and son would be as affectionate as if they were a married couple." He adds that "this kind of relationship is still widespread, despite big changes in lifestyle."[32] Chŏn thus argues that the oedipal complex does not apply to Korean males. It is this historically close relationship between mother and son that blocks any reading of the mother-son relationship in *Mother* as actual incest.[33] Rather, the scene in which Do-joon comes back home after the fateful night and lies beside his mother in the fetal position depicts him as a child.[34]

Similarly, Korean feminist scholar Chŏng Hŭijin argues that gender identity and, in particular, the image of mothers in Korea are different from those of the West. She contends, "Korean contemporary history, characterized by colonial rule and compressed modernity, has produced a uniquely Korean gender identity. A weak, powerless, but violent father; the absence of the father; and the strong, relentless, yet wise mother who maintains silent control behind the father are all images that are very different from Western gender images."[35] In this respect, Korean mothers have been objects of respect, but the core idea of Korean motherhood is absolute conformity to her son's needs and desires.

By taking this mother-son interdependency to an extreme level, *Mother* questions the traditional virtue of sacrificial motherhood in the context of twenty-first-century social conditions. Motherhood in Confucian ideology requires a mother's selfless devotion to educating her children. In the premodern era, an aristocratic family's social status depended on rearing male offspring and educating them to pass the national civil service exam to become high-level government officials. It was solely the mother's responsibility, however, to bring about her sons' academic and professional success. For lower classes with no hope of climbing the social ladder, mothers were expected to devote themselves to supporting the family financially. As Korea transitioned into a modern, industrialized nation with an expanding middle class, however, the Confucian expectation of motherhood underwent a change, although a mother's core obligation of rearing and educating her children (now both sons and daughters) still holds sway. The modern-day mother has become what Park Hong-sik, a Korean scholar of Confucianism, terms a "family manager."[36] She plans and implements her children's daily schedules in a manner designed to achieve the long-term goal of their success on the college entrance exam.

Thus according to Park, the Confucian ideal of the sacrificial mother has been succeeded in modern Korean society by an "education fever" whose goal is sending children to the best universities.[37] The rate of Korean high school students entering college rose from 40 percent in the early 1990s to 84 percent in 2008, with 93 percent of parents expecting their children to pursue higher education.[38]

However, the fierce competition for admission into the best universities has given rise to a culture of selfish familism, fictionalized as reaching a fatal level in Shin Su-won's chilling 2012 film *Pluto* (*Myŏngwangsŏng*).[39] For children to survive this harsh competition, they can no longer be friends with each other. Mothers will do anything to ensure their children beat out their competitors and do not care if their actions hurt other children.

In his book *Familism Is Barbarism*, Korean scholar Lee Tŭkchae traces the origin of selfish familism in Korea to the nation's current political and social situation, which has transferred public responsibilities onto the family unit. He argues that since the financial crisis of 1997, people have had to become more self-centered and to rely mostly on family to survive because Korean society no longer provides any social safety net.[40] Similarly, in her review of *Mother*, Korean education civic activist Kim Myung Shin describes Korea as a "winner-take-all society in which public concern and empathy for others and public interest for the socially weak such as youth and children are lost." Noting that such a society imposes most of the responsibility for maintaining the family's well-being upon mothers, she compares the film's mother, in her nonstop efforts to prove her son's innocence, to the modern-day, middle-class mother who ceaselessly runs to every college fair and private education institution to try to ensure her children's success.[41]

The mother's selfish familism in *Mother*, however, stems from more troubling circumstances than those faced by middle-class mother "managers." Since her failed suicide attempt, the mother has been overprotective of her mentally disabled son. (It is even possible that this poisoning might have caused his mental disability, but the film leaves this question open and unanswered.) Do-joon is completely dependent on her for all aspects of daily life, and he still sleeps with her like a little boy, indicating an infant-like dependency on her, given that his intellectual capacity and maturity are those of a child.

In fact, there are moments in the film that make the audience wonder to what extent Do-joon is aware of what is going on around him. He oscillates between remembrance and amnesia. For instance, when he and his friend Jin-tae are arrested for vandalizing the Mercedes that had struck Do-joon in the earlier hit-and-run incident, Jin-tae is able to escape responsibility by blaming Do-joon; Do-joon can remember the two of them approaching the Mercedes intent on revenge, but he does not remember that Jin-tae alone actually inflicted the damage. Do-joon's intellectual disability and the confusion surrounding his selective memory seem to equate him with the offspring of "manager" mothers: children whose lives have been so closely planned and managed for them that they never become independent, mature adults.

Indeed, Do-joon's selective remembering seems to have been influenced by his mother. She treats him with special acupuncture when she wants him to forget something; she encourages him to apply acupressure to his temples when she wants him to remember. Do-joon's selective memory casts a certain mysteriousness over his character; he is unknowable, even to his mother. At the end of the film, when the mother is about to board the tour bus, Do-joon hands her the acupuncture box she had left in the junkman's burnt house, saying, "Don't leave things behind." The mother is frightened by this gesture, thinking her son must have seen the bloodstain inside the box. However, it is never clear whether Do-joon knows about her committing murder—or even his own. Has he forgotten? Or does he remember, choosing to conceal his knowledge and thus become his mother's accomplice? The ambiguity created by his intellectual (dis)ability casts doubt on the extent of his true innocence.

This mysteriousness of Do-joon creates a cloud of uncertainty over the whole story. Is he another of those human monsters who are let loose in Bong's films? At one point, Do-joon is pictured as hideous, the result of his being beaten by inmates while he is in jail. His bruised face is shown in profile as he accusingly lashes out at his mother. The other inmates have attacked him because he has followed her instruction that he retaliate against those who insult him. Moreover, by meditating to call up memories as she has taught him to do, he tells her he has remembered that she tried to kill him. This pivotal moment signals the mother's failure to keep Do-joon under her protection and control. Nonetheless, the effort to do so drives her every action in the film. The mother belongs to the lowest social strata in Korean society. Therefore, her devotion to Do-joon is not about preparing him to go to the best college and be socially successful. Such a future would be impossible in any case, as Do-joon is intellectually disabled. Rather, this mother's job is to teach Do-joon to stand up to bullies. She must make sure he is able to protect himself from ridicule and from being cast aside as societal "waste," given that Korea does not have a strong welfare system for the disabled.

Thus it is a tragic irony that it is her instruction that ultimately causes Do-joon to commit murder. The mother has been teaching Do-joon to stand up for himself whenever somebody calls him an "idiot" or a "retard." She tells him to hit back twice every time someone hits him once. In effect, she has programmed Do-joon to retaliate violently against anybody who insults him, and this programming kicks in the moment A-jung calls Do-joon an idiot. With his violent response, he kills her.

Consequently, the concept of what "mother" means in postdemocratic Korea is summed up in the question Do-joon's mother asks Jong-pal, the mentally disabled orphan boy who is wrongfully accused of A-jung's murder: "Don't you have a mother?" When Jong-pal answers that he does not, the mother's tears could be ones of relief as much as remorse. Unlike Do-joon, Jong-pal has no mother who will stop at nothing to prove her son's innocence; his lack of such a mother will ensure Do-joon remains free. Here, Do-joon's mother is the

FIGURE 7. *Mother*. The mother visiting the wrongfully accused orphan in jail.

epitome of selfish familism; in effect, her motherly devotion has made her a human monster.

Mother is different from Bong Joon Ho's previous films in several ways. First, it is the first of his films to manifest sexual tension; second, it is the first film he shot in a widescreen format (aspect ratio 2.35:1); third, it is the first film he later released in black and white; and finally, unlike his other films, which take place in very specific locations (the Seoul apartment complex in *Barking Dogs Never Bite*, the rural town of Hwasŏng in *Memories of Murder*, and the Han River in *The Host*), *Mother* is set in an obscure village. The only indicator of the film's time period is the folding cell phones that were in vogue during the mid-2000s. These elements serve to draw attention to the emotional struggle of the mother. The widescreen format heightens the sense of her isolation, and the black-and-white version allows the audience to focus on her without being distracted by the color of her surroundings. Since it is a dark horror story, the screen stripped of color is effective in evoking an eerie feeling. The horror and crime in the film serve as the perfect setting for the colorless images. The mother is not given a name but is called either "Mother" or "Do-joon's mother." Thus like all mothers in Korea, she is defined by her child.[42] The fact that she is not given a name and the setting of a nonspecific time and place suggest that the film is about motherhood as a universal concept. The only instance where a specific prop marks the time period—the ubiquitous cell phone that becomes a crucial tool in solving the mystery—contextualizes the mother's entanglement in neoliberal capitalist Korea.

While *Mother* centers on the character of the mother, many hidden stories lie beneath her traumatic journey. The first half of the film follows the series of events and situations that force her to become a secret investigator to save her son, but the latter half of the film reveals the hidden sexual crime being committed against a poor orphan teenage girl. Social *pujoris* are also exposed and mocked: hypocritical intellectuals, incompetent police, corrupt lawyers, selfish familism, pervasive corruption, and sexual exploitation. Thus the film is a critique of both selfish familism and the system that pushes socially disabled mothers to pursue that familism to the brink of madness.

Barking Dogs Never Bite and *Mother* take controversial looks at morality, engaging in a piercing critique of a contemporary Korean society that produces human monsters. Society has become so cruel, corrupt, and competitive that one can maintain and protect one's family only by exploiting those who are weaker. The films show the ways in which Korean society has lost its moral compass and the manner in which Korean history has contributed to this loss. *Barking Dogs Never Bite* conjures up the memory of the 1980s in the construction boom and materialist culture that decade spawned, and *Mother* takes the traditional mother-son relationship to an extreme to critique the selfish familism it breeds. Both films emphasize the social *pujoris* and moral anomie that surround and affect their characters, money being the curse that leads the protagonists into moral corruption. Because of the hardships the protagonists face and the ambiguity of their moral choices, the audience still feels sympathy for them despite their reprehensible actions.

For both Yoon-ju and the nameless mother, troubled trances represent their efforts to psychically erase their own wrongdoings. Forgetting and amnesia can be read allegorically within the context of Korea's history. As Park Noja argues, amnesia is one of the "biggest enemies" that allow the state to so easily commit violence against its citizens.[43] By violence, Park means the economic violence that has been exacerbated by the neoliberal turn of the twenty-first century and that has replaced, in effect, the torture and murders committed by the state during the years of military dictatorship. *Barking Dogs Never Bite* and *Mother* paint portraits of contemporary Korean citizens whose economic precariousness leads them to moral compromise. Both Yoon-ju and the mother attempt to deal with their corruption by forgetting it. According to Park, such amnesia will ensure the persistence of social *pujoris*. In order to solve the social *pujoris*, the resistance should be persistent. If corruption is repeatedly treated as a short-term scandal and then forgotten without being investigated to the full and persecuting the perpetrators, it adds to creating a moral laxity.

Both films show the extent to which Korean society tolerates immorality. The focus is not on critiquing the incompetence or ineptitude of authorities as in *Memories of Murder* and *The Host*. Rather, *Barking Dogs Never Bite* and *Mother* document the extent to which morality has been driven out of contemporary Korean society. While *Memories of Murder* and *The Host* look back at the historical trauma of the 1980s and its legacy in the current era, *Barking Dogs Never Bite* and *Mother* present Korea's postdemocratic society as one in moral anomie.

5 · BEYOND THE LOCAL
Global Politics and Neoliberal Capitalism in *Snowpiercer* and *Okja*

After making four films set in Korea, Bong Joon Ho took on more ambitious, large-scale global projects with *Snowpiercer* (2014) and *Okja* (2017). Both are sci-fi fantasy action films that involve imaginary settings (the perpetually running train in *Snowpiercer* and a genetically engineered superpig in *Okja*); however, at the same time, they deal with real and current global issues that are being hotly debated worldwide. Global warming is the narrative premise in *Snowpiercer*, and genetic modification and the meat industry are at the heart of *Okja*'s story. Both films maintain neoliberal, global capitalism as the root cause of these problems. Thus Bong has expanded not only the production value of his films but also the scope of the social and political *pujoris* to a global scale. While *Snowpiercer* critiques the widening gap of the rich and poor by depicting a world in which the living conditions of the "haves" in the front section of the train and the "have-nots" in the tail section are extremely divided, *Okja* reveals the corporate greed of a transnational corporate company that forgoes any ethical issues in their pursuit of profits. Additionally, both films portray totalitarian evil in the name of corporation: Wilford Industries in *Snowpiercer* and Mirando Corporation, which runs an Auschwitz-like slaughterhouse and meat factory in *Okja*.

Snowpiercer is Bong's first English-language film and also his first feature film to be set outside Korea (his 2008 short film *Shaking Tokyo* was set in Japan). However, the film was produced with 100 percent investment by the Korean production and distribution company CJ E&M. *Okja* is a bilingual (Korean and English) film whose story takes place in Korea and the United States. It is Bong's first Netflix original film, thus from a funding perspective, it is his first non-Korean film as well. As mentioned previously, all these funding choices were made in order for Bong to keep the creative control of his projects. Because these films aimed at a larger global audience and cast international stars, the uniquely Korean sense of humor—the *piksaris*—are notably absent, and Korean audiences noticed this change, particularly in *Snowpiercer*.

When *Snowpiercer* was released in Korea in August 2013, many film critics and viewers lamented that Bong had lost his Koreanness—in particular, the unique sense of humor that distinguishes a Bong Joon Ho film from others. When it was released in the United States a year later, fans of Bong's films commented that ultimately, the film embodied Koreanness and was uniquely a Bong Joon Ho film. Students in my Korean cinema class described it as very Korean for several reasons: it does not follow mainstream blockbuster conventions; it mixes seemingly disparate elements together; it deals with problems in the social system and the issue of injustice; and above all, it ends in failure, catastrophe, or "half success." In his press conference after the premiere screening in Seoul, Bong himself commented, "In a sense, *Snowpiercer* is also a Korean story,"[1] even though it is his first global project made in English with an international cast and set in a non-Korean space—in an imagined future space, to be exact.

The fact that *Snowpiercer* was both critically and commercially successful abroad as well as in Korea testifies to its transnational appeal, much of which lies in its representation and critique of the inequality between the haves and the have-nots that is expanding globally in the twenty-first century. And it appeals, in a multitude of ways, to variegated audiences with an interest in sci-fi spectaculars and issues of global warming, sustainability, and revolution, among other things. Since these have become global issues, the boundary between the local and the global has collapsed, creating a need for resistance to go beyond the local into a transnational solidarity. At this very conjunction lies the transnational appeal of *Snowpiercer*, which has opened up a possibility for new political cinema in the realm of commercial blockbuster filmmaking.

Snowpiercer is a postapocalyptic sci-fi action film loosely based on the French graphic novel *Le Transperceneige*, by Jacques Lob and Jean-Marc Rochette. The film takes place on a running train after the earth has entered a new ice age due to the failure of attempts to stop global warming. The train *Snowpiercer*, motored by the "eternal engine," is a dystopic Noah's Ark in which the last survivors of humanity live. The society within the train is totalitarian, and the train is divided into two sections by class: the tail section and the front section. The "wretched of the earth" occupy the tail section, and the rich live in the front section. The opposition between the haves and the have-nots is clearly established from the beginning, when the poor in the tail section are subjected to a roll call by armed guards. The sequence is reminiscent of the daily routine of a concentration camp. The film portrays the revolt of the tail-enders, led by a young leader named Curtis. The narrative follows Curtis and his group as they battle their way to the engine room in order to bring about a revolution that would ensure justice and equality for the people in the tail section. In many ways (as I will elaborate later), the film is an allegory of current neoliberal capitalism and embodies a desire to bring justice and equality once and for all, however dear the cost. The film asks, Can we fix this system of inequality, and if so, how? Is an emancipatory revolution possible?

Compared to *Snowpiercer*, *Okja* is a much warmer and lighter action adventure that focuses on the friendship between a teenage Korean girl Mija and a hippopotamus-like giant pig. The adventure takes off when Okja is taken away from Mija by the Mirando Corporation, a company that plans to produce giant pigs for food consumption through genetic modification. Okja's departure triggers the battle between Mija and the members of the Animal Liberation Front on one side and the Mirando Corporation on the other. The film ends with the most hopeful outcome among Bong's films: Mija succeeds in saving Okja even though she and the Animal Liberation Front fail to take down the Mirando Corporation and stop the breeding and slaughtering of superpigs. Although the outcome is opposite that of *The Host*, since the family in that film fails to save their daughter, *Okja* is comparable to *The Host* in many ways. Both films feature a giant animal created by special effects, the stories of these imaginary creatures take place in a very realistic setting, and most of the events happening within the films are modeled on actual realities. Thus the imaginary animals, which in turn are products of very plausible causes, are the tools to depict and critique contemporary social issues. If *The Host* raised the subservient relationship between Korea and the United States in a more political context, *Okja* brings attention to the state of the global economy.

This shift of focus from political power to economic power is symbolized in *Okja*'s parody of the White House Situation Room. When the Mirando Corporation's CEO Lucy Mirando and executives gather together in a conference room to discuss the crisis caused by Mija, the scene is set up to resemble the well-known photograph of the White House situation room during the raid on Osama Bin Laden in 2011. Lucy sits where then secretary of state Hillary Clinton sat covering her mouth and chief Mirando Corporation strategist Frank Dawson in the Obama spot. The sitting positions, props, and clothes are so similar, it is hard to miss the parody.[2] It is a statement that now the corporate power is as strong as or even stronger than the U.S. government in world affairs. The Mirando Corporation is a multinational conglomerate that operates above the government or any political entity.

As *Snowpiercer* was Bong's first science fiction film, he consulted Korean science fiction writer Kim Bo-young when developing his script to make sure various premises of the imaginative story are scientifically plausible. Although the story is based on the French graphic novel, Bong merely took its basic premise and created his own version of the tale, with completely different characters and situations. What he borrowed from the original story was the premise that the earth has entered a new ice age due to global warming, the eternally running train is the only place left for the last human survivors, and there is a divide between the rich in the front section and the poor in the tail. However, the fact that the train runs in a yearly circle, the recurring revolts within the train, and all the specific characters are new. Although the perpetually running train is a very unlikely premise, the film deals with many current issues such as global warming, ecological balance, and economic inequality. The protein blocks made of insects (which are used as a food staple) and the eternal engine (perpetual motor machine) are scientific possibilities. In this way, Snowpiercer creates what H. G. Wells termed "fantasies of possibilities," which would "take some developing possibility in human affairs and work it out so as to develop the broad consequences of that possibility."[3]

In particular, the contrast in living conditions between the tail and front sections reflects the economic inequality of the 1 percent versus the 99 percent, a catchphrase that originated from the Occupy movement's slogan "We are the 99%" in 2011.[4] Since the widening gap between the rich and the poor has been a worldwide social issue due to the global expansion of neoliberal economic policies, the film is remarkably on target for the global mood and has a transnational appeal. The film enjoyed critical acclaim and popularity both within Korea and in the global market. The film was the biggest summer hit in Korea in 2013 and became the all-time second-best box-office hit for a Korean film in the North American market. The film also prompted an active online discussion of the issues raised in the film. As with Bong's monster movie, The Host, Snowpiercer invited a tremendous amount of political reading by film critics and online bloggers, both within Korea and the United States. Reading the film in relation to the neoliberal capitalist system was one of the common themes. Furthermore, as one blogger suggested that the film is good material for sustainability education, real and current issues, including the possibility of a revolutionary class struggle, were discussed by many critics and bloggers.

For Okja, Bong did extensive research on genetically modified food, the Animal Liberation Front, and meat factories. He visited a so-called beef plant in Colorado in 2015. It was a modern factory where more than five thousand cows and pigs are turned into meats every day. What he observed there is represented in the film as the slaughterhouse where superpigs are killed, peeled, and cut into meats in an assembly line. The film portrays this factory scene deliberately to "make it feel like a miserable concentration camp type place, where you just wait to be slaughtered."[5] In this way, the film led the audience to see this meat process from Okja's point of view.

Likewise, much of the film's content is borrowed from and modeled after real events and entities. For example, the M in Mirando Corporation and its green tree logo remind the audience of Monsanto, the world's largest agricultural company whose scientists were among the first to develop genetically modified foods. The Animal Liberation Front actually exists, and although they do battle to stop animal cruelty, they also do raise the question of whether they are "terrorists or freedom fighters" because of their occasional use of violent tactics. Because of that, the ALF was named as a terrorist threat by the U.S. Department of Homeland Security in 2005. The ambiguity of this organization is reflected in the film as ALF's plan to collapse the Mirando Corporation from within by penetrating the company unintentionally puts Okja in an excruciating circumstance of forced mating. Likewise, genetically modified animals are being tested in scientific laboratories, although none are approved for human consumption. Thus the story of *Okja* is not a simple science fiction but something that could become a reality in the not-so-distant future. The success of a rural girl confronting the global conglomerate who strikes her first capitalist deal (exchanging Okja with gold) and comes back home with her beloved pet represents a small but potent image of the radical politics of resistance and protest.

This chapter aims to illustrate the radical politics portrayed in the two films by examining several aspects. First, the chapter will examine the ways in which both *Snowpiercer* and *Okja* create a "new political space" Nancy Fraser argues for to raise issues of global injustice and environmental ethics and to open up the possibility for activism. Second, the chapter will discuss how the train in *Snowpiercer* symbolizes a microcosm of the current neoliberal capitalist system and how both films' transnational appeal can be located in the global expansion of this neoliberalism. Lastly, this chapter will examine how the revolt of the tail section in *Snowpiercer* embodies Walter Benjamin's idea of revolution as well as Jacques Rancière's redefinition of politics and what he terms the "distribution of the sensible" to emphasize the radical politics of subversion in the film.

PUBLIC SCREEN: A NEW POLITICAL SPACE AND ACTIVISM

As Miriam Hansen has shown in her study on the emergence of spectatorship in early cinema,[6] movies have contributed to the public sphere from early on by reaching a much wider and more diverse audience than print media. The *public sphere*, as defined by Jürgen Habermas, is the domain of our social life where citizens as a public "deal with matters of general interest without being subject to coercion" and "express or publicize their views."[7] In the contemporary era, the effectiveness of visual media such as cinema, television, and computers has grown exponentially. Accordingly, the term *public screen* has been coined to take into account the technological and cultural changes that have brought new conditions for politics and activism. This new term recognizes that public discussions take place via "screens." Kevin Michael DeLuca and Jennifer Peeples describe the emergence of the public screen as a new space for discourse, arguing that entertainment TV and movies also constitute alternative venues for participatory politics and public opinion.[8] Sociologists Brian Loader and Dan Mercea use the term "virtual public sphere," arguing that in the digital era, social media offers opportunities for political discussions.[9]

Films labeled blockbusters are often dismissed as being designed to appeal to the lowest common denominator in order to maximize profit. However, *Snowpiercer* and *Okja*, Bong's two most expensive blockbuster films, demonstrate the role of films that go beyond just entertainment and revenues, offering an alternative public sphere that enables democratic capacities for political discussion and critical thoughts on social reality. With his commitment to verisimilitude, Bong Joon Ho has created political blockbusters that have opened up what Miriam Hansen calls an "alternative public sphere," providing a challenge to the ideology advanced by mainstream cinema. *Snowpiercer*'s narrative of a political revolt is in itself a resistance to the status quo. The film provokes political action and redefines the relationship between cinema, politics, and the possibility of instigating activism. The film created a space in the minds of the audience to consider the possibility of the seemingly impossible and to think outside the box. As I will discuss later on, through the character of Namgoong Minsoo, the film offers a new perspective on challenging the status quo and fighting against social inequality: an alternative to capitalism. It is a rare blockbuster movie that calls for a revolution. *Snowpiercer* has proven that a blockbuster film can be subversive while being commercially successful.

The notion of the public screen is effective in describing how *Snowpiercer* and *Okja* have stimulated discussion and conversation on relevant issues associated with our own era. In particular, *Snowpiercer* brings up environmental and global warming issues; sustainability issues; scientific issues such as the eternal engine or perpetual motion; ecological issues; and such political issues as economic inequality, social injustice, and revolution. And *Okja* not only was able to stimulate discussions about genetically engineered food, the meat industry, and corporate responsibilities but went further to make some viewers go vegan and encourage others to eat less meat. All these issues discussed via the internet forum created by these films are at the forefront of politics today. Blockbuster movies are rarely thought of as stimulating intellectual or socially conscious discussion; however, *Snowpiercer* very effectively delivers relevant messages to a large audience about the need for social change and revolution, and *Okja* functions as a catalyst for spontaneous social activism. Both films tie together environmental crisis and capitalism and contribute to the public sphere, as numerous reviews, blogs, web pages, social media posts, and commentaries have been created to offer critiques of and support for their messages.

Snowpiercer was particularly successful in creating an online forum, offering a new, different kind of public sphere. On July 24, 2014, three weeks after *Snowpiercer*'s wide release in the United States, the *New York Times* opened up its online "Room for Debate" with the question "Will Fiction Influence How We React to Climate Change?"[10] The question was based on the popularity of "a subgenre of science fiction that explores the possible, often catastrophic, effects of climate change," which the article termed "cli-fi." Dan Bloom, a blogger who suggested the discussion topic, wrote that the film "gives a sense of climate change's effects on the developing world,"[11] taking the position that cli-fi movies have the power to change people's minds. On his own blog, he selected *Snowpiercer* as the best cli-fi movie of 2014.[12] J. P. Telotte, a professor of film studies who also participated in the online discussion, writes that recent apocalyptic climate films like *Snowpiercer* are filtering into college curricula and being appropriated by scientists and climatologists to introduce the issue to students.[13]

Most of the participants in the NYTimes.com debate agree that movies have the power to bring awareness to climate issues, even though they disagree about the extent to which they will result in action. In particular, movies are increasingly used in classroom settings, including colleges, as an effective educational tool to spark interest in and curiosity about serious issues, such as global warming, in a more familiar way than text-based books. Seth D. Baum, the executive director of the Global Catastrophic Risk Institute, states that *Snowpiercer* is a good text for sustainability education.[14] He posits that the film raises such questions as "Should humanity attempt to engineer its way out of environmental degradation?" and "Can a population survive indefinitely in a small space with no external resource input?"

Snowpiercer lent itself to rich and diverse interpretations after its release both in Korea and the United States. What is interesting about the general response to *Snowpiercer* is that not only film critics and film buffs but also environmentalists, political critics, and other nonfilm people wrote about the film in relation to their area of concern. For example, Jason Mark, the editor of *Earth Island Journal*, writes about the environment in many publications, including the *New York Times*; he dubbed the film "the very first geo-engineering apocalypse movie."[15] Korean political science professor Kim Joon-hyung compares and contrasts *Snowpiercer* and *Elysium* (2013, dir. Neill Blomkamp) in their respective portrayals of extreme inequality and possible solutions from the perspective of a political scientist.[16] On the Rotten Tomatoes review site (where *Snowpiercer* boasts a 95 percent "fresh" rating), 203 critics and 54,425 users participated in the rating; IMDb also carries 486 user reviews.[17] These numbers testify to the film's popularity and show the scope of its potential influence on stimulating discussions.

One of the reasons *Snowpiercer* has inspired a lot of discussion on current issues is partly due to the contribution by the science fiction writer Kim

Bo-young. Kim is known to have helped in the writing of Wilford's talk in the engine room and also in providing a scientific basis for the creation of the train's system. This effort to be more realistic and scientific resulted in one of the many changes from the original graphic novel. In the original comic, the ice age was brought by the use of a climate control weapon; however, in the film, the crisis is more realistically caused by spraying the artificial chemical substance CW-7 into the atmosphere to stop a global warming catastrophe. Thus the new ice age occurs as a result of geoengineering.

The film begins with a voice-over of two reporters narrating the decision by seventy-nine countries to disperse CW-7 into the upper atmosphere "on this day, July 1, 2014," despite the continuing "protests from environmental groups and a number of developing countries." According to their report, scientists claim that CW-7 is "a revolutionary solution to mankind's warming of the planet." The voice-over itself contains significant comments on the current debates about climate issues, which led many reviewers to comment on the topic. First of all, it supports the claim that global warming is a man-made crisis, which some conservatives, including environmentalists, deny. Second, it makes it a current issue by setting the date of the dispersion on July 1, 2014, a very near future from the perspective of the film's release in 2013. Third, it comments on the discrepancy between developed countries and developing countries regarding the climate crisis. At the 2015 United Nations Climate Change Conference held in Paris, many developing countries held protests expressing their anger over the financial plan, which disregarded the fact that the least developed countries face the greatest threat from climate change. Finally, the voice-over sets out the basic premise of the film, clearly positing geoengineering as the major cause of the human catastrophe. Many reviewers took notice of this and labeled *Snowpiercer* a geoengineering apocalypse movie.

In Korea, the film incited heated debates about the probability of the various scientific premises on which the film is based, such as the perpetual motion machine and CW-7. The Kwach'ŏn Science Museum organized a Science Talk Concert titled "*Snowpiercer* and the Future of Humanity" on October 26, 2013. Bong Joon Ho and two science fiction writers who worked with him on the script were invited, and the talk was moderated by Korea's most well-known science fiction critic, Park Sang-joon. Asked about the extent to which a science fiction film should be "scientific," Bong replied that science fiction should be based on science, since the genre is different from fantasy, but not to the extent that it would limit the imagination. In reality, a train might not be the solution for humanity to survive a new ice age; an underground bunker might be a better idea.

In order to make the story plausible, Bong explained that he made the Wilford character a "train *otaku*," obsessed with trains from childhood and thus eventually designing and building the *Snowpiercer* train. To a question about

Yona, who seems to possess the psychic powers of a clairvoyant, Bong mentioned a deleted scene in which Yona says, "I see sound." He went on to explain that just like a "wolf boy" who developed extraordinary ability to see and hear, Yona is a "train baby" who has lived all her life on a train and has developed an extremely keen sense of hearing. One of the audience members claimed that he had calculated the speed of the train as fifty kilometers / thirty miles per hour, which is not fast at all. Bong explained that having the train circulate yearly was important as a setting for the story; when he later heard of the speed, he was disappointed as well. For the perpetual engine, Bong explained that it was modeled after nuclear submarine engines, which last for twenty years. The actual design of the engine in the film was inspired by the nuclear fuel rod.[18] I have not come across any reviewer talking about the protein blocks other than as the food for the tail-enders; however, the use of insects as an alternative source for protein has already become a reality. All these efforts show Bong's commitment to verisimilitude, even when making a science fiction film.

Because of the film's premise, many reviewers, bloggers, and environmentalists discussed it as a cli-fi; however, most of the reviews heralded it as a film dealing with social inequality, the 99 percent and the 1 percent, and neoliberal capitalism and revolution. In sum, the film was received as highly engaging; some reviewers argued that it was "the most political film of the year."[19] Many also described it as an allegory of the present. The most heated discussion revolved specifically around the issue of class warfare and revolution to overthrow the system. As we saw earlier, fierce political debates are not new to Bong's films. *The Host* had ignited an intense discussion in Korea for its comments about Korea's subservient relationship with the United States as well as the inability of the Korean authorities to help the families of the victims of the monster attack.

In Korea, political readings of the film, especially about revolution, outweigh those focused on climate issues. In the Korean context, it is interesting to observe that these various interpretations, discussions, and debates on the radical politics in *Snowpiercer* often led to a debate as to what extent it can be considered a typical Bong Joon Ho film that Korean audiences love. Some argued that Bong had lost his unique sense of humor, which comes from stories and characters deeply rooted in a specifically Korean locality. Although many audiences claimed that they were disappointed in Bong's first attempt at a global film, some argued that the film was as much a typical Bong Joon Ho film as his previous films. For example, Jason Bok, who wrote a long review titled "*Snowpiercer*, 2013: The Train Is the Movie!," argues, "The most Korean (Bong Joon Ho–esque) is the most global." Rejecting the hot debate about the film's Koreanness as meaningless, Bok states that the main story and theme of the film can be applied to many different nations; therefore, under the surface of the multinational appearance of the film, *Snowpiercer* maintains Bong's usual "critical

consciousness about Korean society based on the Korean identity and sensibility."[20] Many other reviewers and bloggers have also argued that the film's story
resonates with the political and social situation that Korea is faced with: increasing social injustice and economic inequality.

References to *Snowpiercer*'s reflection of Korean reality have continued well
beyond the film's release in 2013. On January 4, 2016, the Korean national
newspaper *Hankyoreh* ran an article about Korean young people in their twenties and thirties who have left a life of unemployment or low-wage, part-time
jobs and fierce competition and have chosen to work at menial jobs in Australia.[21] For them, the article states, Korea is *Snowpiercer*. According to the report,
most of the fifteen people interviewed had experienced a harsh job market,
longer hours of work with low wages, and/or company cultures still steeped in
traditional values. They were discovering a new life with leisurely evenings and
better wages in Australia. Even though they were working at menial jobs in meat
factories, restaurants, or furniture delivery, the quality of life was much better.
A twenty-five-year-old female, Paik Younghee (a pseudonym), who works as a
cleaner at the shopping mall, is quoted as saying, "I heard from a seminar that
for young people, Korean society is like *Snowpiercer*. People held onto it out of
fear that if they jump, they will die. But I am outside the train, and I feel relieved.
I am not dead, and at least it is better than inside the train."

Similar comments appeared in a *Washington Post* article on January 31, 2016,
titled "Young South Koreans Call Their Country 'Hell' and Look for Ways Out."
It reported that a "growing number of 20- and 30-somethings, those born with a
'golden spoon' in their mouths, get into the best universities and secure the plum
jobs, while those born with a 'dirt spoon' work long hours in low-paying jobs
without benefits." The cynical terms *golden spoon* and *dirt spoon* are reminiscent
of the "preordained positions" that Mason talks about in *Snowpiercer*: the idea
that your fate is decided by your birth, whether or not you are born to rich and
privileged parents or not. According to the article, these young people call Korea
"Hell Joseon" (after the name of the last kingdom in Korean history, which ended
in 1910). The Hell Joseon group on Facebook "boasts more than 5,000 members
and a dedicated 'Hell Korea' website. . . . [They post] graphic after graphic to
illustrate the awful state of life in Korea: the long working hours, the high suicide
rate and even the high price of snacks." The article adds that there are numerous
online forums that offer advice on ways to escape.[22]

These news articles show how relevant the story of *Snowpiercer* is to Korean
audiences, especially the younger generation. The train in the film has mostly
been interpreted as symbolizing capitalism, particularly neoliberal capitalism;
however, these articles give a new perspective, a new possible interpretation of
seeing the train as Korean society itself. This perspective presents the possibility of escaping from the train, which more and more young Koreans are actually

doing. There is a new life outside of Korea! The millennials in Korea are very different from the young generation of the 1980s, the era of the democratic movement. Although life was harsh and suffocating under military dictatorship, there was hope for change, for revolution, and a belief in the people's ability to bring it about. However, after the economic crisis in the late 1990s, people were losing hope. In this grim situation, *Snowpiercer* urges them to rethink the possibility of change and revolution. The disparity between the wealthy and the poor is not only widening but solidifying, making it almost impossible to climb the economic ladder.

What is implied by the fact that both Korean and American audiences claim that the film portrays a microcosm of their own society? The film portrays a transnational solidarity of the tail-enders. This imagined political space within the diegesis supports Nancy Fraser's idea of going beyond national territories to fight for equality and justice because the discourse of justice based on national sovereignty is no longer valid in an era of globalization.[23] Even in Korea, which used to have a very strong nationalist tendency as a nation of "one ethnicity and one language" (*tanilminjok tanirŏnŏ*), has undergone a drastic change in its demographic since the early 2000s. According to the Korea Immigration Service's 2013 statistics, Korea is now a multicultural and multiracial country, with 3 percent of the population consisting of immigrants, mostly from China and South Asia. The Yonhap News Agency reported that immigrants began to increase in the early 2000s with the trend toward globalization.[24] Most of the immigrants work in manual labor and unskilled jobs, while college-educated Koreans have difficulty finding jobs that they like. Thus as a result of globalization at the local level, the migration pattern is making Korea more diverse and multicultural, a trend that is shared worldwide. Therefore, we could say that Korean society resembles the *Snowpiercer* train in its multiracial population.

Okja raises the question of how effective an entertainment film can be in mobilizing the audience to participate in a social cause. Because it is available on Netflix for streaming, *Okja* has far more viewership (albeit on a smaller screen) than any of Bong's previous films. Thus the response to the film is similarly on a wider scale. Seán McCorry, a cofounder of the Sheffield Animals Research Center and a member of the Vegan Society's Research Advisory Committee, writes in his review of *Okja* that the film "is a timely intervention into debates about the environmental costs of meat production" and compares the film to the popular activist documentary *Cowspiracy* (2014), which had brought the argument that "we need to cut back on meat and dairy production for the sake of the planet" to a wider public in 2014.[25] In Korea, KARA (Korea Animal Rights Advocates), a nonprofit organization that supports animal welfare and deals with animal cruelty, launched a petition, with director Bong Joon Ho's support, to liberate millions of "okjas" from pig stalls. With "Farms Instead of Factories!" as its slogan, the Okja Liberation Project launched a petition on July 5, 2018, less than a week following *Okja*'s release on June 29, 2018. In their statement, they declared, "We should not forget that farm animals are suffering from the capitalist livestock industry," explaining that more than fifteen million pigs are slaughtered every year in Korea.[26] KARA went on to hold public screenings of the film with director Bong Joon Ho present for a Q&A to open up a public forum in which *Okja*'s viewers can freely discuss their concerns.

Okja not only stimulated various animal rights groups to actively seek ways to promote their cause through the film but also convinced many to adopt a vegan diet. A member of PETA (People for the Ethical Treatment of Animals), a nonprofit organization in the United Kingdom, reported on the "11 Things That Happened When People Watched '*Okja*'" on the organization's blog page, referencing numerous Twitter posts of the people who decided to go vegan after watching the film. Some of the eleven things included a woman who noted that she "can't even stand the sight of meat now"; someone tweeted, "If you were already vegan, you went MORE vegan"; yet another said he "decided to stop planning and start doing"; someone else "decided to mentor others"; and a tweet speaking for many readers claimed, "Seriously, this movie changed lives."[27] Bong himself has said he had briefly practiced veganism for a while after visiting the beef plant. PETA also reported in August 2017 that the Google search for the term *vegan* spiked 65 percent after the release of *Okja*.[28] PETA's vice president Colleen O'Brien said in the report, "In July [2017] alone, PETA received more than 21,000 requests for our vegan starter kits—double the number of an average month."[29] *Hankook Ilbo* (The Korea times) also reported on July 2017 that after *Okja*'s release in Korea, social media and online blogs testified to a notable increase in the number of people trying out vegan restaurants for the first time in their lives, and some people confessed that it had become difficult to even look at meat on the table.[30] These kinds of stories are abundant on social media and online blogs.

Thus *Snowpiercer* and *Okja* work to create Fraser's new political space, through cinema, within which the local and the global converge. And at this very conjunction, the film has opened up a new possibility for a political blockbuster movie. The films have created a unique political arena both inside and outside the film text that calls for a radical rethinking of resistance. The local and the global converge around the film and the discourses surrounding the film, and herein lies the transnational appeal of the film.

Furthermore, discussions about the content of the two films often culminate in heated debates regarding the film's endings. For *Snowpiercer*, the questions asked are, Is it hopeful or is it catastrophic? Would humanity prosper with the surviving two children? What does the polar bear at the end symbolize? For *Okja*, the question is, Is this a sad ending where Mija has succumbed to the grips of the Mirando Corporation in order to save just her pet while leaving millions of others to be slaughtered? The audience response seems to divide evenly between hope and despair. However, because of the more radical political content, *Snowpiercer* instigated a more heated debate on the ending.

The entertainment news site Vulture ran an article titled "Let's Talk about the Ending of *Snowpiercer*" on July 11, 2014.[31] The main question concerned what happens to humanity after the train's final crash landing and whether or not the film ends on a hopeful note. The article quotes a Reddit discussion thread where a "slew of dystopian naysayers claim that, unless there are survivors *elsewhere* that Bong Joon Ho decided not to show on film, Tim and Yona are dead meat." Although Bong himself expressed his intention to create a hopeful ending, projecting that Yona and Tim would spread the human race, many viewers argued that the two children would be eaten by the polar bear. Vulture's discussion thread has seventy-nine comments on the film's ending.

On the other hand, many Korean bloggers, like Maltugi, saw it as more of a positive ending. They argued that since the polar bear is at the top of the food chain, it means that the ecological system exists for humanity to survive. Maltugi even argued that there must have been other humans alive outside the train and that the tail-enders had been completely fooled by Wilford that the ice age had virtually wiped out the human race.[32] Some reviewers and bloggers described the train as a twenty-first-century Noah's Ark and the last survivors, Yona and Tim, as the nonwhite Adam and Eve who will restart the human race.

The reviews I have referenced here are only the tip of the iceberg in a vast sea of reviews, commentaries, and blogs in the virtual public sphere. However, they do testify to the variety of ideas and issues contained within the film. While Hollywood blockbusters are considered typical escapism, *Snowpiercer* has achieved status as a new kind of political blockbuster that engages the audience intellectually to confront the issues they face and urges them to think critically and do something about it. It has created a political space both within and outside the film by portraying class warfare in the story and by instigating a lively public discussion outside the text. It also distinguishes itself from Hollywood postapocalyptic blockbusters, like *Elysium* and *The Hunger Games* (2012, dir. Gary Rose) that also deal with inequalities and revolution, in that the change comes by collective action rather than an individual's heroic fight. The idea of political revolution in the film merits an in-depth analysis in relation to its allegorical depiction of our current neoliberalist era.

THE SURPLUS HUMANS: THE TRAIN AS A MICROCOSM OF NEOLIBERAL CAPITALISM IN *SNOWPIERCER*

Whereas Bong's previous films were set in Korea and dealt with the problems of the social system, incompetent government authorities, and injustices against the socially weak in Korea, *Snowpiercer* expands these issues on a global level. The film in many ways presents a political allegory for the global neoliberal system and the increasing inequality within it. The neoliberal economic policies that have been implemented on a global scale since the 1980s during the Reagan era in the United States and the Thatcher era in the United Kingdom are characterized by the deregulation of economies, globalization, and the privatization of governmental responsibilities, which have greatly affected not only the world economy but also people's daily lives.[33] Since these policies were designed to facilitate market expansion and profit for the corporations, they inevitably expanded and intensified the unequal distribution of wealth. As Susan Braedley points out, these "free market" principles of neoliberalism have come to "penetrate social relations: reinscribe, intensify and alter social hierarchies of gender, race and class," creating injustices and inequality.[34]

Sociologist Zygmunt Bauman describes this age of increasing uncertainty as the "liquid times" or "liquid modernity."[35] One of the major consequences of the deregulation policies is the increasing instability of laborers: unemployment and partial employment have increased. These unemployed and underemployed people constitute a population of *surplus humans* within the system. These surplus people are the direct product of unstable working conditions, and it is the existence of surplus humans on the train that makes *Snowpiercer* a poignant political allegory of our own age. Several other elements in the film also support the notion that the world of *Snowpiercer* resembles our own era. For example, Wilford, who has built the train and its eternal engine, is a corporate capitalist who owns Wilford Industries. He exerts absolute power through Minister Mason, his puppet politician who governs the poor of the tail section. This power relationship between the capitalist and politician resembles the current structure of the neoliberal system in which multinational corporations have grown more powerful than national governments. Furthermore, the multinational, multilanguage community on the train characterizes globalization in the neoliberal era. However, it is the surplus humans of the tail section who embody the most salient feature of neoliberal capitalism: the increasing instability of labor conditions and the increasing polarization of haves and have-nots.

The wretched people in the tail section are not a working class in the classical Marxist sense of the term. They do not labor and do not produce goods or services. They are surplus humans in that they have no part in the economic system. It is not that they are unable to work—they are simply deprived of opportunities to work. There are no jobs for them. The few things they do contribute to the train's economy or ecology are entertainment and labor, as in the case of the violinist who was picked up by the guards to perform music for the rich; Paul, who left the tail section to work in the protein block factory; and small children, who keep the engine running. The majority of the tail-enders

FIGURE 8. *Snowpiercer*. Tail-enders look bewildered in the Wilford Industries' colorful classroom.

have no part in the system. They are a population of surplus humans who were not included in the initial design of the train. There was no place for them from the beginning. As Mason puts it in her speech after a little agitation in the tail section over the inspection of children, "There are first-class passengers, economy, and freeloaders like you." They did not buy tickets. Instead, they battled their way onto the train before the earth froze completely after a failed attempt to stop global warming.

The short, animated prequel released online before the debut of the film in Korea depicts the bloody battle between the "freeloaders" to get on the train after the privileged class who bought tickets have boarded.[36] If you don't have the money to buy the expensive tickets, you either fight to get on board or freeze to death. These freeloaders had to fight a bloody war against the military guards and against each other to get on the train. The people in the tail section are the survivors of this battle. However, they are under constant surveillance and have to endure Mason and Wilford's disdain and control. Since Wilford did not have them in his plan for the *Snowpiercer* train, the population has to be regulated and maintained by secretly schemed war or revolt on a regular basis to sustain ecological balance. They are the surplus humans who have to be discarded every now and then. As surplus humans, the people in the tail section correspond to the poor—the 99 percent—who without skills or capital suffer from chronic unemployment or temporary employment under neoliberal capitalism.

The term *surplus* has come to denote "laid off, redundant" in the current global economic order. The term *surplus human* or *superfluous human* itself is nothing new; however, its meaning has evolved over history according to the cultural contexts in which it has been used. The first known use of the term is in nineteenth-century Russian literature. Ivan Turgenev wrote a novella titled *The Diary of a Superfluous Man* in 1850, which has become the archetype for the concept of the superfluous man that has come to identify characters in many other novels. These characters were often born into wealth and the privileged class but felt they did not fit into social norms. They were alienated, outsider figures who were often cynical and bored and led idle lives. These weak outsider men were often juxtaposed with strong women who did fit into society.[37] These characters appeared in many Russian novels before the advent of socialist realist literature in the 1930s.

The term *surplus* was also used to mean "jobless" during the demonstrations of the French jobless movement in the mid-1990s; their slogan was "We're not a surplus, we're a plus."[38] In his afterword to Jacques Rancière's *The Politics of Aesthetics*, Slavoj Žižek indicates that surplus here means "laid off, redundant, reduced to silence in a society that subtracted the jobless from the public accounts, that made them into a kind of residue—invisible, inconceivable except as a statistic under a negative sign."[39] This surplus consists of a "part of society with no properly defined place within it,"[40] which becomes crucial in my later account of the surplus humans in the tail section of the *Snowpiercer* and their revolt as embodying what Rancière termed "the distribution of the sensible" and politics proper. They are the *demos*, the excluded who refuse to stay put in their given place and demand and claim their equal part in the society.

The cultural meaning of *surplus human* became more acute and pervasive in the context of twenty-first-century Korea. Before the 1997–1998 financial crisis, Korean businesses were traditionally based on lifetime employment and a seniority system. However, with the onset of the crisis, they had to downsize and institute massive layoffs. Furthermore, as indicated previously, the crisis facilitated the neoliberal policy of labor market flexibility. According to Statistic Korea, the national statistical agency, the number of temporary workers began to increase each year, and the rate of unemployment, especially for new college graduates and the younger generation (fifteen- to twenty-four-year-olds), rose to 8.1 percent in 2009 and 10 percent in 2015.[41] In the 1990s, the average unemployment rate for the youth was around 5.5 percent. In this context, *surplus human,* or *ingyō ingan* in Korean, acquired a socially and culturally specific meaning that has become a catchword to describe this young generation with little hope for job security or even a hope to get jobs. According to Korean sociologist Choi Tae-sup, the history of labor in Korea is basically a "history of cruelty." The young generation in Korea has been described as the "880,000-won generation" (meaning that they can only earn around 880,000 Korean won—approximately $730—per month on average); the "generation of three give-ups" (most of them giving up relationships, marriage, and children because they cannot afford the high cost); and now, the "generation of four give-ups" (adding jobs to the list). Choi proposes that at the center of these problems lies the labor market flexibilization that intensified with the onset of neoliberal economic policies, which increasingly dismantled job security worldwide.[42]

Choi Tae-sup bases his definition of *surplus humans* on Zygmunt Bauman's notion of "human waste"[43] and focuses on the labor conditions in contemporary Korea: The emergence of a surplus population has to do with the increasing number of people who have the will to join the labor market but are denied opportunities to do so. They are not even losers, because they were not given the chance to compete. Therefore, failure becomes one of the key cultural codes that define the neoliberal capitalist conditions of life, particularly in Korea.

The term *surplus human* was introduced when novelist Son Chang-seop wrote a short story, *Ingyŏ Ingan*, in 1958.[44] The story sketches the aftermath of the Korean War and features characters who have difficulty adjusting to the chaos of the postwar society and live a restless and desolate life. However, a touch of cynicism and self-deprecation is added to the contemporary meaning of the term as it changed to indicate those people who are left behind, those who became losers in the fierce competition imposed by neoliberal policies. *Surplus human* now refers to those who have been pushed aside and marginalized by the system. They want to be successful within the system, but society does not provide jobs or proper places to have a sense of belonging. The winner takes all, and nothing is left for the losers. Unlike, for example, U.S. counterculture youth in the 1960s and the 386 generation of 1980s Korea, these surplus humans are not voluntary outsiders—instead, they were forced out of the system. Thus they have no part in society. As I will elaborate later, "having no part" in the system becomes an important condition in interpreting the revolt of the tail-enders in the film as an act of "dissensus," the real act of politics, in Rancière's term.

The Korean film *Spirit of Jeet Kune Do: Once upon a Time in High School* (2004) introduced the notion of *surplus human* as the keyword for understanding the contemporary era. In the film, the father of the protagonist shouts at his high school son after receiving his failing grades, "If you can't go to college, you are a surplus human. You will become human trash."[45] Failing to go to college means dropping out of the mainstream elite and a successful career. On March 10, 2009, *Dong-a Ilbo* (one of the major national newspapers) ran an article reporting that *surplus human* (*ingyŏ ingan*) is a buzzword for young people in their twenties.[46] The article explains that the term indicates those who failed to get a job and do not have a social role and goes on to assert that the economic recession is the reason.

Sociological studies on this renewed concept of surplus human include *Ingyŏ Sahoi* (Surplus society) and *Sokmul kwa Ingyŏ* (Materialist snob and surplus human), both published in 2013. The books describe the term *surplus humans* as those who have no jobs or place within the system—not voluntarily but because they lost the harsh competition in the job market. Surplus humans are those who tried to succeed in the system but failed. They exist within the system but are not quite won over by the system. Usually they spend all day on computers and games. They are, in a way, harmless. In the United States, the adjective *surplus* is used to indicate those who are rendered jobless and redundant. In *Surplus American: How the 1% Is Making Us Redundant*, published in 2015, Charles Derber and Yale R. Magrass identify a number of groups as "surplus," including the underemployed, people removed from the labor force against their will, and retirees. They argue that increasing numbers of the U.S. public have become part of this surplus population.[47] As these studies show, the surplus population is a major product of the neoliberal economic policies around the world.

Furthermore, the fact that this surplus population in the tail section is multinational and multiracial is very significant in representing globalized neoliberal capitalism. Although the majority of the people on the train speak English, several languages are heard among the population, including French and Japanese. This multilingual community is set up right at the start. When Mason begins her speech about the "shoe on the head" and "the preordained positions" to the tail-section population, her words are translated into French and Japanese until she stops them because they "only got seven minutes." Also, when Curtis and his group free the Korean security specialist Namgoong Minsoo from his prison cell, Namgoong uses a device that translates his Korean into English. The revolt of the surplus population in the tail section is a manifestation of a transnational solidarity to overthrow the system and bring justice. By depicting class warfare within the train, *Snowpiercer* has opened up a space in which discussions and debates about political revolution can proliferate.

Besides the existence of the surplus population on the train, another significant element that makes the film a sharp critique of neoliberal capitalism is the unstoppable train itself. *Snowpiercer* is a film about moving forward, only forward. The story takes place in a train that is perpetually speeding forward, Curtis and the tail-enders move forward to the engine room, Namgoong Minsoo is also pursuing his goal of going forward to the engine room in order to blow the door open to the outside, and Wilford is all about maintaining the engine that keeps the train running forward. The inevitability of the forward progress is presented in a striking ax-fighting scene in which Curtis is caught between going forward to capture Mason or going back to save Edgar (for whom, as we learn later on, he has a sense of debt as well as brotherly love). After a very brief moment of hesitation, Curtis chooses to capture Mason over saving Edgar. Throughout the entire film, there is no moving backward. Everything is told in a linear progression.

This obsession with forward movement in the film fits into its allegorical critique of capitalism. The system of capitalism has to expand and move forward endlessly. This path of endless growth is represented by the forward movement in the film. However, the film demonstrates that this endless forward movement leads to doomed collapse. The train eventually runs out of parts and has to rely on the exploitation of child labor. This is a warning against ever-expanding capitalism. And it is this metaphor of an endless progression and the existence of the surplus population that brings the film closer to a picture of the present.

If the tail-enders symbolize the surplus population, the class warfare portrayed in the film raises questions that are urgent and relevant to our era: How can we reform the current neoliberal system? Is reform even possible? Is a reform within the system possible, or do we need a radical revolution? If a revolution is needed, what kind should it be? What result would it bring? What comes after capitalism? Would a revolution that overthrows capitalism bring the end of humanity? *Snowpiercer* suggests the need for a radical revolution that would mark a complete break from the current system, to the point of risking human extinction. As I have pointed out previously, the film has instigated heated discussions about neoliberal capitalism and its rising economic inequality—in particular, on political revolution that would bring an end to that system in the United States and Korea. The critics' reviews range from "*Snowpiercer* is the most political film of the year"[48] to one that encourages readers to "give the film a shot to see a dramatized microcosm of America" and "Everyone take a closer look at the current state of the class system and the political arena."[49] The review on the World Socialist Web Site, while praising the film's portrayal of "the oppressed and of their uprising," critiques it as sympathetic but "rather superficial." The reviewer, Muhammad Khan, asks, "In our era of unrelenting social tension and global class conflict, what is the value of a perspective that essentially advocates shrinking away from human life and all its problems?"[50] The violent rupture envisioned in the class revolution in *Snowpiercer* is taken quite seriously by critics and audiences alike.

RADICAL POLITICS AND REDISTRIBUTION OF THE SENSIBLE

Snowpiercer is a film about revolution. As I have demonstrated, the film brings up many current issues, including those of environmental crisis. However, it is the revolt of the tail-enders that is at the heart of the film. The revolution of the have-nots is what drives the narrative forward. It is a revolt that not only overthrows the authoritarian power of Wilford but also brings about a radical break from the existing system. Therefore, it is only natural that many reviewers of the film reference revolutionary thinkers from Karl Marx to Antonio Gramsci, Louis

Althusser, Walter Benjamin, and others. However, it is the contemporary French philosopher Jacques Rancière whose reformulation of the relationship between art and politics provides a keen insight into the analysis of the radical politics presented in the film.

The film stunningly visualizes Rancière's redefinition of politics and his notion of the "distribution of the sensible." Rancière's idea of politics proper is based on a clear distinction between the police and politics. For him, what has been usually referred to as politics—the administration of social order by the ruling power—is not politics in the true sense of the term. Rancière calls this governance the "police." Social order is maintained by the police, which entails the distribution of roles and places based on a hierarchy sustained by patterns of inclusion and exclusion. What you can have, do, see, or say is determined by the place you are given in society. In the film, the tail-enders are preordained to the tail section. What they are able to sense (see, hear, taste, touch, smell) and speak is strictly controlled. Thus their knowledge of the world is limited. They live in the tail section with no window to see outside, and they are not allowed to voice their needs, let alone their anger and frustration. They do not even know what their daily food is made of. They are the *demos* (the people), but they do not have any access to the making of the social order. But as they move forward into the front section, what they perceive through their senses expands: they get to know what their food is made of, they see the outside world through the windows, and so on. By revolting against the existing order and abolishing their preordained positions to claim their voice and their part in the social order, they are challenging the existing distribution of the sensible.

The term *sensible* here is the French word, which has a different meaning from the English word. Whereas the English word usually means "having or containing sense or reason," the French word *sensible* means "perceiving through the senses or mind"; therefore, it has to do with cognition and perception.[51] So "sensible" in the "distribution of the sensible" refers to what is captured by the senses. One's perception of the world varies according to where one is positioned in the social order; thus the modes of participation are also determined by those of perception. According to Rancière, political action means revealing the distance between what is distributed to your position and what should be distributed. The real politics is to challenge the police or policing and bring about the redistribution of the sensible. The political subject is not preordained by a specific social status but made through the process. Politics is an act of the people with no role asking for their part in the governing of society. It is about the voiceless claiming their voice. As Slavoj Žižek has summed up, political struggle proper is "not a rational debate between multiple interests, but, simultaneously, the struggle for one's voice to be heard and recognized as the voice of a legitimate partner: when the 'excluded' . . . protested against the ruling elite."[52]

For Rancière, the principle that constitutes politics is democracy, for which equality is not a goal but a premise. And it is not consensus but dissensus that is the fundamental condition of democracy and politics. Democracy is a process of dissensus that creates cracks in the existing social order and the distribution of the sensible. So for Rancière, dissensual aesthetics signifies a rearrangement of the sensible "by confronting the established framework of perception, thought and action with the inadmissible."[53] For him, politics operates in the spaces of dispute, of dissensus.[54] Furthermore, aesthetics is not about studying and defining beauty or art but an artistic practice that has to do with the social distribution of the sensible: what is sensed and perceived. It is a specific sensory experience. Therefore, aesthetics is very close to politics. It is a political system of distributing the senses and perception. It is about to whom the ability to see, speak, and think are distributed.

The revolt by Curtis and the tail-enders—aided by Namgoong—embodies Rancière's politics that disrupts the existing "distribution of the sensible." It realizes Rancière's redefinition of politics, which is about challenging the established order by the excluded, "the part which has no part," in the name of equality and bringing about a redistribution of the sensible. The entire film takes place on a running train in which order is rigidly enforced. The film's theme of social inequality and stratification is clearly conveyed in the visual design of the train, which transforms a vertical, hierarchical social structure into a horizontal one: from the wretched in the tail section, to the front section housing the upper class, to the engine at the head of the train.

At the beginning of the film, the "police order" of the train is clearly established and conveyed by Mason's speech to the tail-enders. Early on, after there is an uproar in the tail section and an angry father whose child has been taken away to the front section loses his arm for punishment, Prime Minster Mason makes a speech. In her long speech, she compares the train's social order to a body with a head and two feet. She emphasizes, "We must each of us occupy our preordained particular position. . . . In the beginning, order was prescribed by your ticket: first class, economy, and freeloaders like you." In the train, this order is eternal and is prescribed by the sacred engine. The tail-enders are shoes and therefore belong to the foot. She shouts, "Know your place. Keep your place. Be a shoe." Mason's speech perfectly fits into Rancière's idea of the "distribution of the sensible." The tail-enders should never, ever covet a place in the head section. These preordained tail-enders have no part in the governing of the train's social system. Therefore, when they reject their preordained place and rise to claim their part and their voice, they are engaging in the real politics that Rancière argues for.

Concurrently, two different ideas of revolution are presented in the film: that of Karl Marx and that of Walter Benjamin. Coincidentally, both ideas use the metaphor of a train. It is well known that historically, the train has been a symbol of modernity, capitalism, and revolution. Karl Marx wrote in 1850, "Revolutions are the locomotives of history."[55] Here, the locomotive symbolizes progress, the linear progression to the classless utopia through class struggle: a modern idea of revolution based on a belief in progress. However, Benjamin contested Marx's idea and wrote, "Perhaps revolutions are an attempt by the passengers on this train—namely, the human race—to activate the emergency brake."[56] Benjamin's idea of revolution is not a linear progression but more of a radical action associated with the sense of urgency and the crisis of the present moment.

In *Snowpiercer*, these two different ideas of revolution are represented in the characters of Curtis and Namgoong Minsoo. Curtis is the leader of the tail-enders' revolt, and Namgoong is the Korean engineer who designed the security system of the train. Thus Curtis and his group need Namgoong in order to open the gates as they plan to move forward to the front. Curtis could be seen as representing Marx's idea, and Namgoong as representing Benjamin's. Curtis's revolution keeps the train running, whereas Namgoong's revolution is about pulling the emergency brake of the running train. As in Bong's previous films, *Snowpiercer* has a dual narrative structure. That is, the story that started off the narrative slowly turns into a different story as the narrative unfolds. In *Snowpiercer*, the narrative starts with the story of Curtis leading the revolt; however, it slowly turns into a story of Namgoong and his radical plan to escape the train. He was the only one who had been observing the outside world when everyone else just believed that it was too cold for humans to survive. He knew that the ice was melting. Therefore, he pretended to be a *kronol* addict in order to collect as much of the drug as possible to explode the gate of the train and escape to the outside world. By blowing up the train, Curtis and Namgoong have brought about a Benjaminian revolution and a radical break from the existing system.

While the story of *Snowpiercer* depicts a struggle between the established order (Wilford Industries) and its excluded (inhabitants of the tail section), the visual design and spatial construction in the film evidence and brilliantly reinforce the notion of the distribution of the sensible. The design of each car of the train reflects the position of the occupants. As Curtis and his followers move forward toward the engine, his perception of the world expands accordingly. His knowledge of how the social order works in the train increases until the crucial yet hidden secret of the train is finally revealed to him in the engine room. He realizes that if the system of the train is maintained, then the exploitation of child labor, the weakest of society, is inevitable. The spaces and things distributed in each carriage offer Curtis and his revolutionary group different sensorial experiences as they pass through to the front.

The order of the train is important because it shapes the progression of the narrative, but, of course, it also reveals how the social system of the train works to maintain the survival of its occupants—in particular, the people in the front section. The train that has run for seventeen years when the story starts is a self-contained, closed ecosystem. Everything needed for the operation of the train and the survival of the people is produced inside the train. The only exception is the ice that the train's front end sucks in to turn into water. As a microcosm of the world and humanity's last resort of survival, the order of the train from the tail to the head section follows the development of civilization: from primitive living conditions in the tail section to the luxurious and decadent abundance in the head section. And what clearly divides the two sections is the use of color and light. Curtis and his group leave the dark, filthy, windowless tail section and travel to the bright, richly colored front section. It is the sensory experience of the visual that brings the truth of the train to light at the end.

On the other hand, *Okja* also depicts anticapitalist resistance on two different levels: by an ordinary girl from the periphery who had no prior experience of a capitalist system and by an organized resistance of the Animal Liberation Front. It is ironic that the film depicts Mija creating a crack, however small, in the system and being able to achieve her goal of saving Okja, while Animal Liberation Front members fail while exposing the frictions within the organization. They are successful in their initial rescue of Okja from the Mirando Corporation in Seoul. Their rescue mission inside the traffic tunnel culminates in a dramatic scene of them leaping from the running truck into the Han River (from where the monster in *The Host* emerged). Through mistranslation/miscommunication, they decide to carry on their mission of infiltrating the Mirando Corporation by taking Okja to New York; accordingly, they flee, leaving Mija and Okja to be captured by the authorities and taken to the Mirando Corporation as part of their plan.

Ironically, Mirando Corporation executives decide to take Mija and Okja to New York to show off their successful breeding of superpigs in their festival.

FIGURE 9. *Okja.* An idyllic moment between Mija and Okja before Okja is taken away.

Thus ALF would have another chance to fight and reveal the dark conspiracies of the Mirando Corporation; however, during their attack on the festival, they are again brutally beaten and captured by the police. They are full of goodwill and dedication but clumsy in the execution of their revolt. On the contrary, Mija succeeds in confronting Mirando CEO Nancy and negotiating Okja out of the slaughterhouse. As in *The Host*, it is the unlikely heroism of a family member desperately trying to save her beloved whatever the cost may be. The Park family in *The Host* fails, but Mija succeeds. She even smuggles out a baby superpiglet in coordination with Okja and the parent pigs. Thus although Mija was not able to save all the superpigs by collapsing the Mirando Corporation's operation, she was able to open up a little door for possible resistance against the neoliberal capitalism.

Snowpiercer and *Okja* are in many respects different from Bong Joon Ho's previous films. They are not specifically Korean stories unfolding in Korean locations. These are his global projects to be made predominantly in the English language and with an international cast. However, they share many important similarities with his previous films: he borrows a genre—science fiction—to make his comments on our present world. *Snowpiercer* is a political allegory about the neoliberal capitalist system and a comment on the need for a radical revolution. *Okja* is a more heartwarming fantasy tale about the love and friendship between a superpig and a rural Korean girl who stops at nothing to save her pig. At the time of their productions, they were both the most expensive blockbusters to date for any Korean film director but at the same time the most political with their allegorical or overt criticism on the unethical greed of the neoliberal corporate culture. Following *The Host*, Bong has made more successful political blockbusters that appealed to a wider global audience.

CONCLUSION
Parasite—A New Beginning?

After two global blockbusters—*Snowpiercer* (2013) and *Okja* (2017)—Bong Joon Ho cowrote, directed, and produced a midsized film, *Parasite* (2019), as his seventh feature. His first solely Korean story in ten years after *Mother* (2009), *Parasite* is a culmination of his previous films, yet at the same time, it is a glimpse of a new beginning in his storytelling. It follows his earlier works in seamlessly blending social commentary into a popular genre film and in telling stories from the point of view of the socially weak; however, it departs from previous films by presenting a more complex and nuanced perspective on the contemporary social world as well as the lives of its inhabitants. The film's story centers on the class conflict between the poor Kim family and the wealthy Park family as members of the Kim family infiltrate the Park household one by one. However, the simple moral dichotomies of rich/evil versus poor/good, particularly prominent in *Snowpiercer* and *Okja*, are noticeably altered to capture multiple layers of contradictions. Thus the film has an equivocal tone heightened by an extreme moral ambiguity.

It is safe to assume that this change is partly due to the fact that Bong has returned to the Korean society he knows so intimately and, more specifically, to the fact that he could fully use his native tongue with which more nuanced expressions are possible. In relation to the moral ambiguity, it is worthwhile to recall that the symptoms of moral corruption in Korean society were already evident in *Barking Dogs Never Bite* (2000) and *Mother*, as detailed in chapter 4. Yoon-ju, the protagonist in *Barking Dogs Never Bite*, is reluctant to bribe his way to a full-time professorial position. He resists but ultimately succumbs to the corrupt practice. The mother in *Mother* finally realizes that she has let an orphan with a mental disability be wrongfully accused of the murder her son committed. Both Yoon-ju and the mother ultimately suffer from a guilty conscience.

However, the Kim family in *Parasite* shows neither moral hesitation nor any sense of guilt. They continue to play the con game naturally and artfully. Ki-Woo even boasts that he does not think forging a college diploma is a crime. From the outset, the family shows no will to fight against social *pujoris* or to change the status quo. Their only goal seems to be to continue working for the Park family as long as they can. In order to achieve this goal, they must forge their identity and frame the previous chauffeur and the house caretaker to get them fired from the Park residence.

Although it is a local drama squarely rooted in Korean realities, *Parasite* is most comparable to *Snowpiercer*, since both films are about the catastrophe caused by class polarization. It is as if *Parasite* is a case study of the issues of neoliberalism and class raised in *Snowpiercer*, looking into the ways in which these issues are played out in the individual lives of the people of Korea specifically. *Snowpiercer* is a universal allegory of the transnational capitalist system and revolution, while *Parasite* is a fable grounded in Korean specificities. If this is the case, what are the Korean realities *Parasite* captures and portrays? We are confronted by a society in which moral corruption and anomie permeate to such an extent that a revolution, as in *Snowpiercer*, is no longer imaginable. This is because the horizontal solidarity among the socially weak that was the driving force of the tail-enders' revolt in *Snowpiercer* is not present in *Parasite*. The tail-enders in *Snowpiercer* unite under the leadership of Curtis and proceed forward to the front section; however, the poor in *Parasite* fight against each other and eventually devolve. This difference is visualized and contrasted through the horizontal space of the train in *Snowpiercer* and the vertical stairs in *Parasite*.

Indeed, horizontal solidarity is one of the constant themes in Bong Joon Ho's films. In *Barking Dogs Never Bite*, part-time lecturer Yoon-ju unites with the apartment's management office employee Hyun-nam to find his lost dog; in *Memories of Murder* (2003), a rural detective and an urban detective cooperate despite their mutual hostility; and the Park family in *The Host* (2006) could finally kill the monster with the help of a homeless man who joined them and poured gasoline over the monster. In *Snowpiercer*, in addition to the tail-enders, security specialist Namgoong Minsoo forms an alliance with Curtis, and Mija in *Okja* cooperates with the members of ALF. The mother in *Mother* is an exception, as she is all by herself in her investigation, but even she is helped by Jin-tae to find out the truth. Most of these alliances and instances of solidarity end in half successes at best, thus making Bong's films pessimistic; however, *Parasite* is the most despairing by showing a world in which the possibility of solidarity is nonexistent. The only source of community and solidarity left in Korea is within the immediate family; however, all three families disintegrate at the end.[1]

Another element that sets *Parasite* apart from Bong's previous films is the disappearance of the system of power from the people's view. This invisibility is what makes horizontal solidarity impossible. In *The Host*, it is the U.S. and the Korean governments that chase the Park family instead of helping them find their daughter, and in *Snowpiercer*, Wilford, who wields his authoritarian power over the tail-enders, and his Wilford Industries are presented as the oppressive system that maintains and reproduces inequality within the train. However, in *Parasite*, no such system or power is revealed. The system is hidden behind the individuals and their struggle. Authorities representing the system do appear in the film, but only briefly and insignificantly on two occasions. First, on the night of the flood, we see a group of flood victims complaining about something to public servants in the gymnasium where a temporary shelter has been set up. Then at the end of the film, when Ki-Woo wakes up at the hospital, he sees a "detective not looking like a detective" and a "doctor not looking like a doctor." They are caricatured and mocked.

Furthermore, Kim Ki-Tek in *Parasite* is different from Park Gang-du in *The Host* and the mother in *Mother*, both of whom had to take things into their own hands because of the indifference, incompetence, or corruption of the authorities. Ki-Tek and his family cannot ask for or expect help from authorities; instead, they must avoid law enforcement because they have committed acts of fraud in order to be hired by the wealthy Park family. Thus the Korean society depicted in *Parasite* is a world of anomie where social norms and morality have collapsed and the socially weak exploit each other. Systemic problems and public corruption are internalized in the characters' actions and experiences.

Since the system as the root cause of the class inequality and its representatives are invisible, it is impossible to conceive of and plan a class revolution in the world of *Parasite*. As Ki-Tek confesses to his son, Ki-Woo, "No plan is the best plan," the poor in *Parasite* are unable to formulate any long-term plans outside their immediate family. In *Snowpiercer*, the tail-enders rise up after a long, secretive planning; however, the Kim family in *Parasite* can only deal with things on an ad hoc basis. They struggle to make ends meet each day, and because they do not have any money, they cannot afford to do any long-term planning. While *Snowpiercer* suggests a glimpse of hope and the possibility of a new world through the subversion of the system and by jumping out of the train, *Parasite* draws the picture of a dog-eat-dog world in which everyone is confused and lost. It puts a magnifying glass over present Korean society and carefully examines the symptoms of catastrophe caused by neoliberal restructuring imposed by the IMF since the 1998 financial crisis. And the most distinctive symptom is moral breakdown.

In *Parasite*, Bong displays what has happened in Korean society in the last twenty years since the neoliberal restructuring: the collapse of the middle class. One of the consequences of this collapse under neoliberal capitalism is the emergence of a surplus population, as discussed in chapter 5. The fact that all four members of the Kim family belong to this jobless surplus population supports the idea that they are the products and symbols of the neoliberal capitalism that intensified in Korea. In particular, Ki-Woo and Ki-Jung are members of a surplus human generation, as they have never been employed; however, Ki-Tek is different. He represents the decline of the middle class that took place after the neoliberal restructuring. Indeed, the film implies that Ki-Tek, Kun-Sae (the basement dweller), and the wealthy Mr. Park all may have belonged to the same middle class in the past. Ki-Tek and Kun-Sae share the same experience of bankruptcy after opening a Taiwanese sponge cake business. The difference between the two is the use of private loans. Kun-Sae, who took out private loans, has to hide in the basement to avoid being hunted down by his creditors, while Ki-Tek could scrape by in the semibasement house folding pizza boxes because he stayed away from the loan sharks.

In the family dining scene at a buffet restaurant, we gather from their dialogue that Ki-Tek failed in his fried chicken business, worked as valet driver in one of the wealthiest villages in Seoul, and opened a Taiwanese sponge cake business, all with no success. He is a clear example of the specifically Korean situation in which many people took the plunge into opening a franchise store believing it to be a sure thing. It is still common for those who chose voluntary early retirement to invest their severance pay in a small franchise business because it is difficult for them to be hired back in the labor market. The franchise business in South Korea has shown a rapid growth after the IMF bailout. According to the Korean Franchise Association's 2017 statistics, there are more than 5,000 franchise headquarters, 220,000 franchise stores, and 1.24 million employees.[2] Inevitably, the competition was fierce, and most of these franchisees failed and fell into poverty, as did Ki-Tek and Kun-Sae in Bong's film. As Ki-Woo often says, "This is symbolic," and indeed, Ki-Tek's family is emblematic of the fall of the middle class in the era of neoliberal capitalism in Korea.

Mr. Park is also a fascinating and symbolic figure, as he and his wife, Yon-Kyo, defy the stereotypical depiction of the rich as villains. We can discern that Mr. Park also once belonged to the middle class from the fact that he and his wife are familiar with the "subway smell." When Mr. Park describes Ki-Tek's odor as "What we smell when we get on the subway," Yon-Kyo replies, "It has been long since I took the subways." Unlike the third-generation CEOs of the Korean chaebol,[3] they were not born with a silver spoon in their mouth. It is very significant, albeit a subtle detail, that Da-song, their son, who was born into a wealthy family, is the first one to detect that Ki-Tek's family members smell alike. Bong, known to pay attention to the smallest details, shows that Mr. Park is the CEO of a successful IT company by using a framed magazine article and an award certificate hanging on the wall of the mansion. Park became a global businessman after receiving an innovation award from an international association for the best use of emerging/new technology in the field of augmented reality in 2017. Younger than Ki-Tek and an IT expert, he has used the system well, but he is a figure who neither leads nor represents the system itself.

Thus Ki-Tek and Kun-Sae on the one hand and Mr. Park on the other represent the two opposing courses the Korean middle class took in the post-IMF era: one was to join the franchise boom but ultimately end up bankrupt and the other was to start up a successful company during the venture business boom and rise to the wealthy class. Of course, as we gather from the film, those who were able to take the second course are a decade younger, good with English, and tech savvy. In this way, the characters in *Parasite* demonstrate how globalized neoliberal capitalism has intervened in the lives of individuals and brought a rapid decline to the middle class of Korea. One thing that is missing is the face of the system behind this class polarization. This disappearance is, in fact, an accurate picture of the current social world in which individuals are considered solely accountable for their successes or failures.

Therefore, the clash between the three families in the film is one in which the grand system is absent and invisible. It is, in essence, a battle between those who share the same root. Mr. Park is superrich, but he is not oppressive and exploitative like Wilford in *Snowpiercer* or greedy and immoral like Lucy Mirando in *Okja*. That is why he and his family are depicted as being nice and naive, thus breaking the stereotypical representation of the rich as evil. They are the nouveau riche of the neoliberal global capitalist system whose wealth is deemed to be of their own merit. Therefore, Mr. Park may be a figure of envy for Ki-Tek and Kun-Sae, but he is not a target of their animosity. He is good enough to allow room for Ki-Tek and Kun-Sae to live off his wealth, and he is a man to whom Kun-Sae pays his "respect."

Thus it comes as a totally unexpected turn of events when Ki-Tek stabs Mr. Park out of unbearable anger. What triggered him to commit this explosive act that would destroy everything for him? In fact, before approaching this climactic scene, the film showed how feelings of humiliation have been heaped upon Ki-Tek. First, his fall from the middle class to the bottom of the social strata provides important background information for understanding his bewildering actions. We can imagine that he must have endured many moments of humiliation and degradation during his downfall. And when he inadvertently overhears Mr. Park's disdain regarding his body odor, a much deeper humiliation hits the core of his sense of self-worth. He learns how his boss thinks about him behind his gentle facade and kind manner.

In this respect, the lovemaking between the Park couple on the night of the flood is one of the most significant in the film. Earlier, when the Kim family was having a party of their own in the empty Park residence, Ki-Tek reacted violently toward his wife, Chung-Sook, when she mocked him by saying that he would flee like a cockroach if the Park family would suddenly return home. Incidentally, the Park family actually does return due to heavy rain, and Ki-Tek has to flee and hide underneath the low coffee table, just like a cockroach. It is in this awkward and humiliating position, with his daughter, Ki-Jung, lying next to him, that he has to endure overhearing the wealthy couple's discussion about his musty odor. The couple tries to describe his smell in all kinds of degrading terms, and then Mr. Park asks his wife, Yon-Kyo, about the "cheap panties" he showed her after he had found them in the back seat of his car because it would arouse him sexually. Ki-Tek knows that he is referring to Ki-Jung's panties. (Ki-Jung had left her panties in the back seat of Mr. Park's car on purpose in order to frame the previous chauffeur of misconduct and get him fired.) And the fact that Ki-Jung is lying right next to him makes it much harder to bear.

This sequence starts with a downward vertical movement of the camera from the Park couple on the sofa to Ki-Tek and Ki-Jung lying beneath the coffee table, thus accentuating the high-class/low-class hierarchy between them. The film then cross-cuts between the unreserved Parks and the awkward Kims. Ki-Tek and Ki-Jung are shown in an overhead shot to convey their embarrassment and degradation. Ki-Tek closes his eyes and pulls up his shirt to his nose when the Parks talk about his odor, but he looks more embarrassed and awkward when Mr. Park mentions "cheap panties." With Ki-Jung lying right next to him, he covers his eyes with his arm. This may well be when the seed for Ki-Tek's explosive action is sown.

Ki-Tek's embarrassment and humiliation are even more provoked the next day when Mr. Park draws a clear line between them as his boss. Despite becoming a flood victim the night before, Ki-Tek gladly helps out Mr. and Mrs. Park on their preparation for Da-song's birthday party on Sunday. However, his goodwill is crushed when Mr. Park reminds him that he is getting paid extra and to think of this somewhat awkward play as part of his job. It is his warning for Ki-Tek to not "cross the line," and it reminds Ki-Tek of his disdain from the night before.

The humiliation that has been building up in Ki-Tek over the course of two days is triggered in a pivotal scene in which Mr. Park holds his nose with an instinctual disgust at dying Kun-Sae. Before he even realizes it, he runs toward Mr. Park and stabs him right in the chest as his anger and resentment explode. In this moment of catastrophe, Ki-Tek finally identifies with Kun-Sae; however, Kun-Sae is dead, and he replaces him as a basement dweller: a "human waste"[4] who has no place above the ground.

The scenes from the night of the flood and Da-song's birthday party mark a point of inflection in Bong's oeuvre. They truly set *Parasite* apart from his previous films. It is his first film to focus on intangible issues of smell and emotion as social products. In *Parasite*, smell functions as the most critical metaphor of class difference. The smell of poverty and the musty "smell of the basement" that brings an instinctual disgust from Mr. Park lay bare the hidden face of the neoliberal capitalist society we live in. There is a stigma to those who fell through the cracks and became outcasts in a world of wealth and privilege, and there is an invisible line between the two worlds.

Here Bong also explores the social aspect of emotion, which is often dismissed as something trivial. The film presents the feelings of humiliation, resentment, and disgust as the predominant emotions of our era. The disgust or disdain for the outcasts, "human waste," and minorities engenders humiliation, shame, and resentment in return. Through the violent reaction of Ki-Tek, the film demonstrates that feelings are also shaped by social forces. Ki-Tek's emotional explosion at the climax represents the rage building up in the outsiders as they are forced further toward the margins. Korean sociologist Kim Chan-ho argues that *momyŏlgam*, the Korean word to describe a feeling of humiliation combined with contempt, is "the core emotion of bitterness that dominates the everyday lives of the Koreans" and that it is "the worst trigger that arouses the feeling of shame."[5] With the global expansion of neoliberal capitalism, the feelings of humiliation and degradation have become a universal experience for the socially weak; however, these are more acutely felt in Korea, where the drive for economic growth has often ignored human rights issues. In contemporary society, *momyŏlgam* is a dangerous feeling that often leads to impulsive actions and vengeance. And in a world of "every man/woman for himself/herself," where the feelings of humiliation and contempt make people vulnerable to outbursts, it is impossible to carry out a rational and well-organized resistance as illustrated in *Snowpiercer*.

Therefore, the class conflict depicted in *Parasite* is different from that of *Snowpiercer*. It is not between the haves and have-nots or the powerful and the powerless but rather a fierce competition and battle among the socially weak. In this film, it is represented as the battle taking place in the Park household between the two poor families. Ki-Tek's family achieves their goal of infiltrating the Park household as employees in the first half of the film. Thus the tension of the film appears to shift to the question of when and how their true identities will be revealed. However, there is an unexpected twist in which the former caretaker, Mun-Kwang, and her husband, Kun-Sae, suddenly and surprisingly become the major obstacle and enemies of the Kims.

The confrontation between these two poor families, a battle in which one or the other must be eliminated, eventually leads to violent murders in broad daylight. When Kun-Sae steps out of the basement, picks up a kitchen knife, and comes out to the front garden, where Da-song's birthday party is going on, it is not Mr. Park but Chung-Sook whom he calls out. The target of his revenge was the Kim family. He kills Ki-Jung but is killed by Chung-Sook, and in the midst of chaos, Ki-Tek kills Mr. Park. All three families meet catastrophic ends; however, without giving the audience a clear sense of who is the perpetrator and who is the victim, the film ends with Ki-Woo's futile fantasy of rescuing his father from the basement.

As such, *Parasite* explores further the issue of class polarization, which *Snowpiercer* had raised, but this time within the concrete realities of Korea. And in so doing, the film achieves a sense of stylistic renewal, and it displays the major traits of Bong's previous films: the motif of misrecognition that triggers the narrative, the narrative of failure that denies the audience of the reassurance of a final resolution, and the foregrounding of vertical spaces Bong seemed to prefer in his previous films. The locality is much richer, with specifically Korean elements that intensify the acute sense of satire as well as the film's verisimilitude. These include, for example, the Taiwanese sponge cake franchise, the *Jjapaguri* noodle (translated as Ram-don in the English subtitles), uniquely Korean spaces such as a semibasement home with a toilet on a high ledge, and other intimate uses of Korean language and sensibilities. In this respect, *Parasite* marks Bong's return to his idiosyncratic filmmaking that is transnational yet nationally specific.

First of all, as in his previous films, it is the motif of misrecognition that drives the narrative forward. However, how that motif is mobilized and operated is distinctly different. As briefly described in the introduction, misrecognitions are actively induced by the members of the Kim family, whereas in previous films, misrecognitions usually happen unintentionally in a chase (Yoon-ju's kidnapping the wrong dog in *Barking Dogs Never Bite* and detectives mistaking a witness as the killer in *Memories of Murder*, for example). *Parasite* pushes the motif of misrecognition to the extreme by creating a situation in which the protagonists are fully utilizing misrecognition by pretension. They pretend to be those they are not. And the film even comments about these pretensions when Ki-Woo asks Da-hye, for whom he is providing tutoring in English, to write an English composition using the word *pretend* at least twice. Da-hye was criticizing her little brother, Da-song, for pretending to be an art genius, but in fact, it is Ki-Woo who is copying his rich college student friend Min-Hyuk. He repeats what Min-Hyuk has said to him and his family and even echoes his plan to date Da-hye once she becomes a college student. In fact, the film's narrative starts with Ki-Woo taking Min-Hyuk's place as Da-hye's English tutor.

Bong's utilization of the motif of misrecognition is at its most Hitchcockian in *Parasite*, since it serves to hide the true identity of the Kim family. However, he takes it in a different direction as the Kim family's ultimate goal differs from that of the titular character in Hitchcock's 1964 film *Marnie*, for example. While Marnie chooses to disappear once she achieves her goal (money), the Kim family plans to keep working for the Park family as long as they can. They even dream of becoming their in-laws. Therefore, the thematic element of misrecognition in *Parasite* does not become a story about delving deeper into the identity problem of the pretender (*Marnie* reveals Marnie's traumatic childhood experience as the cause of her criminal behavior); rather, it is used to bring forth the clash between two poor families. The confrontation is inevitable, since both families want to continue living in the Park residence and each threatens the other with exposure. This conflict further reveals the harsh environment of contemporary Korean society in which the poor and the disfranchised have to battle each other for survival.

The film effectively sets up the motif of misrecognition visually as well right at the beginning. In the semibasement home, Ki-Woo tells his father that he does not think that faking the college diploma is a crime, since he will succeed in entering the university soon. He goes up the stairs and heads to the Park mansion for the interview. Then the camera stays on him as he walks away. When he arrives at the Park's house, the camera follows him from behind as he pushes open the front gate and walks up the stairs and into the sunlight-filled garden. He cannot help but squint at the bright sunlight. This early sequence visually tells the audience that Ki-Woo cannot show his face; he is there to hide his true identity.

Parasite is also distinct from Bong's previous films for its heavy reliance on set design. It is his first film to be shot mostly on a set, unlike his other films set in Korea. With the exception of *Snowpiercer*, which is set in an imaginary train, *Barking Dogs Never Bite*, *Memories of Murder*, *The Host*, and *Mother* were mostly shot on location to capture specifically real places; however, both houses in *Parasite*—the Park family's mansion and the Kim family's semibasement home—were designed and built on set from scratch. The Park mansion was built on an open set, while the Kims' house and its surrounding neighborhood were built within a giant water tank so that the whole neighborhood could be submerged underwater for the flooding scene.

This set design was also very practical in terms of visualizing the class hierarchy through a vertical structure. Bong often used narrow and high vertical spaces in his previous films such as the interrogation room in *Memories of Murder* and the deep sewage in *The Host*. But in *Parasite*, he explicitly uses them to symbolize the class hierarchy. The film effectively demonstrates how one's economic status intervenes and interferes with every aspect of life, including how much sunlight you get and what a heavy rain means. A two-story house filled with bright sunlight through the floor-to-ceiling window (in 2.35:1 aspect ratio!), a semibasement home with limited access to sunlight, and the basement with no sunlight at all represent the economic statuses of the three families. Both the material things—such as houses and windows—and nature, which is supposed to be free for everyone, have different meanings according to where you belong in the social hierarchy.

Ki-Tek's semibasement house represents his precarious position, facing the threat of falling farther down to the basement. The disparity between the

FIGURE 10. *Parasite* storyboard by Bong Joon Ho. Ki-Woo enters the Park mansion (Bong Joon Ho).

wealthy Park family and the poor Kim family is also expressed by the numerous staircases Ki-Tek has to run down with Ki-Woo and Ki-Jung on the night of the flood to get back home from the Parks' rich neighborhood. These outside scenes are shot on location in neighborhoods familiar to Korean audiences. Indeed, as briefly mentioned in the beginning, it is fair to say *Parasite* is the most local of Bong's films to date. His second film to surpass the threshold of ten million ticket sales in Korea since *The Host*, its sense of humor, situations, settings, and dialogue are extremely Korean. Particularly, his tasteful use of dialogue makes the film's black humor more palpable to the Korean audience. It is true that much of the complex nuances are lost in translation; however, the universality of its theme of economic inequality and class polarization, the playful subversions of genre conventions, and above all, the global zeitgeist it captures easily trounce these local specificities. The record-breaking box-office receptions in the United States, France, and elsewhere prove its transnational appeal.[6]

However, it is also true that knowing the Korean cultural codes does open doors for decoding the hidden layers of meaning in the film. For example, Korean audiences will know the references to the Taiwanese Castella (sponge cake) business, since it is well known that those franchises set the fastest bankruptcy record in 2017.[7] So many Taiwanese Castella shops sprang up at the time, making it plausible for the film to have both Ki-Tek and Kun-Sae share the same experience of going bankrupt after opening one of these stores. Also, every Korean knows the *Jjapaguri* noodle and the song Ki-Jung and Ki-Woo sing before entering the wealthy Park's mansion, as it is a common song Koreans often use to memorize things.[8] The film even brings up a historical figure, Admiral Yi Sun-sin, when Yon-Kyo describes to Chung-Sook the table setting she wants for the party as the "crane formation" Yi used in his winning battle against Japanese invasion in the late sixteenth century.[9] The film has numerous cultural references that are familiar and endearing to Korean audiences. And if you are a Bong Joon Ho fan, you would recognize that the university stamp Ki-Jung uses to forge the diploma is that of Bong's alma mater.

Stylistically, *Parasite* pushes the usual traits of Bong's films to a new height, creating a new kind of visual rhythm. His tendency to mix different genres and disparate elements is more intensified, making it even harder to define it into one genre. The tonal shifts are swifter and more unpredictable, as the film moves from being an exhilaratingly funny comedy to a horror, then a thriller, a disaster film, and finally a tragic catastrophe. In terms of narrative structure, *Parasite* is the most nonlinear of Bong's films. As commercial genre films, his previous works unfold in a linear fashion following the progression of events; however, in *Parasite*, the linear progression is often interrupted by flashbacks. The flashbacks are particularly noteworthy in that they are mostly subjective memories or fantasies that add to the overall tone of ambiguity mentioned previously.

Most of the flashbacks are visualizations of what a character remembers or perceives. For example, in one scene, Yon-Kyo describes that Da-song saw a ghost one night when he came down to have another piece of his birthday cake. She explains it as Da-song's illusion, but we learn later on that it was, in fact, Kun-Sae coming up from the basement. In another scene, Mun-Kwang describes one of her happy memories in the Park house as the film shows her dancing with Kun-Sae in the sunlit living room. These subjective memories reflect the tellers' own desires, which means that they may well be their fantasies rather than an objective description of what really happened. The film ends with Ki-Woo's fantasy of buying the house to free his father from the basement. Thus we can see that with *Parasite*, Bong Joon Ho has moved away from his usual aesthetics in various ways.

Bong Joon Ho is one of the most political filmmakers working in commercial genre films today. Not many filmmakers in the world combine cinematic enjoyment and social commentary as successfully as he does. From his debut feature, *Barking Dogs Never Bite*, to his latest film, *Parasite*, Bong has consistently told stories of injustice and hardship from the perspective of the socially weak while at the same time revealing the sociopolitical context of those injustices. His films suggest that the root of the social ills in *Memories of Murder* lies in the 1980s military dictatorship: South Korea's subservient relationship to the United States is at the heart of the social problems in *The Host*, and it is neoliberal capitalism—which in *Snowpiercer* and *Okja* allowed transnational corporations to become giant powers, surpassing the nation—that is to blame for Korea's current inequality and other social disorders.

Barking Dogs Never Bite, *Mother*, and *Parasite* look more closely at individuals' lives rather than on the broader context of the social system; however, the moral dilemma and the choices characters make in each film reveal the structural problems of Korean society. In these films, Bong does not forget to engage with broader questions of social conditions: What makes the characters act that way, and what drives them to the points of physical and moral catastrophe? *Parasite* portrays the cruel realities of contemporary Korean society in which a catastrophe is inevitable when those living in the basement, the subalterns, rise up above the ground. *Parasite* has brought renewed interest in the issue of class in the contemporary world not only in Korea but across the globe after its international release and Oscar sweep. Audiences relate to its story regardless of where they live because of the class polarization, moral decline, and anomie as a result of the globalized neoliberal capitalist system. *Parasite* is a social commentary and a warning about the possibility of the total catastrophe neoliberal capitalism might cause on a global scale. Thus the film allows the audience to think and decide what to do in order to prevent such a disaster. The unique political quality of Bong's genre films lies in the films' abilities to bring the audience to an open "public screen"[10] on the most pressing topical issues of the present.

In *Parasite*, Bong examines and explores the manifold layers of the present neoliberal capitalist system in a more complex and reflexive manner than in his previous works. The protagonists of the film attract audience sympathy to a certain degree; however, their moral conduct is too ambiguous for the audience to support their quest wholeheartedly. It is fair to say that an extreme moral ambiguity dominates the film to a level of confusion. However, ironically, it is precisely this change from his previous films that makes *Parasite* the best film of Bong's to capture the core consequences of our current social and economic system: moral corruption and anomie. The film demonstrates his renewed, keen insight that a perspective based on Manichean dichotomies cannot achieve. Therefore, we can continue to anticipate that Bong Joon Ho will keep on telling new stories from multilayered perspectives as in *Parasite*.

FILMOGRAPHY

The present filmography includes all films—shorts and feature-length films—Bong Joon Ho has directed. Films he did not direct but wrote, produced, or acted in are also included to provide a comprehensive look at Bong's filmic career. Basic information of cast/crew and the romanization of Korean names and film titles are from the Korean Film Database (http://www.kmdb.or.kr) maintained by the Korean Film Archive. For some of his earlier short films, the additional cast/crew information was obtained from the films' opening and ending credits.

Bong has also directed two music videos that are not included in this filmography. In 2000, after directing his first feature film, *Barking Dogs Never Bite*, Bong directed music video *Dan* for singer Kim Don-kyu, starring Bae Doo-na and Park Hae-il. He was also the cinematographer.[1] In 2003, after the success of his second feature film, *Memories of Murder*, Bong directed another music video, *Oeroun Karodŭng* (*Lonely Streetlamp*), sang by Han Young-ae and starring Ryoo Seung-bum and Kang Hye-jung.[2]

Two asterisks (**) denote films in which Bong participated but did not direct.

1993   *White Man* (*Baeksaekin*). Drama. 18 minutes. 16 mm. Color. Director: Bong Joon Ho. Producer: Jegal Yong. Screenwriters: Lee Byung-hoon, Bong Joon Ho. Cinematographer: Yu Seung-ho. Editors: Bong Joon Ho, Chae Eui-byung, Kim Suk-woo, Lee Kyung-won. Cast: Kim Roi-ha, Ahn Nae-sang, Kim Dae-yeop, Lee Sang-yeop (voice).

This is Bong Joon Ho's first short film, which was made during his years at Noramun (Yellow Door), a film club he organized at Yonsei University, Seoul. It was also the first screen acting role for Kim Roi-ha, who would become one of Bong's regular actors. He played the prosecutor in *Incoherence*, the homeless man in *Barking Dogs Never Bite*, Detective Cho Yong-gu in *Memories of Murder*, and the quarantine officer in *The Host*. Kim was a theater actor at the time, and a mutual friend introduced the two.

As the title suggests, *White Man* is a film about an ordinary white-collar worker who picks up a severed human finger on his way to work. The film is mostly without dialogue and conveys the story and its implicit critique of class and labor issues through images, acting, and diegetic sound, particularly TV commercials and news broadcast. Bong's attention to contemporary social issues is evident from this first short film he made.

The film follows an unnamed protagonist as he wakes up in the morning, goes to work, and comes back home. Upon leaving his apartment to go to work, the protagonist picks up a severed index finger dropped near his car in the parking lot. He takes it with him and plays with it as if it is a toy, using it to type, dial, and play guitar, and he even puts a ring on it. He is totally insensitive to whose finger it might be. He comes back home in the evening, turns on the TV, and falls asleep. The newscaster tells that there was a big fight at the parking lot of the high-rise condominium complex when a worker tried to harm the CEO of his company in protest of the lack of compensation for industrial accidents. He had brought his finger that had been severed during the work but dropped it when he got arrested on the spot. Not knowing the truth about the finger, the protagonist casually throws the finger to a dog on the street on his way to work the next morning.

The film already shows the seeds of the major traits that would characterize Bong's later feature films: his eccentric sense of humor and imagination, his concern for the socially weak (in this case, a blue-collar worker), and social commentary. Bong applied to the Korean Academy of Film Arts with this short film and got accepted.

1994   *Memories in My Frame* (*P'ŭreim sogŭi kiŏktŭl*). Drama. 5 minutes. 16 mm. Color. Director: Bong Joon Ho. Screenwriter: Bong Joon Ho. Cinematographer: Jo Yong-gu.

This is Bong Joon Ho's first student film at KAFA, a film school run by the government-sponsored Korean Film Council. This five-minute film tells a simple story of an elementary school boy who, upon returning home from school, finds out that his beloved dog is missing. Disappointed, he places a photo of the dog on his desk, paces around the front gate of the house at night, and even goes around looking for him in his dream. He leaves the door open the next morning when he goes to school in the hopes that the dog returns. Like *White Man*, the film features almost no dialogue. According to Bong, the story is based on his own childhood memory. He writes, "It is a five-minute small film, but I have a strong attachment to it because it contains my own childhood memory."[3] This was his first film featuring a dog and has a similar "dog-goes-missing" story as his later *Barking Dogs Never Bite*.

1994   *Incoherence* (*Chilimyŏllyŏl*). Drama. 31 minutes. 16 mm. 1.33:1. Color. Director: Bong Joon Ho. Screenwriter: Bong Joon Ho.

Cinematographers: Jo Yong-gyu, Son Tae-woong. Editor: Bong Joon Ho. Music: An Hye-suk. Art Direction: Jo Yong-sam. Cast: Kim Roi-ha, Yoo Yeon-soo, Yoon Il-joo, Park Kwang-jin, Im Sang-hyo.

This is Bong Joon Ho's Korean Academy of Film Arts thesis film and the one that made his name known among the Korean film community. Consisting of three episodes and an epilogue, the film is a social satire that mocks intellectuals and opinion leaders' hypocrisy, an issue that would consistently appear in his later films. "Episode 1: A Cockroach" features a professor who reads pornographic magazines and who has a dirty imagination while he presumes an intellectual demeanor in the classroom. The episode makes a strong allusion that the professor is the cockroach of the society. "Episode 2: Outside the Alley" shows a middle-aged man who steals the milk delivered in front of a neighbor's door every morning while jogging around the alley in a residential area. However, the newspaper delivery boy is misrecognized by the owner as the thief. A chase between the middle-aged man and the delivery boy ensues around the alley. Bong's preference for long, narrow spaces is prominent in this episode. "Episode 3: The Night of the Pain" follows a drunken man who attempts to take a dump in a remote corner of an apartment complex. When caught by the janitor and told to go to the basement and to release it on a newspaper, he commits an unimaginable act of revenge. The apartment complex, its basement, and the janitor in this episode reminds us of *Barking Dogs Never Bite*.

These three separate episodes come together in the "Epilogue" in an explosion of social satire. All three of them appear as experts on a TV panel discussion on the subject of moral crisis in Korean society. The audience learns that the milk thief is an editorial writer of a prestigious newspaper, the drunken man a public prosecutor, and the professor an expert on social psychology. They sit there with authority and seriousness debating on the main cause of the moral decay. Again, this short film displays Bong's offbeat sense of humor and satire as well as his biting critique of the hypocrisy of the intellectuals and opinion leaders. The film highlights the incoherent existence in everyday life. The film was invited to the Vancouver International Film Festival and the Hong Kong International Film Festival. The success of this short film eventually led him to direct a feature film.

**1994 *2001 Imagine* (*2001 Imaejin*). Drama. 30 minutes. 16 mm. Color. Director: Jang Joon-hwan. Screenwriter: Jang Joon-hwan. Cinematographer: Bong Joon Ho. Editors: Bong Joon Ho, Jang Joon-hwan. Music: Park Kalin. Art: Cho Young-sam. Cast: Park Hee-soon, An Jin-hui, Kim Kyung-ran.

This is a Korean Academy of Film Arts thesis film directed by Jang Joon-hwan, one of Bong Joon Ho's classmates. Bong is the cinematographer and coeditor of the film. It is a story of a young man who is obsessed with the idea that he is John Lennon reincarnated because he was born at the exact time when Lennon was shot and killed in December 1980. When his mother dies, the protagonist decides it is now time to let the world know he is John Lennon. He plays music, meets his Yoko, and falls in love; however, nobody appreciates his music. After his breakup with Yoko, he believes that he is going to be killed. The film is full of novel imagination and wit, which can be seen in Jang's debut feature, *Save the Green Planet* (2003).

**1996 *7 Reasons Why Beer Is Better Than a Lover* (*Maekchuga aeinboda choŭn ilgopkaji iyu*). Omnibus comedy. 109 minutes. 35 mm. Color. Directors: Kim Yu-jin, Jang Hyun-soo, Chung Ji-young, Park Chul-soo, Park Jong-won, Jang Gil-su, Kang Woo-suk. Producer: Park Chul-soo. Screenwriter: Kim Yu-min. Adaptation: Byeon Won-mi, Bong Joon Ho. Cinematographers: Jeong Han-chul et al. Editor: Park Gok-ji. Music: Byeon Seong-ryong. Art Directors: Cho Yoong-sam, Kim Myung-kyung. Cast: Han Jae-seok, Pang Eun-jin, Sin Hui-jo, Lee Sun-mi, et al. Production Companies: Cinema Service, Park Chul-soo Films.

This is Bong's first participation in a Chungmuro (the Korean equivalent of Hollywood) production, but Bong later expressed that he was embarrassed by it because of the film's unapologetically sexist and vulgar content. As the film title suggests, the film makes comparisons between beer and women and has a lot of lewd and vulgar jokes. The film centers around a young guy named Jonathan who drinks only beer because of his family history with alcohol. He moves from the United States to Korea and tries to find a bride who only drinks beer. The film caught media attention for two reasons: First, when the production was announced, there was a high expectation because seven of the top film directors at the time were collaborating, each directing a fifteen-minute episode that shows the reason beer is better than a lover. However, that expectation turned into scorn when the film was released and became a box office flop. It was even voted by female audiences as the worst film of 1996, catching media attention from the highly negative reviews.

Bong participated in the film as the assistant director for Park Jong-won, one of the most prominent directors at the time. Bong is also credited as one of the story adaptors. According to Bong, "Less than a year of being idle after my graduation from the Korean Academy of Film

Arts, the overwhelming moment of my first slating day has finally come in the winter of December 1995. However, because of what the movie was, I dreaded going to the set, even though I was part of the directing team. I [finally] became a crew member in Chungmuro, but I felt deeply ashamed of myself for being involved in such a movie. I did not go to the theater when it was released. Instead, I watched on video."[4]

**1997 *Motel Cactus* (*Mot'el sŏninjang*). Drama/melodrama. 90 minutes. 35 mm. Color. Director: Park Ki-yong. Executive Producers: Tcha Sung-jai, Kim Seung-bum. Producer: Kim Seon-a. Screenwriters: Park Ki-yong, Bong Joon Ho. Cinematographer: Christopher Doyle. Editor: Ham Sung-won. Music: Cho Joon-hyoung. Art: Choi Jeong-hwa, Oh Jai-won. Cast: Lee Mi-youn, Jin Hee-kyung, Jung Woo-sung, Park Shin-yang. Production Company: Uno Film.

Director Park Jong-won, who worked with Bong on his fifteen-minute episode for *7 Reasons Why Beer Is Better Than a Lover*, introduced him to director Park Ki-yong, and the two worked on the screenplay for this film. He was also hired as the first assistant director. It is Bong's first experience with a feature-length film production. The film received the New Currents Award at the 1997 Busan International Film Festival and a Special Mention Tiger Award at the 1998 Rotterdam International Film Festival.

Motel Cactus is the name of a love hotel in Seoul, where four different intimate encounters occur in room 407, including a woman celebrating her birthday with her boyfriend, young college students who rented the room to shoot a film but end up having sex instead, a drunk older couple using the room for a marathon of lovemaking, and two former lovers coming to the hotel after a funeral to rekindle their old passion but instead are reminded of their old pain. Each couple relates to the same environment differently. The cinematographer, Christopher Doyle, was known at the time for his work with Hong Kong director Wong Kar-wai, and his cinematography brings a delicate sensitivity that is different from many other contemporary Korean films.

**1999 *Phantom, the Submarine* (*Yuryŏng*). Action thriller. 103 minutes. 35 mm. Color. Director: Min Byung-chun. Executive Producer: Tcha Sung-jai. Producer: Kim Seon-a. Original Story: Tcha Sung-jai. Screenwriters: Jang Joon-hwan, Bong Joon Ho, Kim Jong-hoon. Cinematographer: Alex Hong (Hong Kyung-pyo). Editor: Go Lim Pyo. Music: Lee Dong-jun. Art: Hwang In-jun. Cast: Choi Min-soo, Jung Woo-sung, Yoon Joo-sang, Son Byung-ho. Production Company: Uno Film.

Bong became acquainted with producer Tcha Sung-jai when he worked on *Motel Cactus*, which was produced by Tcha's company, Uno Film. Tcha was a rising-star producer at the time, and Uno Film produced many innovative films. Impressed with Bong's short film *Incoherence*, Tcha offered to produce Bong's first feature film, as long as Bong had experience in directing a team and had participated in writing a feature film script. So after working as the first assistant director for *Motel Cactus*, Bong joined the screenwriting team for Uno Film's next project, *Phantom, the Submarine*, together with his KAFA classmate Jang Joon-hwan.[5]

Phantom, the Submarine is a thriller whose story takes place on a nuclear submarine. Released in the same year as *Shiri*, it was one of the first films to apply the idea of Korean-style blockbuster filmmaking, but the result was not up to expectations. The protagonist, Lee Chan-suk, is an elite navy officer; however, he is sentenced to death for killing a deranged superior officer and is "officially" executed. When he wakes up, he finds himself on *Phantom*, South Korea's first and secret nuclear submarine. Everyone onboard is dead on the official registry, since the mission of *Phantom* is top secret. The plan was to investigate reports that the Japanese are building their own nuclear submarine. However, the deputy captain 202 kills the captain and threatens to launch a nuclear strike against Japan, causing chaos and confusion under the deep sea.

Like *Shiri*, *Phantom, the Submarine* is a Hollywood-like film that follows the conventions of the thriller genre. Thus with this film, Bong experienced and practiced writing a script for a conventional genre film. According to Bong,

> The three of us, including Kim Jong-hoon [and Jang Joon-hwan], cowrote the scenario for *Phantom, the Submarine*. All of us had worked as directing crew for *Motel Cactus*. After the filming [of *Motel Cactus*] ended, Tcha Sung-jai, the CEO of Sidus [formerly Uno Film] asked us to write the scenario for his next project of a submarine movie. I helped for two months, working on the first draft, and then I left to work on *Barking Dogs Never Bite*. So as a matter of fact, we can say Jang Joon-hwan is the main writer for *Phantom, the Submarine*. It was a made-to-order project and a part-time job, so it is a bit awkward to say it's my work.[6]

2000 *Barking Dogs Never Bite* (*P'ŭllantasŭŭi kae*). Comedy. 106 minutes. 35 mm, 1.85:1. Color. Director: Bong Joon Ho. Executive Producer: Tcha Sung-jai. Producer: Jo Min-whan. Original Story: Bong Joon Ho. Screenwriter: Bong Joon Ho, Son Tae-ung, Song Ji-ho.

Cinematographer: Jo Yong-gyu. Editor: Lee Eun-su. Music: Jo Seong-woo. Art: Lee Young. Cast: Lee Sung-jae, Bae Doo-na, Kim Ho-jung, Byun Hee-bong, Ko Soo-hee. Production Company: Uno Film.

This is Bong Joon Ho's debut feature film and his only film to fail in the box office. At the time of its release in February 2000, the film's offbeat humor and comic book sensibilities were too unconventional; it was dismissed by film critics as well. However, it received critical recognition outside Korea at international film festivals: it received the FIPRESCI (International Federation of Film Critics) Award at the Hong Kong International Film Festival in April 2000, music composer Jo Seong-woo won the Special Award at the Buenos Aires Film Festival, and producer Jo Min-hwan won Best Newcomer Award at the Munich Film Festival, both in 2001. The film was also reevaluated by Korean film critics as having a unique sense of humor, a distinctive imagination, and a younger generation's sensibilities. The film combined disparate elements together, thus making it hard to pin it down to a specific genre. From its box office failure, Bong learned that films need to be based on familiar genres in order to be commercially successful.

Set in an ordinary apartment complex in Seoul, the film tells a story of Yoon-ju and Hyun-nam. Yoon-ju is a humanities PhD trying to get a full-time faculty position, and Hyun-nam works at the management office of the apartment complex where Yoon-ju lives with his pregnant wife. Frustrated by the noise of a barking dog, Yoon-ju kidnaps a neighbor's dog and hides it in the basement. However, he took the wrong dog, and this misrecognition leads to a series of dogs going missing. When Yoon-ju kidnaps and kills a second dog by throwing it from the rooftop of the high-rise apartment building, Hyun-nam witnesses it from afar and vows to find the dog killer. She does not recognize that Yoon-ju is the killer; rather, various circumstances bring the two together, and they collaborate to find a third missing dog that belongs to Yoon-ju's wife.

While the chase for the dognapper provides action, humor, horror (especially in the basement, where the janitor cooks the dogs and tells horror stories), and comic-book-inspired fantasy scenes, the core conflict in the film lies in Yoon-ju's moral and financial dilemma. If he wants to secure a full-time professor position, he needs to bribe the dean. He is resistant to the idea at first, but will he be able to maintain his moral integrity?

The film demonstrates the seeds of the major characteristics that run through Bong's films: tonal shifts and the mixture of disparate elements, offbeat humor, the concern for realism (he shot the film in the actual apartment complex where he lived with his wife as newlyweds), keen

observations, a critique of social issues and how they affect ordinary
people's lives, and the concern for the losers or the marginalized. The
film is Bong's first collaboration with actor Byun Hee-bong, who would
go on to appear in *Memories of Murder*, *The Host*, and *Okja*.

**2002 *No Blood No Tears* (*P'ido nunmulto ŏpshi*). Action / crime drama. 116 minutes. 35 mm. Color. Director: Ryoo Seung-wan. Executive Producer: Kim
Mi-hee. Producer: Kim Seong-je. Cinematographer: Choi Young-hwan.
Editors: Kim Sang-bum, Kim Jae-beom. Music: Han Jae-gwon. Production Design: Ryu Seong-hui. Special Appearance: Bong Joon Ho (as inter-
rogating detective).

This is the second feature film by director Ryoo Seung-wan, dubbed
as Korean cinema's "action kid." The film is a rare hard-boiled, female
buddy movie in which two women plot to steal money from gangsters
while taking revenge in the process. The film features several well-known
directors as cameos including Bong Joon Ho, Kim Hong-joon and Lee
Moo-young. Bong appears briefly as a detective in a police station early
in the film. Kyung-sun gets into a fight with a drunken male customer
when he tries to seduce her in a sexist manner and ends up in a police
station. They are questioned or rather scolded by an officer who sits at
the desk as he chews gum, as if everything is a bother. Bong plays that
officer with three lines and appears for about thirty seconds. Bong and
director Ryoo Seung-wan are close friends.

2003 *Memories of Murder* (*Sarinŭi Ch'uŏk*). Crime drama / mystery thriller.
131 minutes. 35 mm, 1.85:1. Color. Director: Bong Joon Ho. Execu-
tive Producers: Tcha Sung-jai, No Jong-yun. Producer: Kim Mu-ryeong.
Original Story: Kim Gwang-lim (stage play *Come to See Me* / *Nal Porŏ
Wayo*). Screenwriters: Bong Joon Ho, Shim Sung-bo. Cinematographer:
Kim Hyung Koo. Editor: Kim Sun-min. Music: Iwashiro Taro. Art: Ryu
Seong-hui. Cast: Song Kang-ho, Kim Sang-kyung, Kim Roi-ha, Song Jae-
ho, Byun Hee-bong, Park Hae-il. Production Company: Sidus.

This is Bong Joon Ho's second feature film and his breakthrough film
in Korea. Despite the box office flop of his first film, *Barking Dogs Never
Bite*, Uno Film's Tcha Sung-jai, who believed in Bong's talent, supported
and produced his second project. This story of a serial killer who rapes
and murders women in a rural village is based on a real unresolved case
in Hwasŏng in the 1980s. Many industry insiders suggested that Bong
change the outcome of the investigation in the film to give a sense of
resolution at the end; however, Bong decided to stay true to the real
story. Thus the film goes against accepted conventions of a crime drama

or a detective story right from its conception: that the detectives are not going to capture the serial killer at the end.

Bong's decision to keep the original outcome reflects his desire to make the film more about the 1980s era and less about the serial killer. Thus the main question asked becomes not "Who raped and killed all these women?" but rather "Why were the detectives not able to solve the crime?" Although the ending is already known, the film successfully grabs viewers' attention by constantly defying their expectations.

The film begins with the discovery of the body of the first female victim. The rural police and detectives are clueless and incompetent to successfully lead the investigation. Thus an elite detective is sent from Seoul. The rivalry between the rural detective Park Doo-man (Song Kang-ho) and the city detective Seo Tae-yoon (Kim Sang-kyung) provides the major conflict, tension, and comedic moments. They are polar opposites in their approach to the investigation, but neither is successful in coming up with a solution. As the film unfolds, it becomes evident that it is the oppressive military regime that prevented the detectives from solving the crime and protecting citizens from further harm. The night when they were certain to capture the killer, their call for support was dismissed because all police officers were mobilized to suppress massive protests demanding democracy. Under the surface structure of a mystery genre, the film reveals the systemic violence and the incompetence of the authorities to protect their citizens.

In order to portray the 1980s rural village as realistically as possible, the production team traveled around the whole country to find the perfect location. The Korean Film Archive has a collection of 6,256 negatives of the photographs they took during the location hunt.[7] And Kim Hyung Koo's cinematography and Iwashiro Taro's music add the lyrical yet plaintive atmosphere to the portrayal of the 1980s era.

2004   "Influenza" (*Inp'ŭlluenja*). Mockumentary. 28 minutes. Black and white. Director: Bong Joon Ho. Music: An Hye-suk. Cast: Yoon Je-moon, Ko Soo-hee.

Bong Joon Ho prefers shooting in film than in digital; however, this short film was shot in digital as part of Jeonju International Film Festival's Digital Project 2004 titled "Digital Short Films by Three Filmmakers." *Influenza* is included in the project along with "Mirrored Mind" by Ishii Sogo (Japan) and "Dance Me to the End of Love" by Yu Lik-wai (Hong Kong). What is notable about the film is that the entire film is shot with digital cameras positioned as surveillance cameras. It is a sort of fake documentary that follows a fictional character whose actions are captured by the surveillance cameras. The film consists of ten long takes of the character Cho Hyuk-rae's life as it spirals into that of violence and crime over the period of five years, from 2001 to 2004.

The film starts with Cho standing precariously on a bridge over the Han River with a blank expression. He tries to make a living by selling small goods in the subway, but faced with various forms of violence, he is forced into a corner and eventually resorts to violence himself. He robs money from weak, old people at the ATM machines. And the violence expands and spreads like a virus. The idea of blurring documentaries and fiction, the use of the idea of surveillance cameras, and the themes of violence as a viral influenza all demonstrate Bong's probing eye into Korean society. The film redefines what everyday life means to an ordinary person: constantly being exposed to violence and becoming violent in order to survive. The images caught in the "surveillance camera" show the time and place into which violence and crime are interwoven. And the violence spreads as Cho collaborates with others to carry out a bigger crime. The film positions the viewer into that of a voyeur of violence. The film switches to color as the epilogue set in the present shows people passing by so indifferently. All have become so numb to acts of violence.

2004   "Sink & Rise" (*Shingk'ŭ & raijŭ*). Drama. 6 minutes. Director: Bong Joon Ho. Cinematographer: Je Chang-gyu. Cast: Byeon Hee-bong, Yoon Je-mun, Jeong In-seon.

This six-minute short film is shot as part of *Digital Short Film Omnibus Project Twentidentity* (*I-gong*), a collection of short films directed by ten graduates of the Korean Academy of Film Arts. Bong's *Sink & Rise* is a precursor to his international breakthrough film *The Host* (2006). It is set on the Han River bank and at a snack stand similar to that owned by the family in *The Host*. A man stops by the stand with her daughter to buy her some food. However, since they are short on money, the two quarrel about whether to buy boiled eggs or instant snacks. The father decides to buy the eggs and tells his daughter that when he was little, he would swim in the river, and whenever he got hungry, he would eat the boiled eggs floating on the water. The owner of the stand is intrigued by what he said and argues that he has never heard of such a thing. Upset by his comment, the girl's father makes a bet with the stand owner that if boiled eggs float on the water, the owner would let him have anything he wants from the stand. The father and daughter run toward the river and throw the eggs. This is an amusing short film that shows Bong's sense of humor as well as his wild imagination. The owner of the stand is played by Byun Hee-bong, who repeats the role in *The Host*. Yoon Je-mun, who plays the father, appears in *The Host* as the homeless man who helps the Park family kill the monster as well as in *Mother* (the detective Je-mun) and *Okja* (Park Mun-do).

**2005 *Antarctic Journal* (*Namgügilgi*). Horror / mystery thriller. 114 minutes, 35 mm. Color. Director: Yim Pil-sung. Executive Producers: Tcha Sung-jai, No Jong-yun. Coexecutive Producer: Chae Hoe-seung. Producer: Im Hui-cheol. Original Story: Yim Pil-sung. Screenwriters: Yim Pil-sung, Bong Joon Ho, Lee Hae-jun. Cinematographer: Jung Jeong-hoon. Editor: Kim Sun-min. Music: Kenji Kawai. Cast: Song Kang-ho, Yoo Ji-tae, Kim Gyeong-ik, Park Hee-soon, Yoon Je-moon. Production Company: Sidus.

The director of this film, Yim Pil-sung, is a close friend of Bong Joon Ho. Yim plays the college alumnus of the ex-student activist uncle Park Nam-il in *The Host*. Although they were both student activists, Yim's character, Ttunggebara (meaning "fat Che Guevara"), is now an employee of a high-tech company and betrays Nam-il for money.

Antarctic Journal is Yim's debut feature film, and Bong cowrote it with him. The film is about a South Korean exploration team led by Choi Do-hyung (Song Kang-ho), who sets out to conquer the Pole of Inaccessibility in the Antarctic. One day, they discover an old flag and a journal written by a British exploration team eighty years ago. However, ever since they uncovered this journal, strange things continue to happen, and the exploration becomes a nightmare. According to Yim, Bong contributed one scene because he was spending more time working his own film, *Memories of Murder*, at the time.[8]

2006 *The Host* (*Goemul*). Monster movie / horror / sci-fi thriller. 119 minutes. 35 mm, 1.85:1. Color. Director: Bong Joon Ho. Executive Producers: Choe Yong-bae, Kim U-taek. Producer: Joh Neung-yeon. Screenwriters: Bong Joon Ho, Ha Joon-won, Baek Cheol-hyeon. Cinematographer: Kim Hyung Koo. Editor: Kim Sun-min. Music: Lee Byung-woo. Art / Production Design: Ryu Seong-hui. Cast: Song Kang-ho, Byun Hee-bong, Park Hae-il, Bae Doo-na, Ko A-sung. Production Company: Ch'öngöram.

This is a blockbuster film in terms of both production cost and box office record. The production budget was approximately $10 million (third most expensive Korean film at the time), but half of it was spent on visual effects to create the monster.[9] The film broke the box office record at the time, passing the threshold of ten million ticket sales in just twenty-one days. Internationally, the film became Bong's breakthrough film, earning critical acclaim when it was shown at Cannes Film Festival's Directors' Fortnight section. The film was converted to 3D and screened at the Busan International Film Festival and Chapman University's Busan West Film Festival in 2011.

The film starts as a monster movie as a giant mutant fish emerges from the Han River and wreaks havoc on the riverbank where citizens are enjoying leisure time. In the prologue, the film sets up a perfect premise for a creature to grow in the river: an American mortician working at a U.S. Army camp in Seoul orders his Korean assistant to dump toxic chemicals into the Han River. Bong based this on an actual event, referred to as the McFarland incident, that took place in 2004. However, the genre conventions of a monster movie end here, as the monster reveals its whole body in broad daylight thirteen minutes into the film. After it kidnaps Hyun-seo, a middle school girl and the daughter of dim-witted Park Gang-du, the monster is pretty much confined to a closed space of a sewage works, and it is no longer at the center of the story. The authorities are not pursuing the monster to protect the citizens, but rather they are chasing the Park family, whose daughter has been taken away by the monster and presumed dead.

However, Hyun-seo manages to make a last cell phone call to her dad to let him know she is alive. From that point on, the family members—grandfather, father Gang-du, uncle Nam-il, and aunt Nam-ju—are bent on finding where she is to save her. They escape from the hospital, where they were quarantined, as they were suspected of a virus infection from the monster attack. The family's struggle begins, as the government authorities are chasing them instead of chasing the monster. Will they be able to save Hyun-seo? The film ceases to be a conventional monster flick and turns into a family drama and a critique of the incompetence and unwillingness of the authorities to help and protect the citizens. South Korea's subservient relationship with the United States is also commented upon in this fun yet strongly political blockbuster. In its political commentary, *The Host* shares affinities with *Memories of Murder*, including comments on the legacy of the 1980s era of military dictatorship. The conventions of the monster genre are twisted and subverted within Korea's geopolitical context.

Bong said, "As I watched [pelicans taking fish to their nest in a *National Geographic* documentary], I thought of the kidnapping motif, the idea of the monster carrying away a girl who doesn't die but survives, and the family members who go to rescue her. That's a kidnapping movie plot, you know? . . . My film is closer to the kidnapping film genre."[10]

2007   "Shaking Tokyo" (*Hŭndŭllinŭn Tok'yo*). Drama. 30 minutes. 35 mm, 1.85:1. Color. Director: Bong Joon Ho. Producer: Sadai Yuji. Screenwriter: Bong Joon Ho. Cinematographer: Fukumoto Jun. Art Direction: Isomi Toshiro. Cast: Kagawa Teruyuki, Aoi Yû, Takenaka Naoto.

This is Bong Joon Ho's first film produced outside Korea. The film is shot in Tokyo, Japan, with Japanese actors and crew. It features a *hikikomori* (an agoraphobic man) who has never left his house in ten years. He has not had a conversation with anyone, and he has not touched anyone. He gets his daily necessities by delivery but never looks at the delivery person. One day, the garter belt of the pizza delivery woman catches his eye. For the first time in ten years, he exchanges gazes with someone. At that very moment, an earthquake shakes the house, and the woman collapses. He waits for her again the next day, but instead of meeting her, he is told that she has made her mind up to be a *hikikomori* like him. Shocked, he ventures outside to stop her. He finally succeeds in walking out into the street, but the streets are empty. Everyone had become a *hikikomori*!

An odd love story that shows Bong's ability to weave his keen observations of society into the story of ordinary people. He expresses, through the uniquely Japanese *hikikomori*, his impression of Tokyo as a city of solitude. And the "shaking" in the title implies both the earthquake (Japan is also a land of earthquakes) and the shaking of the heart. The film also displays Bong's sense of humor and novel imagination.

It is part of an omnibus film consisting of three short films set in Tokyo. Titled *Tokyo!*, the omnibus film includes "Interior Design" by Michel Gondry and "Merde" by Leo Carax. The film was screened at the Cannes Film Festival in the Un Certain Regard section.

**2008   *Crush and Blush* (*Missŭ Hongdangmu*). Romantic comedy. 110 minutes. 35 mm. Color. Director: Lee Kyung-mi. Executive Producer: Park Chan-wook. Producer: Lee Min-su. Screenwriter: Lee Kyung-mi, Park Eun-gyo, Park Chan-wook. Cinematographer: Kim Dong-young. Editor: Sin Min-gyeong. Music: Jang Young-gyu. Art: Hwang Ju-hye. Cast: Kong Hyo-jin, Lee Jong-hyuk, Seo U, Hwang-woo Seul-hye, Pang Eun-jin. Production Company: Moho Film.

This is the debut feature film of Lee Kyung-mi, who was Park Chan-wook's assistant director for the 2005 film *Lady Vengeance*. Park's production company, Moho Film, produced the film, and both Park and Bong Joon Ho appear in cameo roles in support of her film. The story is about a plain and unpopular high school Russian-language teacher Misook, who has a crush on one of her colleagues. The problem is she often gets an unsightly deep red flush all over her face. Despite this embarrassing blush, Mi-sook desperately tries to prevent romance between her rival teacher and her crush. Bong appears as one of Mi-sook's classmates at an English-language institute. She has to reeducate herself as an English teacher after Russian classes are canceled. In the scene, he embarrasses and angers Mi-sook by asking her in English, "What subject are you teaching at school now?"

2009   *Mother* (*Madŏ*). Crime drama. 128 minutes. 35 mm, 2.35:1. Color (2009), converted to black and white (2013). Director: Bong Joon Ho. Executive Producer: Moon Yang-gwon. Producers: Seo Woo-sik, Park Tae-jun. Story: Bong Joon Ho. Screenwriters: Park Eun-gyo, Bong Joon Ho. Cinematographer: Alex Hong (Hong Kyung-pyo). Editor: Mun Se-gyeong. Music: Lee Byung-woo. Art / Production Design: Ryu Seong-hui. Cast: Kim Hye-ja, Won Bin, Jin Goo, Yoon Je-moon, Jeon Mi-sun. Production Company: Barunson.

This is the film that allowed the Korean audience to rediscover veteran actress Kim Hye-ja. Kim, who has been touted as a "national mom" due to her roles in TV dramas representing traditional motherhood of unconditional love and sacrifice, is transformed here to a human monster who would do anything to protect her son, even if it means committing murder. However, the audience still feels sympathy for her character because the film sets her up in the beginning as a poor middle-aged single mom struggling to get by while looking after her twenty-eight-year-old, mentally disabled son, Do-joon. When Do-joon is accused of murdering a high school girl, the mother tries everything she could to clear him of the false charge. Faced with the police's unwillingness to reinvestigate, she takes it into her own hands to find the real killer. Thus the film is in a way a combination of *Memories of Murder* (a crime drama set in a rural village) and *The Host* (which has unlikely heroes taking the matter into their own hands to save a family member). The mother succeeds in finding the truth about the murder case, but the outcome is beyond her imagination. By casting against type and developing audience sympathy for the mother character, the film constantly defies audience expectations.

The film raises questions about motherhood and morality. Moral anomie in contemporary Korean society is well presented in the film, in which the socially weak exploit the weaker and get away with it. Also, the issues of sexual exploitation, the hypocrisy of intellectuals, and other social injustices are weaved into this tense crime drama. The film begins with the mother walking into the middle of a field of reeds and ends with her dancing away her pain in a tour bus with other mothers to Lee Byung-woo's music score. Her dance is haunting and brings out mixed and complex feelings.

**2012 *Doomsday Book* (*Illyumyŏlmangbogosŏ*). Sci-fi/fantasy. 113 minutes. Color. Directors: Kim Jee-woon, Yim Pil-sung. Producers: Kang Young-mo, Kim Jeong-hwa. Original Story: Park Seong-hwan, Park Su-min. Screenwriters: Yim Pil-sung, Lee Hwan-hui, Kim Jee-woon, Yang Jong-gyu. Cinematographers: Jo Sang-yuen, Kim Ji-yong, Ha Seong-min. Editors: Nam Na-young, Kim Mi-yeong. Cast: Ryoo Seung-bum, Go Joon-hee, Kim Roi-ha, Lee Kan-hee, Hwang-Hyo-eun.

This is an anthology of three midlength films directed by Kim Jee-woon and Yim Pil-sung. It consists of three episodes with a theme of the apocalypse. Yim directed the first episode, "A Brave New World," and the third episode, "Happy Birthday," and Kim directed the second episode, "The Heavenly Creature." Bong Joon Ho appears in the first episode, which tells the story of the careless treatment of food garbage leading to a zombie apocalypse. Suk-woo is left home alone after all other family members went abroad for vacation. While cleaning the house, he does not take the proper procedure of recycling and just throws away the decaying food in a trash bin. He consumes meat while on a date, but he has strange reactions in his body. The mistreated food bred a zombie virus that is turning the whole world into chaos. Bong appears and plays the guitar in a hilarious scene in which opinion leaders and congressmen participate in a TV panel discussion titled "Mysterious Virus, Is It a Conspiracy?" He represents the Alliance of the Right Perspective, a right-wing activist organization. Wearing a modernized hanbok (Korean traditional clothes), he gives absurd talks about the cause of the virus and then suddenly brings a guitar and immerses himself into playing it to accompany utterly indecipherable talks of a congresswoman.

2013 *Snowpiercer* (*Sŏlgukyŏlch'a*). Sci-fi/fantasy thriller. 125 minutes. 35 mm, 1.85:1. Color. Director: Bong Joon Ho. Executive Producers: Lee Tae-hun, Park Chan-wook. Producers: Park Tae-jun, Choi Doo-ho, Baek Ji-sun, Robert Bernacchi. Original Story: Jacques Lob, Jean-Marc Rochette (*Transperceneige*), Screenwriters: Bong Joon Ho, Kelly Masterson. Cinematographer: Alex Hong (Hong Kyung-pyo). Editors: Steve M. Choe, Kim Chang-ju. Music: Marco Beltrami. Art Direction: Stefan Kovacik. Cast: Chris Evans, Song Kang-ho, Ed Harris, John Hurt, Tilda Swinton, Jamie Bell, Octavia Spencer, Ewen Bremner, Kŏ A-sung. Production Companies: Moho Film, Opus Pictures.

This is Bong Joon Ho's first global project in English and also his first film to be shot almost entirely on a set. The shooting took place at Barrandov Studios in Prague, Czech Republic. The cast is also international and includes Chris Evans, John Hurt, and Tilda Swinton as well as Korean actors Song Kang-ho and Ko A-sung. However, the funding for the film came from Korean sources, making it the most expensive Korean film to date, with the production cost of approximately $40 million. Its worldwide box office gross is over $86 million.[11]

The story is based on the 1982 French graphic novel *Le Transperceneige*; however, Bong's adaptation is quite different from the original story. What *Snowpiercer* borrowed from *Le Transperceneige* is the central idea that there is a perpetually running train in which the last survivors of a new ice age reside, that the train is divided into front and tail sections, and that there is a protagonist who tries to move to the front section to reach the engine. The premise is the same, but the story and characters of the film version are completely different. Bong's film is more politically charged, with the people in the tail section aspiring to bring a revolution within the train led by their leader, Curtis. They are fed up with the poor food and the filthy living conditions of the tail section. Will they revolt against the mighty Wilford, who designed the train and runs it with an iron grip? The train is linear, and there is no turning back once they embark on this revolution.

According to the Korean Film Archive, *Snowpiercer* is officially the last Korean film to be shot in 35 mm film. All film-processing labs are closed down, and in the 2010s, the print era came to an end with a rapid expansion of digital multiplexes. Ironically, even though *Snowpiercer* was shot in 35 mm, it had to be converted to digital because no theater was able to project it in print.[12]

**2014 *Sea Fog* (*Haemu*). Drama/thriller. 110 minutes. 35 mm. Color. Director: Shim Sung-bo. Executive Producers: Joh Neung-yeon, Kim Tae-wan, Bong Joon Ho. Producer: Han Sang-beom. Original Story: Kim Min-jeong. Screenwriters: Shim Sung-bo, Bong Joon Ho. Cinematography: Alex Hong (Hong Kyung-pyo). Editors: Kim Sang-bum, Kim Jae-beom. Cast: Kim Yoon-suk, Park Yu-cheon, Han Ye-ri, Moon Sung-keun, Kim Sang-ho. Production Companies: Haemu, Ease Pictures, Off Screen, July Film, Louis Pictures.

This is the directing debut film for Shim Sung-bo, who cowrote *Memories of Murder*. Bong Joon Ho produced and cowrote the film. It is a story of six crew members of a fishing boat who, to make up for their failure to return with a full load of fish, decide to smuggle illegal immigrants from China to Korea. However, as they face a heavy fog, rain, and waves, things do not go as planned. The film is an adaptation of a stage play of the same title that was based on a real-life event of a human trafficking tragedy that took place in Yeosu, a port city in the southwestern region of the Korean peninsula.

2017   *Okja* (*Okcha*). Fantasy adventure. 120 minutes. Digital. Color. Director: Bong Joon Ho. Executive Producers: Collin Creighton, Sarah Esberg, Pauline Fischer, Samuel Yeunju Ha, Kim Woosang, Christina Oh, Brad Pitt, Stan Wlodkowski. Producers: Bong Joon Ho, Choi Dooho, Dede Gardner, Lewis Taewan Kim, Ted Sarandos, Woo-sik Seo. Coproducers: Tilda Swinton, Sandro Kopp. Story: Bong Joon Ho. Screenwriters: Bong Joon Ho, Jon Ronson. Cinematography: Darius Khondji. Editors: Han Meeyeon, Yang Jin-mo. Production Design: Lee Ha-jun, Kevin Thompson. Music: Jung Jaeil. Cast: Tilda Swinton, Paul Dano, Ahn Seo-hyun, Byun Hee-bong, Yoon Je-moon, Steven Yeun. Production Company: Plan B Entertainment.

This is Bong Joon Ho's first film funded by a non-Korean production company. Netflix gave Bong $50 million with total creative freedom, and Brad Pitt's production company, Plan B, produced the film. The only condition was to film it digitally. Thus *Okja* is Bong's first digital feature film. The title *Okja* is the name of a genetically modified superpig bred by the Mirando Corporation, aiming to produce massive amounts of meat for public consumption. Mirando had sent out twenty-six piglets to farmers around the world to raise for ten years and then compete in a superpig contest. Mija's grandfather was chosen as the Korean breeder, and that is how Okja came to live with Mija in a remote mountain village in Korea.

Thirteen-year-old Mija grew up with Okja. They are inseparable, and Mija believes Okja is going to live with them forever after her grandfather pays off her uncle, who occasionally comes to check up on Okja. She does not know about the contest and thus does not suspect at all when a group of people (from the Mirando Corporation) come to visit and see Okja. However, when she discovers Mirando has taken away Okja, she vows to bring her back, and thus begins her grand adventure to Seoul and then to New York. She is fearless in her determination to get Okja back, and during her pursuit, she becomes involved with the Animal Liberation Front, who has a plan to destroy the Mirando Corporation from the inside by sending Okja to their factory with a video-recording device attached. However, their plan does not go as they had planned, and Mija has to confront the CEO of the Mirando Corporation at a slaughterhouse where Okja is to be killed. Will she able to save Okja?

Like other films by Bong, *Okja* also interweaves a biting critique of social issues into a blockbuster genre film: this time, about corporate greed, genetically modified food, and above all, the appalling conditions of a meat factory farm. The film initiated discussions about these issues in numerous online sites, blogs, and social media, and some of the viewers even converted to veganism. The film also became the center of controversy at the Cannes Film Festival. A French theater chain protested that films that will not be released in French theaters should not be included in the festival's competition section. The film was also boycotted by the major theater chains in Korea.

2019   *Parasite (Gisaengchung)*. Black comedy thriller. 132 min. Digital, 2.35:1. Color. Director: Bong Joon Ho. Executive Producers: Bang Ok-kyung, Miky Lee, Park Myeong-chan. Producers: Bong Joon Ho, Kwak Sin-ae, Moon Yang-kwon. Coproducer: Lee Joohyun. Screenwriters: Bong Joon Ho, Han Jin-won. Cinematographer: Alex Hong (Hong Kyung-pyo). Editor: Yang Jinmo. Production Design: Lee Ha-jun. Music: Jung Jaeil. Cast: Song Kang-ho, Lee Sun-kyun, Jo Yeo-jeong, Choi Woo-sik, Jang Hye-jin, Park So-dam, Lee Jeong-eun, Park Myeong-hoon. Production Companies: Barunson E&A, CJ Entertainment.

Bong Joon Ho returns to the familiar territory of a Korean story and the Korean language precisely a decade after *Mother* (2009). He builds on the theme of class division and conflict portrayed in his global sci-fi project *Snowpiercer* (2013), setting this film firmly in contemporary Korean realities. While *Snowpiercer* expressed the class issue in a horizontal structure of a perpetually moving train with the poor battling their way to the front, *Parasite* captures the consequences of the widening gap between the haves and have-nots in a vertical metaphor of upstairs and downstairs. Premiering at the Cannes International Film Festival, the film received the Palme d'Or, becoming the first Korean film to receive the coveted award and then went on to win four major awards at the 2020 Oscars, including Best Picture, Best Director, Best International Feature Film, and Best Screenwriting.

As the working title of *Décalcomanie* ("decalcomania") suggests, the film starts with the story of two families who look alike (parents with one son and one daughter) but have completely different class statuses in Korea: one is superrich (the Park family), and the other is poor, with all four members unemployed (the Kim family). In the first half of the film, all four members of the Kim family succeed in conning their way into the Park family as tutors, a chauffeur, and a live-in housemaid. They fake their résumés and pretend to be strangers to one another. When the tension builds on whether or when they will get caught, the story makes a completely unexpected turn, and the story of the two families becomes that of three. The complete surprise is the existence of a man (the husband of the former housemaid) who has been living in the secret basement of the Park house. Now the conflict intensifies between the two poor families, and their confrontation eventually leads to a total catastrophe for all three families.

Parasite can be described as a compressed version of Bong's previous films, but at the same time, it also represents a departure from them. First of all, unlike his previous films mostly shot on location, it is almost entirely shot on sets. The Parks' mansion and the Kims' semi-basement house are meticulously designed to capture the stark contrast between the high and the low. Their vertical connection is highlighted on the night of the flood, when the film depicts the water flowing over from the Park neighborhood down to the lowland village of the Kim family. The camera follows the Kim family as they run toward their home. What distinguishes the film the most from his previous films is its intense portrayal of moral anomie in contemporary Korean society. The stereotypical depiction of the rich as evil and the poor as plain victims is subverted. Unlike Yoon-ju in Barking Dogs Never Bite or the mother in Mother, the Kim family shows no moral remorse in their wrongdoings. The film captures the economic and moral consequences of twenty years of neoliberal economic policies Korea had to adopt due to the IMF bailout in 1997. The structure or larger system of social ills is no longer visible, and individuals are left on their own to find their means for survival. The lack of the use of authorities as the antagonists to the socially weak is the film's stark departure from Bong's previous work. Now the socially weak fight one another.

NOTES

INTRODUCTION

1. With a population of fifty-one million in South Korea, the sale of ten million tickets is considered a milestone and a hit in the domestic market.

2. *The Host* was invited to the Directors' Fortnight at the Cannes Film Festival and received rave reviews from critics. It was also sold to eleven countries at the Cannes film market for $2.3 million, a record international sale for a Korean film at the time. Nam Sangsŏk, "Yŏnghwa *Koemul* K'anesŏ hop'yŏng" [*The Host* acclaimed at Cannes], SBS News, May 25, 2006, http://news.sbs.co.kr/news/endPage.do?news_id=N1000124318&plink=TIT&cooper=SBSNEWS.

3. In July and August 2008, Korean Film Archive organized a retrospective of Korean monster movies to commemorate the revival of the genre with the success of Bong's *The Host* and Shim Hyung-rae's *D-War* (2007). Besides *The Host* and *D-War*, the retrospective included ten films: *Yongary, Monster from the Deep* (1967), the most famous of the earlier films; *Big Monster Wangmagwi* (1967); the animated *The War of Great Monsters* (1972); *APE* (1976); *Flying Dragon Attack* (1984); and other films of the 1980s and 1990s. It also included the famous *Pulgasari* (1985), a North Korean film directed by South Korean filmmaker Shin Sang-ok, who was kidnapped with his actress wife, Choi Eun-hee, by North Korean leader Kim Jong-il. Shin made several films in North Korea between 1978 and 1986; "Koesudaebaekkwa: Han'guk koesuga Onda" [Monster encyclopedia: Korean monsters are coming], Korean Film Archive, July 29–August 5, 2008, https://www.koreafilm.or.kr/cinematheque/programs/PI_00287.

4. The producer of Bong's first two feature films was Tcha Sung-jai, one of the leading producers of New Korean Cinema in the early 2000s. He took Bong under his wing after seeing his thesis film *Incoherence* (1994). He hired him as one of the assistant directors of *Motel Cactus* (1997) and as one of the screenwriters of *Phantom, the Submarine* (1999). It is a well-known anecdote that when Bong's *Barking Dogs Never Bite* flopped at the box office, Tcha told Bong that he knew it was going to bomb but also that Bong would make a great second film. Tcha also supported Bong's original vision for *Memories of Murder* against all negative reactions from industry insiders.

5. Constantine Spyrou, "Netflix's Revolutionary New Film 'Okja' Is Causing People to Go Vegan," *Foodbeast* (blog), July 5, 2017, https://www.foodbeast.com/news/okja-reactions/.

6. Hong Sŏngrok, "Pong Chunho, 'Hyŏnshilchŏgin koemul mandŭnŭn'ge kwan'gŏniŏtchyo'" [Bong Joon Ho, "Making a realistic monster was the key"], *Hankyoreh Shimun*, June 8, 2006, http://www.hani.co.kr/arti/PRINT/130433.html.

7. Pak Kyŏnghŭi, "70Hoe K'anyŏnghwaje: Pong Chunho kamdogŭi yŏktae K'an pangmun'gi" [70th Cannes Film Festival: Director Bong Joon Ho's past visits to Cannes], *MaxMovie*, May 19, 2017, http://news.maxmovie.com/321029.

8. The English words *absurdities* and *irrationalities* do not accurately capture the nuanced meaning of the Korean word *pujori*, which implies some degree of corruption. The notion of *pujori* is discussed in detail in chapter 3.

9. *Chronotope* is a term coined by the Russian literary theorist Mikhail Bakhtin to indicate the spatial/temporal frame in a narrative. It plays a key role in the production of meaning.

10. I use the term *postdemocratic* Korea to indicate the period after democratization in the late 1980s. In his book *The Failure of Socialism in South Korea 1945–2007* (New York: Routledge, 2015), Yunjong Kim uses the terms "pre-democracy era" and "post-democracy era" to distinguish between the military dictatorship that ended in 1987 and the era of parliamentary democracy. Some scholars use the term *postauthoritarian* to indicate the postdemocratic period, as Young-a Park does in *Unexpected Alliances: Independent Filmmakers, the State, and the Film Industry in Postauthoritarian South Korea* (Stanford, Calif.: Stanford University Press, 2014).

11. See chapter 1.

12. Homi K. Bhabha, *The Location of Culture* (Abingdon, Va.: Routledge, 2004), 55.

13. In *The Field of Cultural Production*, ed. Randal Johnson (New York: Columbia University Press, 1993), Pierre Bourdieu develops a theory that situates art within the social conditions of its time as well as in the broader context of power structure.

14. Pierre Bourdieu, *Rules of Art: Genesis and Structure of the Literary Field*, trans. Susan Emanuel (Stanford, Calif.: Stanford University Press, 1996), xix.

15. C. Wright Mills, *The Sociological Imagination* (New York: Oxford University Press, 2000), Kindle.

CHAPTER 1 A NEW CULTURAL GENERATION

1. The short documentary can be found on the Korea Youth Media Festival website: *Pong Chunholŭl ch'achasŏ* [Searching for Bong Joon Ho], 2015, directed by Chŏng Harim, I Chiyŏn, and Pak Kŏnsik, http://kymf.ssro.net/mth/contest/contest.do?no=1770&cmd=view&kind=movie&order=a&gubun=&ktype=workname&kword=%EB%B4%89%EC%A4%80%ED%98%B8&pageNo=&s_session=15.

2. In "Tongsitae Hankuk yŏnghwaesŏ chakkachuŭiŭi sangŏpchŏk suyong yangsang" [The commercial embrace of auteurism in contemporary Korean films], Sung Jinsoo explores the ways in which auteurist marketing started in the early 2000s, when Korean directors began to receive international recognition, winning prizes at international film festivals. The paper examines Bong Joon Ho and the marketing of *Snowpiercer* in 2013 as one of the case studies. Sung argues that the auteur marketing of *Snowpiercer*, which actively utilized Bong's popularity and commercial potential, reinforced and constructed an even bigger aura of an auteur around Bong, equating the film with the director instead of the stars. Sung Jinsoo, "Tongsitae Hankuk yŏnghwaesŏ chakkachuŭiŭi sangŏpchŏk suyong yangsang" [The commercial embrace of auteurism in contemporary Korean films], *Yŏnghwayŏn'gu*, no. 63 (March 2015): 161–194.

3. From April 24 to June 23, 2013, the Korean Film Archive (KOFA) conducted a survey of sixty-two Korean film scholars, critics, and industry people to select the one hundred greatest Korean films. The survey was done on all the feature films released in theaters between the early years of silent film and December 31, 2012. KOFA announced the result in February 2014; "2014 Han'gukyŏnghwa 100Sŏn" [100 greatest Korean films 2014], KMDb, https://www.kmdb.or.kr/db/list/42.

4. Christina Klein, "Why American Studies Needs to Think about Korean Cinema, or Transnational Genres in the Films of Bong Joon-ho," *American Quarterly* 60, no. 4 (2008): 873.

5. Arjun Appadurai, "Disjuncture and Difference in the Global Cultural Economy," *Theory, Culture & Society* 7, no. 2 (1990): 295–310.

6. Jonathan Rutherford, *Identity: Community, Culture and Difference* (London: Lawrence and Wishart, 1990), 211.

7. In *The Genius of the System: Hollywood Filmmaking in the Studio Era* (New York: Henry Holt, 2015), Thomas Schatz examines major filmmakers during Hollywood's golden age and argues for the importance of the producer in the Hollywood system.

8. Roland Barthes's 1967 essay "The Death of the Author" and Michel Foucault's 1969 essay "What Is an Author?" profoundly changed the critical approaches to film authorship in the 1970s. Barthes removed the author from the center of literary studies by arguing that we should focus on the texts rather than authors. Foucault also affirms the disappearance of the author from modern literature and proposed a new concept of "author function," the idea that the author plays a discursive role in a given society.

9. David A. Gerstener and Janet Staiger, *Authorship and Film* (New York: Routledge, 2003), 52.

10. Seung-hoon Jeong and Jeremi Szaniawski, eds., *The Global Auteur: The Politics of Authorship in 21st Century Cinema* (London: Bloomsbury Academic, 2016), 1.

11. Angie Han, "The Weinstein Co. Cutting 'Snowpiercer' Because Americans Are Stupid," /Film (blog), August 6, 2013, http://www.slashfilm.com/the-weinstein-co-cutting-snowpiercer-because-americans-are-stupid/.

12. Ben Child, "*Snowpiercer* Director Reportedly Furious about Weinstein English-Version Cuts," *Guardian*, October 8, 2013, https://www.theguardian.com/film/2013/oct/08/snowpiercer-director-english-cuts-bong-joon-ho.

13. "Free Snowpiercer," Change.org, last modified August 19, 2014, https://www.change.org/p/free-snowpiercer.

14. Sonia Kil, "Bong Joon-ho on Working with Netflix and the Controversy over 'Okja' at Cannes," *Variety*, May 16, 2017, http://variety.com/2017/film/news/bong-Joon-Ho-working-with-netflix-controversy-okja-cannes-1202428394/.

15. Zack Sharf, "'Okja' Rejected by 93% of South Korean Movie Theaters over Netflix Controversy," *IndieWire*, June 7, 2017, http://www.indiewire.com/2017/06/okja-south-korea-rejected-netflix-bong-joon-ho-1201838682/.

16. Chungmuro is the name of a street located in central Seoul. Since the 1960s it has been known as the street of the Korean film industry. With the emergence of New Korean Cinema, which accompanied a profound transformation of the film industry, many film production companies moved to Kangnam district. However, the name Chungmuro still symbolizes the Korean film industry.

17. Chris Berry, "Full Service Cinema: The Korean Cinema Success Story (So Far)," *Text and Context of Korean Cinema: Crossing Borders*, ed. Young-Key Kim-Renaud, R. Richard Grinker, Kirk W. Larsen, Washington, DC: George Washington University, *Sigur Center Asia Paper*, no. 17 (2002): 7, https://www2.gwu.edu/~sigur/assets/docs/scap/SCAP17-KoreanCinema.pdf.

18. According to the Korean Film Council, the domestic market share of homemade films was consistently over 50 percent since 2004, except between 2008 and 2010, which showed declines to 42.1 percent (2008), 48.8 percent (2009), and 46.5 percent (2010). It peaked at 63.8 percent in 2006, the year in which Bong's *The Host* broke the box office record. Korea is one of only four countries in which domestic films' market share is above 50 percent; the other three are the United States, India, and Japan; "2014nyŏndop'an Han'gukyŏnghwayŏn'gam" [Korean film yearbook 2014], Korean Film Council, last modified April 4, 2018, https://www.kofic.or.kr/kofic/business/rsch/findPublishDetail.do?boardNumber=40&flag=1&pubSeqNo=2058.

19. *New Korean Cinema* is not a term coined within the Korean film industry or Korean film academia; it was first used as the title of an edited volume, *New Korean Cinema*, published in 2005 by New York University Press. Edited by Chi-Yun Shin and Julian Stringer, the book included a collection of essays on contemporary Korean films that explored the changes that brought the Korean cinema's rise to prominence in the early 1990s. Darcy Paquet's book *New Korean Cinema* charts the rebirth of Korean cinema between the 1980s and the mid-2000s and attributes the arrival of New Korean Cinema "sometime during the 1990s"; Darcy Paquet, *New Korean Cinema: Breaking the Waves* (New York: Wallflower, 2009), 3. Korean film scholars still do not use the term *New Korean Cinema*. Some scholars such as Moon Jae-cheol use the term "post-'Korean New Wave'"; Moon Jae-cheol, "Pyŏnhwadoen shigansŏnggwa taejungŭi chŏngsŏ: Nyuweibŭ ihuŭi yŏnghwae nat'anan kwagŏŭi imiji" [Chronotope and structure of feeling: Images of the past in the post-"Korean new wave" films], *Journal of Popular Narrative* 9, no. 2 (December 2003): 64–87.

20. Young-a Park, *Unexpected Alliances: Independent Filmmakers, the State, and the Film Industry in Post-authoritarian Korea* (Stanford, Calif.: Stanford University Press, 2015), 82.

21. Homi K. Bhabha, "Of Mimicry and Man: The Ambivalence of Colonial Discourse," in *The Location of Culture* (London: Routledge, 2004), 66–84. Homi Bhabha uses the term "colonial mimicry" to explain the colonized subjects' imitation of the culture of the colonizer.

22. In her book *Hankuk yŏnghwa yŏksa* [History of Korean cinema], Kim Mihyŏn distinguishes between the 1990s and the 2000s in terms of the rise of auteur cinema in Korea. She classifies the 1990s as the era during which auteur directors began to make their first feature films: Park Chan-wook's *Moon Is the . . . Sun's Dream* (1992), Hong Sang-soo's *The Day a Pig Fell into a Well* (1996), Kim Ki-duk's *Crocodile* (1996), and Lee Chang-dong's *Green Fish* (1997). Kim groups Bong Joon Ho with these directors as Korean auteurs who rose to prominence globally. Kim Jee-woon also made his debut feature, *The Quiet Family*, in 1998. And Kim classifies the years after 2000 as the era of commercial auteurism in which the Korean film industry succeeded in systematically transforming itself. The rise of the multiplexes also contributed to the growth of the domestic film market. She defines *commercial auteurism* as "a balanced combination of commercial success and auteur traits"; Kim Mihyŏn, *Han-kuk yŏnghwa yŏk-sa* [History of Korean cinema] (Seoul: K'ŏmyunik'eisyŏnbuksŭ, 2014), Ridibooks.

23. Karl Mannheim, "The Problem of Generations," in *Karl Mannheim: Essays*, ed. Paul Kecskemeti (London: Routledge, 1972), 276–322, http://marcuse.faculty.history.ucsb.edu/classes/201/articles/27MannheimGenerations.pdf.

24. Yuk Sŏngch'ŏl, "Sarinŭi Ch'uŏk kamdok Pong Chunho, kŭ-ga kunggŭmhada" [Let's get to know Bong, the director of *Memories of Murder*], *Wŏlgan ch'amyŏsahoe*, June 1, 2003, http://www.peoplepower21.org/Magazine/715011.

25. *Otaku* is a Japanese term coined for the young fans of popular culture—animation, manga, and sci-fi—that began to form in Japan in the 1970s.

26. Bong recommended the original Japanese manga *Oldboy* to Park Chan-wook, who adapted it to make his international breakthrough film *Oldboy*. The comic book store that he had been a regular customer for a long time also gained popularity when Bong became one of the most successful film directors in Korea.

27. Chu Sŏngch'ŏl, ed., *Tebwiŭi sun'gan: Yŏnghwagamdong 17ini tŭllyŏjunŭn naŭi ch'ŏngch'un punt'ugi* [Debut moment: Seventeen film directors tell their struggles as youth] (Seoul: P'urŭnsup, 2014).

28. *MaxMovie*, ed., *Pong Chunho* [Bong Joon Ho] (Seoul: K & Group, 2017), 177.

29. Jung Ji-youn, ed., *Bong Joon-ho*, trans. Colin A. Mouat (Seoul: Seoul Selection, 2008), Kindle.

30. Pak Ilyŏng, *Sosŏl-ga Kubossiŭi ilsaeng: Kyŏngsŏng modŏnboi Pakt'aewŏnŭi sasaenghwal* [The life of the novelist Kubo: The private life of Pak T'ae-Won, the modern boy of Seoul] (Seoul: Munhakkwa Chisŏngsa, 2016), back cover.

31. Christina Klein's article, "The AFKN Nexus: US Military Broadcasting and New Korean Cinema," traces the history and programming of the American Forces Korean Network (AFKN) in Korea and explores the ways in which the AFKN, during the military regime years of the 1970s and 1980s, provided young Koreans with an alternative media culture that may have helped the emergence of the genre-oriented New Korean Cinema; Christina Klein, "The AFKN Nexus: US Military Broadcasting and New Korean Cinema," *Transnational Cinemas* 3, no. 1 (2012): 19–39.

32. He attended Yonsei University, one of the top private universities in Korea. In *Parasite*, the seal Ki-Jung used to forge a college diploma for her brother, Ki-Woo, was actually that of his alma mater.

33. They named their film club "Yellow Door," after the color of their club office door.

34. Chu, *Tebwiŭi sun'gan*, 186.

35. Kim Hyung Koo (cinematographer), interview by author, September 19, 2016.

36. Darcy Paquet, *New Korean Cinema: Breaking the Waves* (New York: Wallflower, 2012), Kindle.

37. Chu, *Tebwiŭi sun'gan*, 196.

38. Mun Sŏk, "Jangjunhwangwa Jigureul jikyeora tansaenggi 2" [Jang Junhwan and the birth of *Save the Green Planet* 2], *Cine 21*, March 21, 2003, http://www.cine21.com/news/view/?mag_id=17945.

39. In his book *New Korean Cinema: Breaking the Waves* (London: Wallflower, 2009), Darcy Paquet gives a detailed account of the new changes in the Korean film industry as well as the changes in Korean society in the 2000s.

40. Japanese cartoons began to be aired on Korean network TV in the early 1960s. Upon the liberation from Japanese imperialism in 1945, Japanese popular culture had been banned in Korea. When Korea and Japan reestablished their diplomatic relationship in 1965, Japanese songs, films, and anime were still officially banned, but TV networks were allowed to air Japanese cartoon series, although they could not acknowledge that they were Japanese products. They were dubbed in Korean, so many children never knew they were Japanese. These cartoon series were extremely popular. The members of the 386 generation were toddlers in the 1960s and thus grew up watching these cartoons.

41. Yŏnhamnyusŭ, "'Okcha' Pong Chunho gamdok manhwa *K'onan* yŏjaai pŏjŏn mandŭlgo ship'ŏtta'" [*Okja* director Bong Joon Ho, "I wanted to make a girl version of the cartoon *Future Boy Conan*"], *Hankyoreh Shinmun*, May 21, 2017, http://www.hani.co.kr/arti/culture/culture_general/795537.html.

42. Thomas Elsaesser, "The Pathos of Failure: American Films in the 1970s," in *The Last Great American Picture Show: New Hollywood Cinema in the 1970s*, ed. Alexander Horwath, Noel King, and Thomas Elsaesser (Amsterdam: Amsterdam University Press, 2004), 168–169.

CHAPTER 2   CINEMATIC "PERVERSIONS": TONAL SHIFTS, VISUAL GAGS, AND TECHNIQUES OF DEFAMILIARIZATION

1. "Chŏnŭn pyŏnt'aeimnida" [I am a pervert], YouTube video, 2:21, "CJENM," July 30, 2013, https://www.youtube.com/watch?v=BldTZ6JO400.

2. *Merriam-Webster Collegiate Dictionary*, s.v. "pervert," https://unabridged.merriam-webster .com/collegiate/pervert.

3. Viktor Shklovsky, "Art as Technique," in *Literary Theory: An Anthology*, ed. Julie Rivkin and Michael Ryan (Malden, Mass.: Wiley-Blackwell, 2017), 8–14.

4. Stéphane Delorme and Jean-Philippe Tessé, "L'art du piksari," *Cahiers du cinéma* 618 (2006): 47–49.

5. Hwang Tuchin, "Modǔn tongneenǔn chǒnsǒri innǔn pǒp: *Madǒ*ǔi chin'gyǒngsansu, chin'gyǒnggǒnch'uk, chin'gyǒngyǒnghwa" [Every village has a legend: *Mother's chin'gyǒng* landscape, *Chin'gyǒng* architect, *Chin'gyǒng* movie], *Cine 21*, November 25, 2010, http://www .cine21.com/news/view/?mag_id=63746.

6. Huh Moonyung, "Making Genre Films in the Third World: *Memories of Murder* and *The Host*, Genre and Local Politics," in *Bong Joon-ho*, ed. Jung Ji-youn (Seoul: Seoul Selection, 2008), 43.

7. In their 1969 manifesto, "Towards a Third Cinema," Argentinian filmmakers Octavio Getino and Fernando Solanas used the term "first cinema" to indicate Hollywood cinema. Latin American third cinema rejects both the first cinema and the second cinema (European art cinema) to create collective, revolutionary films.

8. Christina Klein, "Why American Studies Needs to Think about Korean Cinema, or, Transnational Genres in the Films of Bong Joon-ho," *American Quarterly* 60, no. 4 (2008): 872–873.

9. Béla Bálazs and Erica Carter, eds., *Béla Bálazs: Early Film Theory: Visible Man and the Spirit of Film* (New York: Berghahn Books, 2011), 98.

10. Bálazs and Carter, 100.

11. Mun Sǒk, "Pong Chunho gamdogǔi *Koemul* p'ǔrip'ǔrodǒksyǒn 2" [Director Bong Joon Ho's preproduction of *The Host 2*], *Cine 21*, March 15, 2005, http://www.cine21.com/news/ view/?mag_id=29050.

12. Kim Chinkyǒng, "Kyǒmjaehwabǒp soge nat'anan kǔndaesǒnge kwanhan koch'al: sǒgu insangjuǔihwabǒpkwaǔi pigyorǔl chungshimǔro" [The modernity in Kyomjae's painting style: Focusing on comparative studies with the Western Impressionist painting], *Yang-ming Studies* 36 (2013): 338.

13. Hwang, "Modǔn tongneenǔn chǒnsǒri innǔn pǒp."

14. Chu Sǒngch'ǒl, "Saeroun enjinǔl changch'ak'aetta: 'Pong Chunhoǔi segye'wa *sǒlgukyǒlch'a*ǔi tok'ing, kǔ kyǒlgwanǔn . . ." [New engine installed: The result of the docking of 'Bong Joon Ho's world' and the *Snowpiercer* . . .], *Cine 21*, August 5, 2013, http://www.cine21 .com/news/view/?mag_id=74031.

15. "Okja chejangnot'ǔ" [Okja production note], *Cine 21*, accessed August 27, 2018, http:// www.cine21.com/movie/info/?movie_id=46441.

16. Bong Joon Ho et al., "Chǔlgǒun hoksa'ǔi shiganiǒtchi" [It was a fun time of exhaustion], interview by Chu Sǒngch'ǒl, *Cine 21*, October 14, 2009, http://www.cine21.com/news/view/ ?mag_id=58231.

17. Bong Joon Ho, *Koemul meik'ing puk* [Illustrated journal of the making of *The Host*] (Seoul: 21Segibuksǔ, 2006), 66.

18. Bong, 66.

19. Bong told this story during the Busan West Film Festival at Chapman University in 2011. He explained that the improvised action was captured in its entirety thanks to his experienced DP Kim Hyung Koo, who kept on filming despite Song Kang-ho's unexpected kick. It startled Kim Sang-kyung, who suspected that Bong and Song had planned this behind his back. Thus he had some sore feelings about it before he realized that it was solely Song's improvisation.

20. Han Mira, "Pong Chunho yŏnghwaŭi naerŏt'ibŭ konggani kannŭn chijŏnghakchŏng ŭimie kwanhan yŏn'gu" [Research on geopolitical meanings of narrative spaces in Bong Joon Ho's films], *Yŏnghwayŏn'gu* 63 (2015): 286.

21. Steve D'Katz, *Film Directing Shot by Shot: Visualizing from Concept to Screen* (Waltham, Mass.: Focal, 1991), 19.

22. Im Sŏnae, Han'gukyŏnghwa sŭt'oribodŭ [Storyboarding in Korean cinema] (Seoul: Communication Books, 2012).

23. *Okja* is Bong's first film to have locations in three different countries: Korea, the United States, and Canada. The story takes place in Korea and the United States, but the cliff scene at the beginning of the film in which Okja saves Mija from falling off the cliff in the Korean countryside was actually shot in Canada.

CHAPTER 3   SOCIAL *PUJORIS* AND THE "NARRATIVES OF FAILURE": TRANSNATIONAL GENRE AND LOCAL POLITICS IN *MEMORIES OF MURDER* AND *THE HOST*

1. In his interview with Yonhap News after the release of his sci-fi film *Snowpiercer*, Bong Joon Ho said, "Having to leave Korean time and space was the biggest challenge," referring to the fact that for the first time, he "did not include anything particularly Korean and erased any locality"; Im Mina, "Pong Chunho, 'Han'guk shigonggan ttŏnan yŏnghwa . . . kajang k'ŭn tojŏn'" [Bong Joon Ho, "Film beyond the Korean time and space . . . the biggest challenge"], *Yonhap News*, July 23, 2013, http://www.yonhapnews.co.kr/entertainment/2013/07/23/1102000000AKR20130723166200005.HTML.

2. "Top 10 des années 2000," *Cahiers du cinéma*, https://www.cahiersducinema.com/produit/top-10-des-annees-2000/.

3. "The Host," Rotten Tomatoes, http://www.rottentomatoes.com/m/the_host_2007/.

4. Namhee Lee, *The Making of Minjung: Democracy and the Politics of Representation in Korea* (Ithaca, N.Y.: Cornell University Press, 2007), 2.

5. Gi-wook Shin and Kyung Moon Hwang, eds., *Contentious Kwangju: The May 18 Uprising in Korea's Past and Present* (New York: Rowman and Littlefield, 2003), xvii. This number was announced by Martial Law Command on June 2, 1980; however, the exact numbers are still not known. *Kyunghyang Shinmun*, one of Korea's national newspapers, reported on July 13, 2015, that 207 were dead; 2,392 were wounded; and more than 910 were missing; Wŏn, Hŭipok, "5·18 Kwangju minjung hangjaeng, Han'guk minjujuŭi undongŭi pich'i toeda" [May 18 Kwangju democratic struggle becomes the light of Korea's democratic movement], *Kyunghyang*, July 13, 2015, http://news.khan.co.kr/kh_news/khan_art_view.html?art_id=201507111446581.

6. Dennis Wainstock, *Truman, MacArthur and the Korean War: June 1950–July 1951* (New York: Enigma Books, 2013), xvi.

7. Choi Jung Woon, *Owŏrŭi sahoegwahak* [Social science of May] (Seoul: Owŏrŭi Pom, 2012), Ridibooks.

8. In his interview with *Cineaste*, Bong Joon Ho describes the family in *The Host* as "lovable losers." He explains, "The audience was emotionally attached to the family from the very beginning of the film. It is one thing that the nation is not able to do what they have to do, and it is another thing that lovable loser characters are incompetent in the film"; Kevin B. Lee, "The Han River Horror Show: Interview with Bong Joon-ho," trans. Ina Park and Mina Park, *Cineaste* 32, no. 2 (2007), https://www.cineaste.com/spring2007/interview-with-bong-joon-ho.

9. "Yŏktae paksŭop'isŭ" [All-time box office], Korean Film Council, http://www.kobis.or .kr/kobis/business/stat/boxs/findDailyBoxOfficeList.do.

10. Shim Jae-myung, Paekchiyŏnŭi P'ip'ŭl INSIDE Ep. 382 [Paek Chiyŏn's People INSIDE, Episode 382]: "Shimjaemyŏng taep'yo, Sŏlgukyŏlch'a Pong Chunho kamdokŭl noch'ida" [Producer Shim Jae-myung missed an opportunity to work with director Bong Joon Ho of *Snowpiercer*], YouTube video, 1:47, "CJENM," August 13, 2013, https://www.youtube.com/watch ?v=K-Sybqzsum4. In the interview, Shim Jae-myung, one of the top producers in the Korean film industry, explains her decision to turn down the chance to invest in Bong Joon Ho's *The Host*: "When I read the script of *The Host*—they did not ask us to produce the film, but we had a chance to invest in the film—I was not sure [it would work]. I was skeptical about the possibility of a sci-fi, fantasy, and thriller film [succeeding] in Korean cinema and of creating a monster that had never been seen before."

11. In his Q&A about *Memories of Murder* at the Busan West Film Festival held at Chapman University on November 12, 2011, Bong described in detail his newspaper research of the Hwasŏng serial murder case and how it informed the direction the screenplay took.

12. When Bong Joon Ho went to the London Film Festival in 2000 with his debut feature, *Barking Dogs Never Bite*, he visited a bookstore and bought the graphic novel *From Hell* by Alan Moore (author) and Eddie Campbell (illustrator) (Marietta, Ga.: Top Shelf Productions, 2012) in the Jack the Ripper section.

13. Kim Yŏnghŭi and Im Pŏm, "Yŏnghwa taedam: Nuarŭ pŏmjoeyŏnghwaro kwanshimmori, Pakch'anuk- Pong Chunho kamdok" [Cine-talk: Park Chan-wook and Bong Joon Ho, spotlight on their noir crime movies], *Cine 21*, April 26, 2003, http://www.cine21.com/news/ view/mag_id/18591.

14. Korean audiences are familiar with the outcome of the notorious Hwasŏng serial killer case, and non-Korean audiences are given the information via the title sequence, which states the film is based on a true story.

15. In the actual Hwasŏng serial killer case, this is the date the naked corpse of the second victim was discovered in a ditch.

16. Christina Klein, "Why American Studies Needs to Think about Korean Cinema, or, Transnational Films of Bong Joon-ho," *American Quarterly* 60, no. 4 (2008): 881–882.

17. Max Weber, "Politics as a Vocation," in *Max Weber's Complete Writings on Academic and Political Vocations*, trans. Gordon C. Wells (New York: Algora, 2008), Kindle.

18. To re-create the historical period of the 1980s for *Memories of Murder*, Bong conducted an extensive search all over Korea to find locations; he would end up shooting at over fifty locations.

19. Kim Hŭigyŏng, "'Sarinŭi Ch'uŏk' Pong Chunho gamdok: 8onyŏndaerŭl chimyŏngsubaehandat" [Bong Joon Ho's *Memories of Murder*: The 1980s on the wanted list], *DongA Ilbo*, April 3, 2003, http://news.donga.com/3/all/20030403/7930795/1.

20. Joseph Jonghyun Jeon, "Memories of Memories: Historicity, Nostalgia, and Archive in Bong Joon-ho's *Memories of Murder*," *Cinema Journal* 51, no. 1 (2011): 75–94.

21. According to *Pressian*, the "McFarland incident" was revealed when a Korean assistant reported to the environmental organization Green Korea that, on February 9, 2000, the American mortician Albert McFarland ordered him to pour 480 old bottles of formaldehyde into the drain. He refused twice, but McFarland insisted, saying, "Do what the fuck I tell you. Are you stupid?" After dumping the toxic chemical and inhaling the gas, the assistant was ill for three weeks. Three months later, he reported the incident to a superior. It took five years to convict McFarland, whose sentence was only forty-five days of salary reduction. He was allowed to continue working in the mortuary and was even promoted. This incident drew

public attention to environmental contamination by U.S. forces in Korea; Kang Yanggu, "*Koemul* t'ansaengshik'in 'Maekp'allaendŭ sagŏn'ŭn iraetta" [The truth of the McFarland incident that inspired *The Host*], *Pressian*, July 31, 2006, http://www.pressian.com/news/article.html?no=33075.

22. Susan Sontag, "The Imagination of Disaster," in *Against Interpretation and Other Essays* (New York: Picador, 1966), 209–210.

23. Sontag, 213.

24. In his interview with the film magazine *Cine 21*, Bong explains that when he was in high school around 1986 or 1987, he saw from his bedroom window, which looks across the Han River, "a dark creature climbing up a bridge post." He vowed, "If I become a film director, I will make a film about people fighting a monster from the Han River"; Mun Sŏk, "Pong Chunho kamdogŭi *Koemul* p'ŭrip'ŭrodŏksyŏn 1" [Director Bong Joon Ho's preproduction of *The Host* 1], *Cine 21*, March 15, 2005, http://www.cine21.com/news/view/mag_id/29049.

25. Responses like these are common in Korean culture. In his talk on *The Host* with film scholar and critic Kim Soyoung, Bong Joon Ho states, "These people [like Hyun-seo and Gang-du from *The Host*] are alienated from the system, and they are not helped; however, nobody blames the system. Instead, they internalize and individualize the disaster. Aren't Korean people like this? For example, the victims of the Daegu subway disaster did not blame the system. Instead, most of them were blaming themselves. 'If I were richer, if I had bought my child a car when he/she got into college, then he/she wouldn't have died.' Disasters come more from structural problems, but the family in *The Host* reacts the same way"; Kim Ŭnhyŏng and Chŏn Jŏngyun, "*Koemul* Pongchunho kamtok, yŏnghwap'yŏnglonka Kimsoyŏng kyosu taetam" [Director Bong Joon Ho of *The Host* talks with film critic Kim Soyoung], *Cine 21*, July 12, 2006, http://www.cine21.com/news/view/mag_id/39944.

26. Choi Jang Jip, *Minjuhwa ihuŭi minjujuŭi: Han'guk minjujuŭiŭi Posujŏk Kiwŏn'gwa Wigi* [Democracy after democratization: The conservative origin and the crisis of Korean democracy] (Seoul: Humanista, 2010), 161.

27. Keun S. Lee, "Financial Crisis in Korea and IMF: Analysis and Perspective," presentation, Merrill Lynch Center for the Study of International Financial Services and Markets, New York, February 27, 1998, http://www.hofstra.edu/pdf/biz_mlc_lee1.pdf.

28. Choi, *Minjuhwa ihuŭi minjujuŭi*, 265.

29. The term comes from sociologist Emile Durkheim. In his book *Suicide: A Study in Sociology*, Durkheim observed that during the 1873 financial crisis in Vienna, the number of suicides immediately rose; he contends, "Economic crises have an aggravating effect on the suicidal tendency." Anomie is the temporary condition of social deregulation, and anomic suicide is that which results from such deregulation; Emile Durkheim, *Suicide: A Study in Sociology* (1897; repr., New York: Free Press, 1997), 241. For the *DongA Ilbo*, see Special Coverage Team, "Shimch'ŭngbunsŏk chasal: IMF chik'u 42%-2003nyŏn kyŏnggich'imch'e ttae 27%kŭpchŭng" [In-depth analysis of suicide: 42 percent increase immediately after IMF—27 percent increase during the 2003 recession], *DongA Ilbo*, last modified September 27, 2009, http://news.donga.com/3/all/20070215/8407797/1.

30. Newsis reported that Korean netizens were claiming on major online movie sites that *The Host* reminds them of the Kwangju Uprising. The U.S. Army pouring the toxic chemicals into the river, the isolation of the people on the riverbank, the monster's attack on the civilians, and the Molotov cocktails were some of the elements the netizens listed as the bases for this interpretation; Newsis, "Yŏnghwa *Koemul*, 5.18 talmŭn kkol(?)" [Film *The Host*, similar to May 18?], *Chosŏndatk'ŏm*, last modified August 8, 2006, http://news.chosun.com/site/data/html_dir/2006/08/08/2006080870375.html.

31. Ssinek'ŭra, "*Koemul*: koemurŭi chŏngch'e! (Pong Chunhoga sumgyŏnoŭn sangjingdŭl)" [*The Host*: The identity of the monster! (The symbols Bong Joon Ho has hidden [in the film])], *Naŭi yŏnghwap'yŏng* (blog), June 15, 2007, http://m.blog.naver.com/melt21/140038980340.

32. In the interview I conducted on July 14, 2017, in Seoul, Bong explained that the dialogue was removed during the revision of the original script. He added that even though it was not included in the film, the Park family had the background story of being the evictees from the Sanggye-dong.

33. National Institute of the Korean Language, *P'yojun'gugŏdaesajŏn* [Standard Korean dictionary], https://stdict.korean.go.kr/main/main.do.

34. Fredric Jameson, *Postmodernism: Or, the Cultural Logic of Late Capitalism* (Durham, N.C.: Duke University Press, 1992), 51.

CHAPTER 4   MONSTERS WITHIN: MORAL AMBIGUITY AND ANOMIE IN *BARKING DOGS NEVER BITE* AND *MOTHER*

1. Chang Kyung-sup, "Compressed Modernity and Its Discontents: South Korean Society in Transition," in *Economy and Society* 28, no. 1 (1999): 51.

2. Similar concepts such as "compressed growth" and "rapid development" are commonly used to describe the accelerated modernization process Korea went through in the postwar period.

3. Chang, "Compressed Modernity," 51.

4. Choi Chang-ryol, *Taehanmin'gukŭl malhanda* [Speaking of the Republic of Korea] (Seoul: Idambukseu, 2012), Ridibooks.

5. Alvin Toffler, *Future Shock* (New York: Bantam Books, 1970), 1.

6. Nancy Abelmann, *The Melodrama of Mobility: Women, Talk, and Class in Contemporary South Korea* (Honolulu: University of Hawaii Press, 2003), 281. Through her early 1990s interviews with Korean women in their fifties and sixties, Nancy Abelmann chronicled how a compressed modernity unfolded in the lives of ordinary women.

7. Ernst Bloch developed the notion of *noncontemporaneity* (*Ungleichzeitigkeit*) in his 1962 book, *The Heritage of Our Times* (1962; repr., Cambridge: Polity, 1991), in which he tries to explain the rise of fascism in Germany.

8. Cho Hae-joang, "Taehanmin'gung sahoeŭi kŭnŭl" [Shadow in the Korean society], in *Han'gugin, Urinŭn Nuguin-ga* [Koreans, who are we?], ed. P'ŭllat'onak'ademi (Seoul: 21Segibuksŭ, 2016), Ridibooks. Cho lists aging population, low birth rate, low growth rate, overeducation, growth without employment, youth unemployment, and polarization as the side effects of compressed growth.

9. Cho Hae-joang, "'You Are Entrapped in an Imaginary Well': The Formation of Subjectivity within Compressed Development—a Feminist Critique of Modernity and Korean Culture," quoted in Abelmann, *Melodrama of Mobility*, 283.

10. Chang Wŏnho, "Han'guksahoeŭi pulshin, wŏninŭn ŏdie innŭn'ga?" [What is the cause of distrust in Korean society?], in *Taehanmin'gukŭn todŏkchŏgin'ga?*, ed. Kim Misook (Seoul: Tongashia, 2009), 112.

11. Chang, "Compressed Modernity," 51.

12. A term coined by Robert Flank and Philip Cook in their book of the same title. It is used to indicate a polarization under neoliberal society; Robert Flank and Philip Cook, *The Winner-Take-All Society: Why the Few at the Top Get So Much More than the Rest of Us* (New York: Penguin, 1996).

13. Kang Jun-man, *Urinŭn wae irŏk'e sanŭn'gŏlkka* [Why do we live this way?] (Seoul: Inmwulkwa Sasangsa, 2014). Ridibooks.

14. Kang.

15. Chang, "Compressed Modernity," 34.

16. Ahn Byung-wook, "Han'gungminjuhwaundonge taehan P'yŏnggawa Inshigŭi Chŏnhwanŭl Wihayŏ" [For a change in the evaluation and conception of Korea's democratization movement], *Yŏksawa Hyŏnshil* 77 (2010): 40.

17. On October 6, 2014, the daily *Hankook Ilbo* reported that Korea maintained the highest suicide rate among OECD member nations for the last ten years, with an average of 40 people committing suicide a day. Korea's suicide rate counts to 28.5 per 100,000 people, more than twice the OECD nations' average of 12.1 per 100,000 people. It also reported that the family suicide rate in Korea is the world's highest and that these high suicides rates occurred since the 2008 world financial crisis; Kim Chi-jung, "10nyŏn nŏmge OECD chasallyul 1wi . . . Idaero nwadul kŏn'ga" [No. 1 suicide rate among OECD nations over ten years: Just leaving it this way?], *Hankook Ilbo*, October 6, 2014, https://www.hankookilbo.com/v/8a588d67540b4b61818405f3eea489fa.

18. When Bong Joon Ho visited Chapman University in November 2011 for a retrospective of his films, I conducted an interview with him. When I asked him what "Koreanness" is to him, his answer was simple: "*Pujori.*"

19. Im Kwon-Taek has made films that have revived and revisited traditional Korean culture and its heritage, including *Sopyonje* (1993), *Festival* (1995), *Chunhyang* (2000), *Chihwaseon* (2002), and *Hanji* (2011). Often, his films are associated with the uniquely Korean notion of "han," feelings of regrets or unresolved grief, as manifested in traditional Korean art such as *pansori*, a subject of both *Sopyonje* and *Chunhyang*. For in-depth discussions of the Koreanness in Im's films, see David E. James and Kyung Hyun Kim, eds., *Im Kwon-Taek: The Making of a Korean National Cinema* (Detroit: Wayne State University Press, 2002).

20. *P'yojun'gugŏdaesajŏn* [Standard Korean dictionary], https://stdict.korean.go.kr/main/main.do.

21. In the *Merriam-Webster Collegiate Dictionary*, the full definition of the adjective *absurd* is (1) "ridiculously unreasonable, unsound, or incongruous"; (2) "having no rational or orderly relationship to human life: meaningless; also lacking order of value"; (3) "dealing with the absurd . . . or with absurdism." The definition of the noun *absurd* is "the state or condition in which human beings exist in an irrational and meaningless universe and in which human life has no ultimate meaning—usually used with *the*"; *Merriam-Webster Collegiate Dictionary*, s.v. "absurd," https://unabridged.merriam-webster.com/collegiate/absurd. Neither definition carries the meaning of a fraudulent act.

22. Pang Hyŏnch'ŏl, "Han'guk kongmuwŏn pujŏngbup'ae segye 4wi: KDI 'P'yeswaejŏk imyongje-do ttaemun" [Korea's public official corruption ranks fourth in the world: KDI, "Due to closed hiring system"], *Chosun Biz News*, October 10, 2013, http://biz.chosun.com/site/data/html_dir/2013/10/09/2013100903125.html.

23. *Hankook Ilbo* reported on April 19, 2011, that Michael Sandel's book *Justice: What's the Right Thing to Do?* has sold more than one million copies, the first humanities book to reach that threshold; Nam Kyŏnguk, "*Chŏngŭiran Muŏshin-ga* 100manbu tolp'a: Wae?" [*Justice: What's the Right Thing to Do?* exceeds 1 million sales: Why?], *Hankook Ilbo*, April 19, 2011, http://www.hankookilbo.com/v/e2f4e5ec04f8432abbe7d539f2bfob6a. On June 5, 2012, the *Wall Street Journal* reported that Michael Sandel himself has gained a "celebrity status" in Korea, attracting a large crowd of fifteen thousand at his discussion held at a university's amphitheater. Citing Seoul's Asan Institute survey, the *Wall Street Journal* adds that 74 percent of respondents said

Korean society was unfair, whereas Sandel's own survey showed that 38 percent of Americans felt that their society was unfair. One of the attendees of the discussion was quoted as saying, "We developed very fast and we just valued money and material things for so long. Nowadays we are strengthening our emotions and ethics," testifying the need for social justice; Evan Ramstad, "U.S. Professor on Fairness Is a Hit in Seoul," *Wall Street Journal*, June 5, 2012, http://www.wsj.com/articles/SB10001424052702303506404577445841573895570. Sandel's book was translated to Korean with a simple title of *What Is Justice?*

24. Pak Noja, *Pigurŭi shidae* [The era of servility] (Seoul: Hankyoreh, 2014), 5–10.

25. He was asked to donate a large sum of money to be hired full time. The *Kat'ollingnyus* [*Catholic Newspaper*] reported on May 31, 2010, that Sŏ Chŏngmin, a forty-five-year-old adjunct professor at Chosun University, had committed suicide and left a note asking for an investigation into the university's chronic ills. The newspaper added that since 1998, there have been eight known cases of adjunct professor suicides, and the article criticized the corruption in the hiring process; Han Sangpong, "'Che-ga tangshinŭi chongimnikka?': Taehakkangsa yusŏ namgigo chasal" ["Am I your slave?": A college adjunct commits suicide, leaving a death note], *Kat'ollingnyusŭ*, May 31, 2010, http://www.catholicnews.co.kr/news/articleView.html?idxno=3603.

26. Bong chose the actual apartment complex where he lived during his first three years of marriage.

27. The legendary Korean independent documentary *Sanggyedong Olympics* (1988) chronicles the struggle of the poor residents of Sanggye-dong, a village in Seoul, who were forcibly evicted from their underdeveloped residential area by the city to build apartment complexes as part of the beautification for the Seoul Summer Olympics. The Parks in *The Host* are evictees of this Sanggye-dong.

28. Many dog owners living in apartment complexes have their dogs undergo vocal-cord removal surgery so they don't disturb their neighbors. It shows the way in which having a pet presents a dilemma between communal living and animal cruelty. The pet owners believe the surgery would reduce the chance of neighbor disputes; however, it is an act of animal cruelty.

29. Bong Joon Ho, "'Madŏ nŭn nae ch'oech'oŭi pon'gyŏk seksŭyŏnghwada': Pong Chunho kamdokŭl mannada" [*Mother* is my first serious sex movie": Meeting with director Bong Joon Ho], interview by Hŏ Kicha, *Ddanji Ilbo*, June 10, 2009, http://www.ddanzi.com/?mid=ddanziNews&search_target=title&search_keyword=%ED%98%B8&page=7&m=1&document_srl=618215.

30. K. Maja Krakowiak and Mary Beth Oliver, "When Good Characters Do Bad Things: Examining the Effect of Moral Ambiguity on Enjoyment," *Journal of Communication* 62, no. 1 (2012): 118. The article also states that viewers expect "morally correct endings for these characters" and expect "a criminal to get caught" (121), but Bong's films, including *Barking Dogs Never Bite* and *Mother*, deny these expectations.

31. One of the common features in Korean TV dramas is the conflict between a possessive mother-in-law and her daughter-in-law with the son/husband caught in the middle.

32. Chŏn Inkwŏn, *Namjaŭi T'ansaeng* [Birth of a man] (Seoul: P'urŭnsup, 2003), 73–74.

33. This idea that a "mother is not a woman" is traditionally prevalent in Korea. However, her repressed sexuality in the film, her spying on Jin-tae during sexual intercourse, the depiction of her extremely intimate relationship with Do-joon, and sleeping next to him in an intimate distance make their relationship seem incestuous. The needle in the thigh has a connotation of a widow in traditional Confucian culture overcoming her sexual desire.

34. This then switches to the crime scene, in which A-jung is shown hanging from the balcony of the house. The scene of her death juxtaposed against the scene of Do-joon sleeping

with his mom creates a sort of split-screen effect. This allusion to Do-joon's possible crime is so subtle that it often goes unnoticed.

35. Chŏng Hŭijin, *P'eminijŭmŭi tojŏn* [The feminism's challenge], 3rd ed. (Seoul: Gyoyangin, 2015), 70.

36. Park Hong-sik, "Kajŏnggyoyuk tamdangjarosŏŭi chŏnŏpchubu yŏk'algwa kajŏngmunje" [The role of housewives as home educators and family issues], *Yugyosasang munhwa yŏn-gu* 30 (2007): 313–340.

37. Park, "Kajŏnggyoyuk tamdangjarosŏŭi chŏnŏpchubu yŏk'algwa kajŏngmunje."

38. "South Korea's Education Fever Needs Cooling," *Business Insider*, October 25, 2013, http://www.businessinsider.com/south-koreas-education-fever-needs-cooling-2013-10.

39. The film is set in an elite high school that goes through an investigation of the murder of one of its students. It depicts the intense competition for college entrance among top students and reveals the cruelty of a secret circle that only the best students may join. The students and their parents—especially their mothers—are only focused on their success.

40. Lee Tŭkchae, *Kajokchuŭinŭn Yamanida* [Familism is barbarism] (Seoul: Sonamu, 2001). In the book, Lee defines this system of selfish familism as a "family-nation system" that is equivalent to fascism brought by the nation's violence.

41. Kim Myŏngsin, "Ttwigo tto ttwinŭn i ttangŭi modŭn madŏdŭrege" [To all the mothers of this land who keep running and running], *Pressian*, June 12, 2009, http://www.pressian .com/news/article.html?no=95340.

42. In the film, she is called by others as just "Mother" or "Do-joon's mother." In Korea, when a woman has a child or children, she is no longer called by her name; she is usually called "so-and-so's mom." Mothers are defined by their child/children.

43. Pak, *Pigurŭi shidae,* 109.

CHAPTER 5   BEYOND THE LOCAL: GLOBAL POLITICS AND NEOLIBERAL CAPITALISM IN *SNOWPIERCER* AND *OKJA*

1. Bong Joon Ho, "Pong Chunho, *Sŏlgukyŏlch'a'*, inlyu pop'yŏnchŏk kach'i talun chakp'um" [Bong Joon Ho, *Snowpiercer* dealing with universal values], YouTube video, 2:06, "YTN NEWS," July 22, 2013, https://www.youtube.com/watch?v=ZanPOCMg_2w. Bong Joon Ho commented about the nature of the non-Koreanness of the film: "In previous films like *Memories of Murder*, *Mother*, and *The Host*, I have always based the story on a specifically Korean situation, time period, and locations like the Han River. *Snowpiercer* was the first film without those guidelines, [so] I felt a little empty. However, the film deals with a very universal theme, the human drama about the poor versus the rich, the powerless versus the power unfolding within a running train. So I thought this is very much [a] universal story, and because of that, it is also a Korean story."

2. The comparison of the two photos was uploaded on Twitter by Hunter Harris, the associate editor of Vulture, on June 28, 2017, the day *Okja* began streaming on Netflix in the United States, and went viral; Hunter Harris (@hunterharris), "okja is delightful and grim and this is my favorite part," Twitter, June 28, 2017, 9:44 a.m., pic.twitter.com/Y8uBNgPnNZ.

3. H. G. Wells, "Preface to the 1921 Edition," in *The War in the Air: And Particularly How Mr. Bert Smallways Fared While It Lasted* (Harmondsworth, U.K.: Penguin, 1967), 7, quoted in Keith M. Johnston, *Science Fiction Film: A Critical Introduction* (London: Berg, 2011), 1.

4. The Occupy movement followed in the wake of Occupy Wall Street, which began on September 17, 2011, in New York City. It attracted widespread attention and spawned worldwide protests against social and economic inequality.

5. *Okja*'s VFX supervisor Erik De Boer's interview, quoted from Simon Ward, *Okja: The Art and Making of the Film* (London: Titan Books, 2018), 138.

6. Hansen argues, "The cinema constitutes a public sphere of its own, defined by particular relations of representation and reception"; Miriam Hansen, *Babel and Babylon: Spectatorship in American Silent Film* (Cambridge, Mass.: Harvard University Press, 1994), 7.

7. Steven Seidman, ed., *Jürgen Habermas on Society and Politics: A Reader* (Boston: Beacon, 1989), 231.

8. Kevin Michael DeLuca and Jennifer Peeples, "From Public Sphere to Public Screen: Democracy, Activism, and the 'Violence' of Seattle," *Critical Studies in Media Communication* 19, no. 2 (2002): 125–151.

9. Brian Loader and Dan Mercea, "Networking Democracy? Social Media Innovations and Participatory Politics," *Information, Communication & Society* 14, no. 6 (2011): 757–769.

10. "Room for Debate: Will Fiction Influence How We React to Climate Change?," *New York Times*, July 29, 2014, http://www.nytimes.com/roomfordebate/2014/07/29/will-fiction -influence-how-we-react-to-climate-change.

11. Dan Bloom, "Movies Like *Snowpiercer* Can Sound the Alarm," *New York Times*, last modified July 30, 2014, http://www.nytimes.com/roomfordebate/2014/07/29/will-fiction -influence-how-we-react-to-climate-change/movies-like-snowpiercer-can-sound-the-alarm.

12. Dan Bloom, "THE CLIFFIES 2014—Cli Fi Movie Awards—Winners List—Awards Program Tagline 'Can Cli Fi Movies Save the Planet?,'" *Blogspot* (blog), November 1, 2014, http://korgw101.blogspot.com/2014/11/the-cliffies-2014-nominations-are-in.html.

13. J. P. Telotte, "Science Fiction Reflects Our Anxieties," *New York Times*, last modified July 30, 2014, http://www.nytimes.com/roomfordebate/2014/07/29/will-fiction-influence -how-we-react-to-climate-change/science-fiction-reflects-our-anxieties. Increasingly at universities and colleges, nonfilm courses use movies to raise and discuss social issues. Chapman University's honors program has courses like "Controversial Issues in Biology," "Anime and War," and "Disney: Gender, Race, and Religion" that use films as their main texts.

14. Seth D. Baum, "Film Review: *Snowpiercer*," *Journal of Sustainability Education* 7 (2014), http://www.jsedimensions.org/wordpress/content/film-review-snowpiercer_2014_12/.

15. Jason Mark, "In Review: *Snowpiercer*," *Earth Island Journal*, July 19, 2014, http://www .earthisland.org/journal/index.php/elist/eListRead/in_review_emsnowpiercer_em/.

16. Kim Joon-hyung, "*Snowpiercer, Elysium* and the Land We Live In," Mirezi.com, September 2, 2013, http://www.mirezi.com/2013/09/column-3_4118.html.

17. *Snowpiercer* (2013), IMDb.com, April 23, 2015, http://www.imdb.com/title/tt1706620/.

18. The Q&A on the scientific premises of the film is from "Kwahakchŏng kŏmjŭng chinach'imyŏn yŏnghwa chaemiŏpchi annayo?" [Doesn't too much scientific verification make movies boring?], DongAScience.com, October 27, 2013, http://www.dongascience .com/news/view/2796.

19. Joe Carter, "How to Understand *Snowpiercer*," *Action Institute Powerblog* (blog), July 18, 2014, http://blog.acton.org/archives/70893-understand-snowpiercer.html. Jonah Goldberg agreed: "On *Snowpiercer* (SPOILERS)," *National Review*, July 23, 2014, http://www .nationalreview.com/corner/383523/snowpiercer-spoilers-jonah-goldberg. Carter's review has sixty-six comments.

20. Jason Bok, "Sŏlgukyŏlch'a 2013, Kich'anŭn Yŏnghwada!" [*Snowpiercer*, 2013: The train is a movie!], *The Bok* (blog), September 17, 2013, http://blog.naver.com/environment9/ 30176057667.

21. Hwang Boyeon, "Ch'ŏngnyŏnege Han'gukŭn 'sŏlgukyŏlch'a . . . ssigukttang wasŏ trchŏnyŏginnŭn sam'" [For the young, Korea is *Snowpiercer*: Having "life with an evening"

in a foreign land], *Hankyoreh Shimun*, January 4, 2016, http://www.hani.co.kr/arti/society/society_general/724550.html.

22. Anna Fifield, "Young South Koreans Call Their Country 'Hell' and Look for Ways Out," *Washington Post*, January 31, 2016, https://www.washingtonpost.com/world/asia_pacific/young-south-koreans-call-their-country-hell-and-look-for-ways-out/2016/01/30/34737c06-b967-11e5-85cd-5ad59bc19432_story.html.

23. Nancy Fraser, *Scales of Justice: Reimagining Political Space in a Globalizing World* (New York: Columbia University Press, 2010).

24. Hyŏn Yŏngpok, "Ch'eryu oegugin 150 manmyŏng ch'ŏt tolp'a—tamunhwa, tainjonghwa kasok" [Foreign immigrants exceed 1.5 million for the first time: Multicultural, multiracialization accelerates], *Yonhap News*, June 10, 2013, http://www.yonhapnews.co.kr/politics/2013/05/28/0503000000AKR20130528133900372.HTML.

25. Seán McCorry, "*Okja*: A Film That Provides Food for Thought on 'Sustainable' Meat Production," Conversation, June 28, 2017, https://theconversation.com/okja-a-film-that-provides-food-for-thought-on-sustainable-meat-production-80088.

26. KARA (Korea Animal Rights Advocates), "K'ara, kamgŭmt'ŭl ch'ubang wihae Pong Chunho gamdokkwa Okcha haebang p'ŭrojekt'ŭ torip" [KARA launches Okja Liberation Project with director Bong Joon Ho to eliminate pig stalls], press release, July 5, 2017, https://www.ekara.org/report/press/read/8828.

27. Alanna Ramsier, "11 Things That Happened When People Watched 'Okja,'" *PETA* (blog), June 30, 2017, https://www.peta.org/blog/okja-turning-people-vegan/.

28. Anna Starostineetskaya, "*Okja* Release Spikes 'Vegan' Google Searches by 65%," *VegNews*, August 6, 2017, https://vegnews.com/2017/8/okja-release-spikes-vegan-google-searches-by-65-percent.

29. Starostineetskaya.

30. Kim Sŏro, "Yŏnghwa 'okchaoka shikt'ang wie kajyŏon pyŏnhwanŭn" [Changes the movie Okja brought to the table], *Hankook Ilbo*, July 10, 2017, https://www.hankookilbo.com/News/Read/201707101357235400.

31. Lindsey Weber, "Let's Talk about the Ending of *Snowpiercer*," Vulture, July 11, 2014, http://www.vulture.com/2014/07/snowpiecer-movie-discussion.html.

32. Maltugi, "Sŏlgukyŏlch'a majimak changmyeon pukkŭkkomi yŏnghwaŭi modŭn'gŏsŭl sŏlmyŏnghanda" [The polar bear in the last scene of Snowpiercer explains everything], *Hŭkkwa ssiat* (blog), August 6, 2013, http://maltugi.blogspot.com/2013/08/blog-post_6.html.

33. Susan Braedley and Meg Luxton, eds., *Neoliberalism and Everyday Life* (Montreal: McGill-Queen's University Press, 2010).

34. Braedley and Luxton, 6.

35. Zygmunt Bauman, *Liquid Times: Living in an Age of Uncertainty* (Cambridge: Polity, 2006). He describes the ways in which capitalism has evolved from the "solid" phase of welfare statism to the "liquid" phase of neoliberalism.

36. "*Snowpiercer* R-Rated Animated Prequel (2013)—Chris Evans Movie HD," YouTube video, 5:33, "FilmIsNow Movie Trailers," July 23, 2013, https://www.youtube.com/watch?v=DrvBy5_aFOA.

37. Ellen Chances, "The Superfluous Man in Russian Literature," in *The Routledge Companion to Russian Literature*, ed. Neil Cornwell (London: Routledge, 2002), 111–122.

38. Brian Holmes, "Hieroglyphs of the Future: Jacques Rancière and the Aesthetics of Equality," *Cabinet* 4 (2001), http://www.cabinetmagazine.org/issues/4/Hieroglyphs.php.

39. Slavoj Žižek, "The Lessons of Rancière," in *The Politics of Aesthetics*, by Jacques Rancière, trans. Gabriel Rockhill (London: Continuum, 2007), 76.

40. Žižek, 70.

41. Korea's national statistical agency, Statistic Korea, provided the national index of unemployment rate; "Ch'wiŏpcha su/shirŏmnyul ch'ui" [Trend in the number of the employed/unemployment rate], *e-narachip'yo* [E-national index], http://www.index.go.kr/potal/main/EachDtlPageDetail.do?idx_cd=1063.

42. Choi Tae-sup, *Ingyŏ sahoi* [Surplus society] (Seoul: Woongjin Knowledge House, 2013).

43. In his book *Wasted Lives: Modernity and Its Outcasts* (Oxford: Polity, 2004), Polish sociologist Zygmunt Bauman argues that the superfluous population of migrants, refugees, and other outcasts is the result of the quest for economic progress in the era of uncertainty he describes as "liquid modernity."

44. Son Chang-seop, "Ingyŏ In'gan," in *Ingyŏ In'gan* (Seoul: Minŭmsa, 2005), Ridibooks. This short story is considered one of the finest literary works of the 1950s; capturing the social mood in the immediate postwar period in Korea, it tells the story of three young men who spends time with each other chatting all day. The protagonist, Manki, is a dentist, but the other two are jobless and full of angst and despair.

45. *Malchukkŏri Chanhoksa* [*Spirit of Jeet Kune Do: Once Upon a Time in High School*], directed by Yoo Ha, produced by Tcha Sung-jai and No Jong-yun, production company Sidus, and distributed by CJ Entertainment, 2004.

46. Ch'oe Hyŏnchŏng, "Chŏlmŭn Ch'ŭngŭi Chajo Sŏkkin Yuhaengŏ Ingyŏin'gan" ["Surplus Human," a self-deprecating word in vogue among the young], *DongA Ilbo*, March 20, 2009, http://news.donga.com/3/all/20090310/8706013/1.

47. Charles Derber and Yale R. Magrass, *Surplus American: How the 1% Is Making Us Redundant* (New York: Routledge, 2012).

48. Carter, "How to Understand *Snowpiercer.*"

49. Curtis M. Parvin, "Are Social Classes on the Right Track? A Review of 'Snowpiercer' (2013)," *Rhode Island Liberator* (blog), November 14, 2014, https://riliberator.wordpress.com/2014/11/14/are-social-classes-on-the-right-track-a-review-of-snowpiercer-2013/.

50. Muhammad Khan, "*Snowpiercer*: A New Ice Age and Its Consequences," World Socialist Web Site, October 8, 2014, https://www.wsws.org/en/articles/2014/10/08/snow-008.html.

51. *Merriam-Webster Collegiate Dictionary*, s.v. "sensible," accessed March 17, 2016, http://www.merriam-webster.com/dictionary/sensible.

52. Žižek, "Lesson of Rancière," 69.

53. Jacques Rancière, *The Politics of Aesthetics* (London: Continuum, 2007), 85.

54. Rancière, 51.

55. Karl Marx, "The Class Struggles in France, 1848–1850," in *Marx & Engels Collected Works*, vol. 10, *Marx and Engels 1849–51*, ed. Karl Marx and Frederick Engels (Chadwell Heath, U.K.: Lawrence and Wishart Electric Book, 2010), 122, http://www.hekmatist.com/Marx%20Engles/Marx%20&%20Engels%20Collected%20Works%20Volume%2010_%20M%20-%20Karl%20Marx.pdf.

56. Walter Benjamin, "Paralipomena to 'On the Concept of History,'" in *Selected Writings*, vol. 4, *1938–1940*, ed. Howard Eiland et al., trans. Edmund Jephcott et al. (Cambridge, Mass.: Harvard University Press, 2003), 402.

CONCLUSION

The romanization of the characters' names in *Parasite* follows the English-translated version of the script.

1. For the detailed discussion of familism in South Korea, see chapter 4.

2. Kim Yong-woon, "[IMF 20nyŏn yut' ongjindan] Kŏriro naemollin kajangdŭl: Kamaengjŏm chŏnsŏngshidae yŏrŏtchiman" [(IMF 20 years distribution analysis) thrown onto the street: It was the heyday of franchise business but . . .], edaily, November 21, 2017, https://www.edaily.co.kr/news/read?newsId=03240646616128016&mediaCodeNo=257& OutLnkChk=Y.

3. The term chaebol literally means "wealth clique" in Korean. It refers to giant conglomerates such as Samsung, LG, and Hyundai, each of which forms a group with a large number of diverse affiliate companies. They are called chaebol in order to convey the specifically Korean characteristics. They are often run and controlled by the families of the companies' founders, and the ownership and management rights are often inherited. Most of the founding companies of the chaebols started during the 1940s and 1950s, after the independence from Japan's colonial rule. Thus most of the chaebol groups are currently run by the third-generation CEOs.

4. See chapter 5 for a more detailed discussion of Zygmunt Bauman's notion of "human waste" and surplus population in the age of neoliberalism.

5. Kim Chan'ho, Momyŏlgam: Kuryokkwa Chonŏbŭi Kamjŏngsahoehak [Sense of humiliation: Sociology of emotions of shame and dignity] (Seoul: Munhakkwa Chisŏngsa, 2014).

6. On its opening weekend in October 2019, Parasite set several box office records in the United States, including the largest per-screen average for a foreign language film and the best per-screen haul since La La Land; Dave McNary, "Bong Joon-ho's 'Parasite' Posts Powerful Opening in North America," Variety, October 13, 2019, https://variety.com/2019/film/news/ box-office-parasite-bong-joon-ho-1203368957/. It also set French box-office records in September 2019 by becoming the most successful Cannes-winning film in fifteen years; Agence France-Presse, "Parasite Sets French Box-Office Record," Straits Times, September 24, 2019, https://www.straitstimes.com/lifestyle/entertainment/parasite-sets-french-box-office -record.

7. I Osŏng, "Taeman k'asŭt'era mollakŭn chŏnghaejin sunsŏyŏtta" [The fall of Taiwanese castella was inevitable], SisaIN, April 11, 2017. https://www.sisain.co.kr/news/articleView.html ?idxno=28805. According to this article, the Taiwanese Castella boom started in late 2016 with seventeen different franchises with more than four hundred stores opening up nationwide. Most of the businesses collapsed in April 2017 from fierce competition and a media scandal involving a malpractice case.

8. Jjapaguri is a popular recipe (some describe it as a "people's recipe") that mixes two different types of instant noodles: black bean noodle (Jjapagetti) and spicy seafood-flavored noodle (Nŏguri). And the title of the original song is "Toktonŭn uri ttang" (Dokdo is our land). Composed in 1982 to raise people's awareness of the island, it became one of the most beloved songs for its easy melody and historical significance. The island has been under a territorial dispute between Korea and Japan for many decades.

9. Admiral Yi Sun-sin (1545–1598) is one of the most celebrated figures in Korean history. In 1597, he led a naval battle against Japan, named the Battle of Myeongyang. Despite being outnumbered 133 warships to 13, he saved Korea from the Japanese invasion. He is famous for designing the turtle ship used in the battle as well as the crane-wing formation of the battleships. The 2014 Korean historical blockbuster film The Admiral: Roaring Currents depicts the events surrounding this battle.

10. For a detailed discussion of the notion of the "public screen," see chapter 5.

FILMOGRAPHY

1. The music video is available on YouTube: "Dan-Kim Don-kyu," YouTube video, 4:33, "myjukebox8090," May 6, 2012, https://www.youtube.com/watch?v=tuCZW6Ptpgg.

2. "Han Young-ae- Oeroun Karodŭng MV 2003" [Lonely Streetlamp MV 2003], YouTube video, 3:41, "Old Kpop Ch'uŏgŭi myubi," October 20, 2016, https://www.youtube.com/watch?v=7ZBDbf6RWmw.

3. "Bong Joon Ho," KMDb, http://www.kmdb.or.kr/db/per/00001843.

4. Chu Sŏngch'ŏl, ed., *Tebwiŭi sun'gan: Yŏnghwagamdong 17ini tŭllyŏjunŭn naŭi ch'ŏngch'un punt'ugi* [Debut moment: Seventeen film directors tell their struggles as youth] (Seoul: P'urŭnsup, 2014), 196.

5. Jang would later direct his debut feature film, *Save the Green Planet* (*Chigurŭl Chik'yŏra*), with Tcha Sung-jai in 2003.

6. Bong Joon Ho, "'80nyŏndae 'kkoraji'rŭl poyŏjugo ship'ŏtta': [Int'ŏbyu 1] Yŏnghwa *Sarinŭi Ch'uŏk* Pong Chunho kamdok" ["I wanted to show the status of the 1980s": (Interview 1) director Bong Joon Ho on *Memories of Murder*], interview with Kim Yong-un and Kang Hyun-sik, OhmyNews, October 31, 2003, http://star.ohmynews.com/NWS_Web/OhmyStar/at_pg.aspx?cntn_cd=a0000151049.

7. Sŏ Hyein, "*Sarinŭi Ch'uŏk* (Pong Chunho, 2003): Myŏngjakŭl mandŭn ch'ŏt pŏntchae maedŭp" [*Memories of Murder* (Bong Joon Ho, 2003): The first step to making a classic], *Yŏnghwach'ŏn'guk*, August 20, 2018, http://www.kmdb.or.kr/story/179/4776.

8. Yim Pil-sung, "Chejagilchi: Namgŭgilgi" [Production diary: *Antarctic Journal*], *P'illŭmmeik'ŏsŭ K'ŏmyunit'i*, May 14, 2005, https://www.filmmakers.co.kr/production_2004010500/23821.

9. Jung Ji-youn, ed., *Bong Joon-ho*, trans. Colin A. Mouat (Seoul: Seoul Selection, 2008), 134.

10. Jung, 129.

11. "Snowpiercer," Box Office Mojo, accessed April 23, 2015. https://www.boxofficemojo.com/movies/?id=snowpiercer.htm.

12. "Sŏlgukyŏlch'a" [*Snowpiercer*], KMDb, accessed April 23, 2015. http://www.kmdb.or.kr/db/kor/detail/movie/K/14111.

BIBLIOGRAPHY

Abelmann, Nancy. *The Melodrama of Mobility: Women, Talk, and Class in Contemporary South Korea*. Honolulu: University of Hawaii Press, 2003.

Agence France-Presse. "Parasite Sets French Box-Office Record." *Straits Times*, September 24, 2019. https://www.straitstimes.com/lifestyle/entertainment/parasite-sets-french-box-office -record.

Ahn, Byung-wook. "Han'gungminjuhwaundonge taehan p'yŏnggawa inshigŭi chŏnhwanŭl wihayŏ" [For a change in the evaluation and conception of Korea's democratization movement]. *Yŏksawa hyŏnshil* 77 (2010): 17–38.

Appadurai, Arjun. "Disjuncture and Difference in the Global Cultural Economy." *Theory, Culture & Society* 7, no. 2 (1990): 295–310.

Bakhtin, Mikhail M. "Forms of Time and of the Chronotope in the Novel: Notes toward a Historical Poetics." In *Narrative Dynamics: Essays on Time, Plot, Closure and Frames*, edited by Brian Richardson, James Phalen, Peter Rabinowitz, 15–24. Columbus: Ohio State University Press, 2002.

Bálazs, Béla, and Erica Carter, eds. *Béla Bálazs: Early Film Theory: Visible Man and the Spirit of Film*. New York: Berghahn Books, 2011.

Barthes, Roland. "The Death of the Author." In *Image-Music-Text*, translated by Stephen Heath, 142–148. New York: Hill and Wang, 1978.

Baum, Seth D. "Film Review: *Snowpiercer*." *Journal of Sustainability Education* 7 (2014): 1.

Bauman, Zygmunt. *Liquid Times: Living in an Age of Uncertainty*. Cambridge: Polity, 2006.

———. *Wasted Lives: Modernity and Its Outcasts*. Cambridge: Polity, 2004.

Benjamin, Walter. "Paralipomena to 'On the Concept of History.'" In *Selected Writings*. Vol. 4, *1938–1940*, edited by Howard Eiland and Michael W. Jennings, translated by Edmund Jephcott et al., 401–411. Cambridge, Mass.: Harvard University Press, 2003.

Berry, Chris. "Full Service Cinema: The Korean Cinema Success Story (So Far)." In *Text and Context of Korean Cinema: Crossing Borders*, edited by Young-key Kim-Renaud, R. Richard Grinker, and Kirk W. Larsen. Washington, DC: George Washington University, *Sigur Center Asia Paper*, no. 17 (2002): 7–16. https://www2.gwu.edu/~sigur/assets/docs/scap/ SCAP17-KoreanCinema.pdf.

———. "'What's Big about the Big Film?': 'De-westernizing' the Blockbuster in Korea and China." In *Movie Blockbusters*, edited by Julian Stringer, 217–229. London: Routledge, 2003.

Bhabha, Homi K. *The Location of Culture*. New York: Routledge, 2004.

Bloch, Ernst. *The Heritage of Our Times*. Cambridge: Polity, 1991.

Bloom, Dan. "THE CLIFFIES 2014—Cli Fi Movie Awards—Winners List—Awards Program Tagline 'Can Cli Fi Movies Save the Planet?'" *Blogspot* (blog), November 1, 2014. http://korgw101.blogspot.com/2014/11/the-cliffies-2014-nominations-are-in.html.

———. "Movies Like *Snowpiercer* Can Sound the Alarm." *New York Times*, last modified July 30, 2014. http://www.nytimes.com/roomfordebate/2014/07/29/will-fiction-influence-how -we-react-to-climate-change/movies-like-snowpiercer-can-sound-the-alarm.

Bok, Jason. "Sŏlgukyŏlch'a 2013, kich'anŭn yŏnghwada!" [*Snowpiercer*, 2013: The train is a movie!]. *The Bok* (blog), September 17, 2013. http://blog.naver.com/environment9/30176057667.

Bong Joon Ho. "Chŏnŭn pyŏnt'aeimnida" [I am a pervert]. YouTube video, 2:21. "CJENM," July 30, 2013. https://www.youtube.com/watch?v=BldTZ6JO400.

———. "'8onyŏndae 'kkoraji'rŭl poyŏjugo ship'ŏtta': [Int'ŏbyu 1] Yŏnghwa *Sarinŭi Ch'uŏk* Pong Chunho kamdok" ["I wanted to show the status of the 1980s": (Interview 1) Director Bong Joon Ho on *Memories of Murder*]. Interview with Kim Yongun and Kang Hyŏnsik. Ohmynews, October 31, 2003. http://star.ohmynews.com/NWS_Web/OhmyStar/at_pg.aspx?cntn_cd=a0000151049.

———. *Koemul meik'ing puk* [Illustrated journal of the making of *The Host*]. Seoul: 21Segibuksŭ, 2006.

———. "'*Madŏ* nŭn nae ch'oech'oŭi pon'gyŏk seksŭyŏnghwada': Pong Chunho kamdokŭl mannada" ["*Mother* is my first serious sex movie": Meeting with director Bong Joon Ho]. Interview with Kim Yongun and Kang Hyŏnsik. *Ddanji Ilbo*, June 10, 2009. http://www.ddanzi.com/?mid=ddanziNews&search_target=title&search_keyword=%ED%98%B8&page=7&m=1&document_srl=618215.

———. "Pong Chunho, *Sŏlgukyŏlch'a*', inlyu pop'yŏnchŏk kach'i talun chakp'um" [Bong Joon Ho, *Snowpiercer* dealing with universal values]. YouTube video, 2:06. "YTN NEWS," July 22, 2013. https://www.youtube.com/watch?v=ZanPOCMg_2w.

Bong Joon Ho, Kim Jŏng, and Min Kyu-dong. "Chŭlgŏun hoksa'ŭi shiganiŏtchi" [It was a fun time of exhaustion]. Interview by Chu Sŏngch'ŏl. *Cine 21*, October 14, 2009. http://www.cine21.com/news/view/?mag_id=58231.

Bourdieu, Pierre. *The Field of Cultural Production*. Edited by Randal Johnson. New York: Columbia University Press, 1993.

———. *The Rules of Art: Genesis and Structure of the Literary Field*. Translated by Susan Emanuel. Stanford, Calif.: Stanford University Press, 1996.

Box Office Mojo. "Snowpiercer." Accessed April 23, 2015. https://www.boxofficemojo.com/movies/?id=snowpiercer.htm.

Braedley, Susan, and Meg Luxton, eds. *Neoliberalism and Everyday Life*. Montreal: McGill-Queen's University Press, 2010.

Business Insider. "South Korea's Education Fever Needs Cooling." October 25, 2013. http://www.businessinsider.com/south-koreas-education-fever-needs-cooling-2013-10.

Cahiers du cinéma. "Top 10 des années 2000." Accessed November 8, 2015. https://www.cahiersducinema.com/produit/top-10-des-annees-2000/.

Carter, Joe. "How to Understand *Snowpiercer*." Action Institute Powerblog (blog), July 18, 2014. http://blog.acton.org/archives/70893-understand-snowpiercer.html.

Chances, Ellen. "The Superfluous Man in Russian Literature." In *The Routledge Companion to Russian Literature*, edited by Neil Cornwell, 111–122. London: Routledge, 2002.

Chang, Dŏkchin. "Apch'uksŏngjang 50nyŏn, mulchilchuŭijadŭrŭi kakchadosaeng sahoe namgyŏ" [50 years of compressed growth resulted in materialists' society of every man for himself]. Interview by Kim Hyeyŏng. *Hankook Ilbo*, October 29, 2015. https://www.hankookilbo.com/News/Read/201510292029348871.

Chang, Dŏkchin, Kim Hyŏnshik, Kim Tuhwan, and Ch'oe Hyeji. *Apch'uksŏngjangŭi kogohak* [The archaeology of the compressed growth]. Seoul: Hanul, 2017.

Chang, Kyung-sup. "Compressed Modernity and Its Discontents: South Korean Society in Transition." *Economy and Society* 28, no. 1 (1999): 30–55.

Chang, Wŏnho. "Han'guksahoeŭi pulshin, wŏninŭn ŏdie innŭn'ga?" [What is the cause of the distrust in Korean society?]. In *Taehanmin'gukŭn todŏkchŏgin'ga?* [Is Korea moral?], edited by Kim Misook, 172–195. Seoul: Tongashia, 2009.

Change.org. "Free *Snowpiercer*." Last modified August 19, 2014. https://www.change.org/p/free-snowpiercer.

Child, Ben. "*Snowpiercer* Director Reportedly Furious about Weinstein English-Version Cuts." *Guardian*, October 8, 2013. https://www.theguardian.com/film/2013/oct/08/snowpiercer-director-english-cuts-bong-joon-ho.

Ch'oe Hyŏnchŏng. "Chŏlmŭn Ch'ŭngŭi Chajo Sŏkkin Yuhaengŏ 'Ingyŏin'gan'" ["Surplus human," a self-deprecating term in vogue among the young]. *DongA Ilbo*, March 20, 2009. http://news.donga.com/3/all/20090310/8706013/1.

Cho Hae-joang. "Taehanmin'gung sahoeŭi kŭnŭl" [Shadow in the Korean society]. In *Han'gugin, Urinŭn Nuguin-ga?* [Koreans, who are we?], edited by P'ŭllat'onak'ademi. Seoul: 21Segibuksŭ, 2016. Ridibooks.

Choi, Jang Jip. *Minjuhwa ihuŭi minjujuŭi: Han'guk minjujuŭiŭi posujŏk kiwŏn'gwa wigi* [Democracy after democratization: The conservative origin and the crisis of Korean democracy]. Seoul: Humanista, 2010.

Choi, Jung Woon. *Owŏrŭi sahoegwahak* [Social science of May]. Seoul: Owŏrŭi Pom, 2012. Ridibooks.

Choi, Tae-sup. *Ingyŏ sahoi* [Surplus society]. Seoul: Ungjinjishik'ausŭ, 2013.

Choi Chang-ryol. *Taehanmin'gukŭl malhanda* [Speaking of the Republic of Korea]. Seoul: Idambukseu, 2012. Ridibooks.

Chŏn, Inkwŏn. *Namjaŭi T'ansaeng* [Birth of a man]. Seoul: P'urŭnsup, 2003.

Chŏng, Harim, I Chiyŏn, and Pak Kŏnsik. *Pong Chunholŭl ch'achasŏ* [Searching for Bong Joon Ho]. Video, 21:12. 2015. http://kymf.ssro.net/mth/contest/contest.do?no=1770&cmd=view&kind=movie&order=a&gubun=&ktype=workname&kword=%EB%B4%89%EC%A4%80%ED%98%B8&pageNo=&s_session=15.

Chŏng, Hŭijin. *P'eminijŭmŭi tojŏn* [The feminism's challenge]. 3rd ed. Seoul: Gyoyangin, 2015.

Chu Sŏngch'ŏl. "Saeroun enjinŭl changch'ak'aetta: 'Pong Chunhoŭi segye'wa sŏlgukyŏlch'aŭi tok'ing, kŭ kyŏlgwanŭn . . ." [New engine installed: The result of the docking of "Bong Joon Ho's world" and the *Snowpiercer* . . .]. *Cine 21*, August 5, 2013. http://www.cine21.com/news/view/?mag_id=74031.

———, ed. *Tebwiŭi sun'gan: Yŏnghwagamdong 17ini tŭllyŏjunŭn naŭi ch'ŏngch'un punt'ugi* [Debut moment: Seventeen film directors tell their struggles as youth]. Seoul: P'urŭnsup, 2014.

Cine 21. "Okja chejangnot'ŭ" [Okja production note]. Accessed August 27, 2018. http://www.cine21.com/movie/info/?movie_id=46441.

Crouch, Colin. *Post-democracy*. Malden, Mass.: Polity, 2004.

Dargis, Manohla. "It Came from the River, Hungry for Humans (Burp)." *New York Times*, March 9, 2007. https://www.nytimes.com/2007/03/09/movies/09host.html.

Delorme, Stéphane, and Jean-Philippe Tessé. "L'art du piksari." *Cahiers du cinéma* 618 (2006): 47–49.

DeLuca, Kevin Michael, and Jennifer Peeples. "From Public Sphere to Public Screen: Democracy, Activism, and the 'Violence' of Seattle." *Critical Studies in Media Communication* 19, no. 2 (2002): 125–151.

Derber, Charles, and Yale R. Magrass. *Surplus American: How the 1% Is Making Us Redundant*. New York: Routledge, 2012.

Derrida, Jacques. *Limited Inc.* Translated by Jeffrey Mehlman and Samuel Weber. Evanston: Northwestern University Press, 1988.

D'Katz, Steve. *Film Directing Shot by Shot: Visualizing from Concept to Screen.* Waltham, Mass.: Focal, 1991.

DongAScience.com. "Kwahakchŏng kŏmjŭng chinach'imyŏn yŏnghwa chaemiŏpchi annayo?" [Doesn't too much scientific verification make movies boring?], October 27, 2013. http://www.dongascience.com/news/view/2796.

Durkheim, Emile. *Suicide: A Study in Sociology.* New York: Free Press, 1997.

Ďurovlčová, Nataša, and Garrett Stewart. "Amnesia of Murder: *Mother.*" *Film Quarterly* 64, no. 2 (2010): 64–68.

Elsaesser, Thomas. "The Pathos of Failure: American Films in the 1970s." In *The Last Great American Picture Show: New Hollywood Cinema in the 1970s,* edited by Alexander Horwath, Noel King, and Thomas Elsaesser, 279–292. Amsterdam: Amsterdam University Press, 2004.

Fifield, Anna. "Young South Koreans Call Their Country 'Hell' and Look for Ways Out." *Washington Post,* January 31, 2016. https://www.washingtonpost.com/world/asia_pacific/young -south-koreans-call-their-country-hell-and-look-for-ways-out/2016/01/30/34737c06 -b967-11e5-85cd-5ad59bc19432_story.html.

FilmIsNow Movie Trailers. "*Snowpiercer* R-Rated Animated Prequel (2013)—Chris Evans Movie HD." YouTube video, 5:33. July 23, 2013. https://www.youtube.com/watch?v= DrvBy5_aFOA.

Fischer, Russ. "There Is Only One Cut of 'Snowpiercer,' Which Opens Wide This Week." */ Film* (blog), July 1, 2014. https://www.slashfilm.com/snowpiercer-cut/.

Flank, Robert, and Philip Cook. *The Winner-Take-All Society: Why the Few at the Top Get So Much More than the Rest of Us.* New York: Penguin, 1996.

Foucault, Michel. "What Is an Author?" In *Language, Counter-memory, Practice: Selected Essays and Interviews,* edited by Donald F. Bouchard, 113–138. Ithaca, N.Y.: Cornell University Press, 1977.

Fraser, Nancy. *Scales of Justice: Reimagining Political Space in a Globalizing World.* New York: Columbia University Press, 2010.

Gerstener, David A., and Janet Staiger, eds. *Authorship and Film.* New York: Routledge, 2003.

Goldberg, Jonah. "On *Snowpiercer* (SPOILERS)." *National Review,* July 23, 2014. http://www .nationalreview.com/corner/383523/snowpiercer-spoilers-jonah-goldberg.

Han, Angie. "The Weinstein Co. Cutting 'Snowpiercer' Because Americans Are Stupid." */ Film* (blog), August 6, 2013. https://www.slashfilm.com/the-weinstein-co-cutting -snowpiercer-because-americans-are-stupid/.

Han, Mira. "Pong Chunho yŏnghwaŭi naerŏt'ibŭ konggani kannŭn chijŏnghakchŏng ŭimie kwanhan yŏn'gu" [Research on geopolitical meanings of narrative spaces in Bong Joon Ho's films]. *Yŏnghwayŏn'gu* 63 (2015): 259–287.

Han Sangpong, "'Che-ga tangshinŭi chongimnikka?': Taehakkangsa yusŏ namgigo chasal" ["Am I your slave?": A college adjunct commits suicide leaving a death note]. *Kat'ollingnyusŭ,* May 31, 2010. http://www.catholicnews.co.kr/news/articleView.html ?idxno=3603.

Hansen, Miriam. *Babel and Babylon: Spectatorship in American Silent Film.* Cambridge, Mass.: Harvard University Press, 1994.

Harris, Hunter (@hunterharris). "Okja is delightful and grim and this is my favorite part." Twitter, June 28, 2017, 9:44 am. pic.twitter.com/Y8uBNgPnNZ.

Holmes, Brian. "Hieroglyphs of the Future: Jacques Rancière and the Aesthetics of Equality." *Cabinet* 4 (2001). http://www.cabinetmagazine.org/issues/4/Hieroglyphs.php.

Hong, Sŏngrok. "Pong Chunho, 'Hyŏnshilchŏgin koemul mandŭnŭn'ge kwan'gŏniŏtchyo'" [Bong Joon Ho, "Making a realistic monster was the key"]. *Hankyoreh Shimun*, June 8, 2006. http://www.hani.co.kr/arti/PRINT/130433.html.

Hsu, Hsuan L. "The Dangers of Biosecurity: *The Host* and the Geopolitics of Outbreak." *Jump Cut* 51 (2009). http://www.ejumpcut.org/archive/jc51.2009/Host/text.html.

Huh, Moonyung. "Making Genre Films in the Third World: *Memories of Murder* and *The Host*, Genre and Local Politics." In *Bong Joon-ho*, edited by Jung Ji-youn, translated by Colin A. Mouat. Seoul: Seoul Selection, 2008. Kindle.

Hwang, Boyeon. "Ch'ŏngnyŏnege Han'gukŭn 'sŏlgukyŏlch'a ... igukttang wasŏ 'chŏnyŏginnŭn sam'" [For the young, Korea is *Snowpiercer*: Having 'Life with an Evening' in a foreign land]. *Hankyoreh Shimun*, January 4, 2016. http://www.hani.co.kr/arti/society/society_general/724550.html.

Hwang, Tuchin. "Modŭn tongneenŭn chŏnsŏri innŭn pŏp: *Madŏ*ŭi chin'gyŏngsansu, chin'gyŏnggŏnch'uk, chin'gyŏngyŏnghwa" [Every village has a legend: *Chin'gyŏng* landscape, *chin'gyŏng* architect, *chin'gyŏng* movie in *Mother*]. *Cine 21*, November 25, 2010. http://www.cine21.com/news/view/?mag_id=63746.

Hyŏn Yŏngpok. "Ch'eryu oegugin 150 manmyŏng ch'ŏt tolp'a—tamunhwa, tainjonghwa kasok" [Foreign immigrants exceed 1.5 million for the first time: Multicultural, multiracialization accelerates]. *Yonhap News*, June 10, 2013. http://www.yonhapnews.co.kr/politics/2013/05/28/0503000000AKR20130528133900372.HTML.

Im, Mina. "Pong Chunho, 'Han'guk shigonggan ttŏnan yŏnghwa ... kajang k'ŭn tojŏn'" [Bong Joon Ho, "Films beyond the Korean time and space ... the biggest challenge"]. *Yonhap News*, July 23, 2013. https://www.yna.co.kr/view/AKR20130723166200005.

Im, Sŏnae. "Han'gukyŏnghwa sŭt'oribodŭ" [Storyboarding in Korean cinema]. Seoul: K'ŏmyunik'eisyŏnbuksŭ, 2012.

I Osŏng. "Taeman k'asŭt'era mollakŭn chŏnghaejin sunsŏyŏtta" [The fall of Taiwanese castella was inevitable]. *SisaIN*, April 11, 2017. https://www.sisain.co.kr/news/articleView.html?idxno=28805.

James, David E., and Kyung Hyun Kim, eds. *Im Kwon-Taek: The Making of a Korean National Cinema*. Detroit: Wayne State University Press, 2002.

Jameson, Fredric. *Postmodernism: Or, the Cultural Logic of Late Capitalism*. Durham, N.C.: Duke University Press, 1992.

Jeon, Joseph Jonghyun. "Memories of Memories: Historicity, Nostalgia, and Archive in Bong Joon-ho's *Memories of Murder*." *Cinema Journal* 51, no. 1 (2011): 75–94.

Jeong, Seung-hoon, and Jeremi Szaniawski, eds. *The Global Auteur: The Politics of Authorship in 21st Century Cinema*. London: Bloomsbury Academic, 2016.

Johnston, Keith M. *Science Fiction Film: A Critical Introduction*. London: Berg, 2011.

Jung Ji-youn, ed. *Bong Joon-ho*. Translated by Colin A. Mouat. Seoul: Seoul Selection, 2008. Kindle.

Kang, Jun-man. *Urinŭn wae irŏk'e sanŭn'gŏlkka* [Why do we live this way?]. Seoul: Inmwulkwa Sasangsa, 2014. Ridibooks.

Kang, Yanggu. "*Koemul* t'ansaenghshik'in 'Maekp'allaendŭ sagŏn'ŭn iraetta" [The truth of the McFarland incident that inspired *The Host*]. *Pressian*, July 31, 2006. http://www.pressian.com/news/article/?no=33075.

KARA (Korea Animal Rights Advocates). "K'ara, kamgŭmt'ŭl ch'ubang wihae Pong Chunho gamdokkwa Okcha haebang p'ŭrojekt'ŭ torip" [KARA launches Okja Liberation Project with director Bong Joon Ho to eliminate pig stalls]. Press release, July 5, 2017. https://www.ekara.org/report/press/read/8828.

Khan, Muhammad. "*Snowpiercer*: A New Ice Age and Its Consequences." World Socialist Web Site, October 8, 2014. https://www.wsws.org/en/articles/2014/10/08/snow-008.html.

Kil, Sonia. "Bong Joon-ho on Working with Netflix and the Controversy over 'Okja' at Cannes." *Variety*, May 16, 2017. https://variety.com/2017/film/news/bong-joon-ho-working-with-netflix-controversy-okja-cannes-1202428394/.

Kim, Chan'ho. *Momyŏlgam: Kuryokkwa Chonŏbŭi Kamjŏngsahoehak* [Sense of humiliation: sociology of emotions of shame and dignity]. Seoul: Munhakkwa Chisŏngsa, 2014.

Kim, Chinkyŏng. "Kyŏmjaehwabŏp soge nat'anan kŭndaesŏnge kwanhan koch'al: sŏgu insangjuŭihwabŏpkwaŭi pigyorŭl chungshimŭro" [The modernity in Kyomjae's painting style: Focusing on comparative studies with the Western Impressionist painting]. *Yangming Studies* 36 (2013): 329–370.

Kim, Hŭigyŏng. "'Sarinŭi Ch'uŏk' Pong Chunho kamdok: 8onyŏndaerŭl chimyŏngsubaehanda" [Bong Joon Ho's *Memories of Murder*: The 1980s on the wanted list]. *DongA Ilbo*, April 3, 2003. http://www.donga.com/news/article/all/20030403/7930795/1.

Kim, Joon-hyung. "*Snowpiercer, Elysium* and the Land We Live In." Mirezi.com, September 2, 2013. http://www.mirezi.com/2013/09/column-3_4118.html.

Kim, Mihyŏn. *Han-kuk yŏng-hwa yŏk-sa* [History of Korean cinema]. Seoul: K'ŏmyunik'eisyŏnbuksŭ, 2014. Ridibooks.

Kim, Ŭnhyŏng, and Chŏn Jŏngyun. "*Koemul* Pong Chunho kamtok, yŏnghwap'yŏnglonka Kimsoyŏng kyosu taetam" [Director Bong Joon Ho of *The Host* talks with film critic Kim Soyoung]. *Cine 21*, July 12, 2006. http://www.cine21.com/news/view/mag_id/39944.

Kim, Yŏnghŭi, and Im Pŏm. "[Yŏnghwa taedam] Nuarŭ pŏmjoeyŏnghwa-ro kwanshimmori, Pakch'anuk- Pong Chunho kamdok" [Cine-talk: Park Chan-wook and Bong Joon Ho, spotlight on their noir crime movies]. *Cine 21*, April 26, 2003. http://www.cine21.com/news/view/?mag_id=18591.

Kim, Yongun. "[IMF 20nyŏn yut' ongjindan] Kŏriro naemollin kajangdŭl: Kamaengjŏm chŏnsŏngshidae yŏrŏtchiman" [(IMF 20 years distribution analysis) thrown onto the street: It was the heyday of franchise business but...]. *edaily*, November 21, 2017. https://www.edaily.co.kr/news/read?newsId=03240646616128016&mediaCodeNo=257&OutLnkChk=Y.

Kim, Yunjong. *The Failure of Socialism in South Korea: 1945–2007.* New York: Routledge, 2015.

Kim Chi-jung. "1onyŏn nŏmge OECD chasallyul 1wi... Idaero nwadul kŏn'ga" [No. 1 suicide rate among OECD nations over ten years: Just leaving it this way?]. *Hankook Ilbo*, October 6, 2014. https://www.hankookilbo.com/v/8a588d67540b4b61818405f3eea489fa.

Kim Myŏngsin. "Ttwigo tto ttwinŭn i ttangŭi modŭn madŏdŭrege" [To all the mothers of this land who keep running and running]. *Pressian*, June 12, 2009. http://www.pressian.com/news/article.html?no=95340.

Kim Sŏro. "Yŏnghwa 'okchaoka shikt'ang wie kajyŏon pyŏnhwanŭn" [Changes the movie *Okja* brought to the table]. *Hankook Ilbo*, July 10, 2017. https://www.hankookilbo.com/News/Read/201707101357235400.

Klein, Christina. "The AFKN Nexus: US Military Broadcasting and New Korean Cinema." *Transnational Cinemas* 3, no. 1 (2012): 19–39.

———. "Why American Studies Needs to Think about Korean Cinema, or Transnational Genres in the Films of Bong Joon-ho." *American Quarterly* 60, no. 4 (2008): 871–893.

Korean Film Archive. "Koesudaebaekkwa: Han'guk koesuga onda" [Monster encyclopedia: Korean monsters are coming]. July 29–August 5, 2008. https://www.koreafilm.or.kr/cinematheque/programs/PI_00287.

———. "*Sŏlgukyŏlch'a*" [*Snowpiercer*]. http://www.kmdb.or.kr/db/kor/detail/movie/K/14111.

———. "2014 Han'gukyŏnghwa 100Sŏn" [100 greatest Korean films 2014]. https://www.kmdb.or.kr/db/list/42.

Korean Film Council. *2014nyŏndop'an Han'gukyŏnghwayŏn'gam* [Korean film yearbook 2014]. Last modified April 4, 2018. https://www.kofic.or.kr/kofic/business/rsch/findPublishDetail.do?boardNumber=40&flag=1&pubSeqNo=2058.

———. "Yŏktae paksŭop'isŭ" [All-time box office]. Last modified November 8, 2013. http://www.kobis.or.kr/kobis/business/stat/boxs/findDailyBoxOfficeList.do.

Krakowiak, K. Maja, and Mary Beth Oliver. "When Good Characters Do Bad Things: Examining the Effect of Moral Ambiguity on Enjoyment." *Journal of Communication* 62, no. 1 (2012): 117–135.

Lee, Keun S. "Financial Crisis in Korea and IMF: Analysis and Perspective." Presentation, Merrill Lynch Center for the Study of International Financial Services and Markets, New York, February 27, 1998.

Lee, Kevin B. "The Han River Horror Show: Interview with Bong Joon-ho." Translated by Ina Park and Mina Park. *Cineaste* 32, no. 2 (2007). https://www.cineaste.com/spring2007/interview-with-bong-joon-ho.

Lee, Namhee. *The Making of Minjung: Democracy and the Politics of Representation in Korea.* Ithaca, N.Y.: Cornell University Press, 2007.

Lee, Tŭkchae. *Kajokchuŭinŭn yamanida* [Familism is barbarism]. Seoul: Sonamu, 2001.

Loader, Brian, and Dan Mercea. "Networking Democracy? Social Media Innovations and Participatory Politics." *Information, Communication & Society* 14, no. 6 (2011): 757–769.

Maltugi. "Sŏlgukyŏlch'a majimak changmyeon pukkŭkkomi yŏnghwaŭi modŭn'gŏsŭl sŏlmyŏnghanda" [The polar bear in the last scene of *Snowpiercer* explains everything]. *Hŭkkwa ssiat* (blog), August 6, 2013. http://maltugi.blogspot.com/2013/08/blog-post_6.html.

Mannheim, Karl. "The Problem of Generations." In *Karl Mannheim: Essays*, edited by Paul Kecskemeti, 276–322. 1952. Reprint, London: Routledge, 1972. http://marcuse.faculty.history.ucsb.edu/classes/201/articles/27MannheimGenerations.pdf.

Mark, Jason. "In Review: *Snowpiercer*." *Earth Island Journal*, July 19, 2014. http://www.earthisland.org/journal/index.php/elist/eListRead/in_review_emsnowpiercer_em/.

Marx, Karl. "The Class Struggles in France, 1848–1850." In *Marx & Engels Collected Works.* Vol. 10, *Marx and Engels 1849–51*, edited by Karl Marx and Frederick Engels, 45–146. Chadwell Heath, U.K.: Lawrence & Wishart Electric Book, 2010. http://www.hekmatist.com/Marx%20Engles/Marx%20&%20Engels%20Collected%20Works%20Volume%2010_%20M%20-%20Karl%20Marx.pdf.

MaxMovie, ed. *Pong Chunho* [Bong Joon Ho]. Seoul: K & Group, 2017.

McCorry, Seán. "*Okja*: A Film that Provides Food for Thought on 'Sustainable' Meat Production." Conversation, June 28, 2017. https://theconversation.com/okja-a-film-that-provides-food-for-thought-on-sustainable-meat-production-80088.

McNary, Dave. "Bong Joon-ho's 'Parasite' Posts Powerful Opening in North America." *Variety*, October 13, 2019. https://variety.com/2019/film/news/box-office-parasite-bong-joon-ho-1203368957/.

Mills, C. Wright. *The Sociological Imagination*. New York: Oxford University Press, 2000. Kindle.

Moon, Jae-cheol. "Pyŏnhwadoen shigansŏnggwa taejungŭi chŏngsŏ: Nyuweibŭ ihuŭi yŏnghwae nat'anan kwagŏŭi imiji" [Chronotope and structure of feeling: Images of the past in the post-'Korean-New-Wave' films]. *Journal of Popular Narrative* 9, no. 2 (2003): 64–87.

Moon, So-jeong. "Han'guk kajokpyŏndongŭi yŏksajŏk maengnagesŏ sangsanghan *Madŏŭi* kajokyongmang" [Rethinking the *Mother* in the historical context of Korean family]. *Yŏsŏnghakyŏn-gu* 19, no. 2 (2010): 97–118.

Moore, Alan. *From Hell*. Illustrated by Eddie Campbell. Marietta, Ga.: Top Shelf Productions, 2012. Kindle.

Mun, Sŏk. "Jangjunhwangwa *Jigureul jikyeora tansaenggi 2*" [Jang Junhwan and the birth of *Save the Green Planet* 2]. *Cine 21*, March 21, 2003. http://www.cine21.com/news/view/?mag_id=17945.

———. "Pong Chunho gamdogŭi *Koemul* p'ŭrip'ŭrodŏksyŏn 1" [Director Bong Joon Ho's preproduction of *The Host 1*]. *Cine 21*, March 15, 2005. http://www.cine21.com/news/view/mag_id/29049.

———. "Pong Chunho gamdogŭi *Koemul* p'ŭrip'ŭrodŏksyŏn 2" [Director Bong Joon Ho's preproduction of *The Host 2*]. *Cine 21*, March 15, 2005. http://www.cine21.com/news/view/?mag_id=29050.

Nam, Sangsŏk. "Yŏnghwa *Koemul* K'anesŏ hop'yŏng" [*The Host* acclaimed at Cannes]. *SBS News*, May 25, 2006. http://news.sbs.co.kr/news/endPage.do?news_id=N1000124318&plink=TIT&cooper=SBSNEWS.

Nam Kyŏnguk. "Chŏngŭiran Muŏshin-ga 100manbu tolp'a: Wae?" [*Justice: What's the Right Thing to Do?* exceeds 1 million sales: Why?]. *Hankook Ilbo*, April 19, 2011. http://www.hankookilbo.com/v/e2f4e5ec04f8432abbe7d539f2bfob6a.

National Institute of the Korean Language. *P'yojun'gugŏdaesajŏn* [Standard Korean dictionary]. http://stdict.korean.go.kr/search/searchView.do.

Newsis. "Yŏnghwa *Koemul*, 5.18 talmŭn kkol(?)" [Film *The Host*, similar to May 18?]. Chosŏndatk'ŏm. Last modified August 8, 2006. http://news.chosun.com/site/data/html_dir/2006/08/08/2006080870375.html.

New York Times. "Room for Debate: Will Fiction Influence How We React to Climate Change?" July 29, 2014. http://www.nytimes.com/roomfordebate/2014/07/29/will-fiction-influence-how-we-react-to-climate-change.

Pak, Hyemyŏng, and Kim Sohŭi. "'*Sarinŭi Ch'uŏg'*ŭi kamdok, pip'anja, chijijaga kajin 3kang taedam" [Triangle conversation between the director, critic, and supporter of *Memories of Murder*]. *Cine 21*, May 2, 2003. http://www.cine21.com/news/view/?mag_id=18684.

Pak, Kyŏnghŭi. "70Hoe K'anyŏnghwaje: Pong Chunho kamdogŭi yŏktae K'an pangmun'gi" [70th Cannes Film Festival: Director Bong Joon Ho's past visits to Cannes]. *MaxMovie*, May 19, 2017. http://news.maxmovie.com/321029.

Pak, Noja. *Pigurŭi Shidae* [The era of servility]. Seoul: Hankyoreh, 2014.

Pak Ilyŏng. *Sosŏl-ga Kubossiŭi ilsaeng: Kyŏngsŏng modŏnboi Pakt'aewŏnŭi sasaenghwal* [The life of the novelist Kubo: The private life of Pak T'ae-won, the modern boy of Seoul]. Seoul: Munhakkwa Chisŏngsa, 2016.

Pang, Hyŏnch'ŏl. "Han'guk kongmuwŏn pujŏngbup'ae segye 4wi: KDI 'P'yeswaejŏk imyongje-do ttaemun" [Korea's public official corruption ranks fourth in the world: KDI, "Due to closed hiring system"]. *Chosun Biz News*, October 10, 2013. http://biz.chosun.com/site/data/html_dir/2013/10/09/2013100903125.html.

Paquet, Darcy. *New Korean Cinema: Breaking the Waves.* New York: Wallflower, 2009.

Park, Hong-sik. "Kajŏnggyoyuk tamdangjarosŏŭi chŏnŏpchubu yŏk'algwa kajŏngmunje" [The role of housewives as home educator and family issues]. *Yugyosasang munhwa yŏn-gu* 30 (2007): 313–340.

Park, Young-a. *Unexpected Alliances: Independent Filmmakers, the State, and the Film Industry in Postauthoritarian South Korea.* Stanford, Calif.: Stanford University Press, 2014.

Parvin, Curtis M. "Are Social Classes on the Right Track? A Review of 'Snowpiercer' (2013)." *Rhode Island Liberator* (blog), November 14, 2014. https://riliberator.wordpress.com/2014/11/14/are-social-classes-on-the-right-track-a-review-of-snowpiercer-2013/.

Ramsier, Alanna. "11 Things That Happened When People Watched '*Okja*.'" PETA (blog), June 30, 2017. https://www.peta.org/blog/okja-turning-people-vegan/.

Ramstad, Evan. "U.S. Professor on Fairness Is a Hit in Seoul." *Wall Street Journal*, June 5, 2012. http://www.wsj.com/articles/SB10001424052702303506404577445841573895570.

Rancière, Jacques. *The Politics of Aesthetics.* London: Continuum, 2017.

Rotten Tomatoes. "*The Host*." Accessed April 25, 2016. http://www.rottentomatoes.com/m/the_host_2007/.

Rutherford, Jonathan. "The Third Space: Interview with Homi Bhabha." In *Identity: Community, Culture and Difference*, 207–221. London: Lawrence and Wishart, 1990.

Schatz, Thomas. *The Genius of the System: Hollywood Filmmaking in the Studio Era.* New York: Henry Holt, 2015.

Seidman, Steven, ed. *Jürgen Habermas on Society and Politics: A Reader.* Boston: Beacon, 1989.

Sharf, Zack. "'*Okja*' Rejected by 93% of South Korean Movie Theaters over Netflix Controversy." *IndieWire*, June 7, 2017. https://www.indiewire.com/2017/06/okja-south-korea-rejected-netflix-bong-joon-ho-1201838682/.

Shim, Jae-myung. Paekchiyŏnŭi P'ip'ŭl INSIDE Ep. 382 [Paek Chiyŏn's People INSIDE, Episode 382]: "Shimjaemyŏng taep'yo, *Sŏlgukyŏlch'a* Pong Chunho kamdokŭl noch'ida" [Producer Shim Jae-myung missed an opportunity to work with director Bong Joon Ho of *Snowpiercer*]. YouTube video, 1:47. "CJENM," August 13, 2013. https://www.youtube.com/watch?v=K-Sybqzsum4.

Shin, Chi-Yun, and Julian Stringer, eds. *New Korean Cinema.* New York: New York University Press, 2005.

Shin, Gi-wook, and Kyung Moon Hwang, eds. *Contentious Kwangju: The May 18 Uprising in Korea's Past and Present.* New York: Rowman and Littlefield, 2003.

Shklovsky, Viktor. "Art as Technique." In *Literary Theory: An Anthology*, edited by Julie Rivkin and Michael Ryan, 8–14. Malden, Mass.: Wiley-Blackwell, 2017.

Sŏ Hyein. "*Sarinŭi Ch'uŏk* (Pong Chunho, 2003): Myŏngjakŭl mandŭn ch'ŏt pŏntchae maedŭp" [*Memories of Murder* (Bong Joon Ho, 2003): The first step to making a classic]. *Yŏnghwach'ŏn'guk*, August 20, 2018. http://www.kmdb.or.kr/story/179/4776.

Solanas, Fernando, and Octavio Getino. "Towards a Third Cinema." *Cinéaste* 4, no. 3 (1970–1971): 1–10.

Son Ch'angsŏp. *Ingyŏ ingan* [*Surplus human*]. Seoul: Minŭmsa, 2005.

Sontag, Susan. "The Imagination of Disaster." In *Against Interpretation and Other Essays*, 209–225. New York: Picador, 1966.

Special Coverage Team. "Shimch'ŭngbunsŏk chasal: IMF chik'u 42%-2003nyŏn kyŏnggich'imch'e ttae 27%kŭpchŭng" [In-depth analysis of suicide: 42 percent increase immediately after IMF—27 percent increase during the 2003 recession]. *DongA Ilbo.* Last modified September 27, 2009. http://news.donga.com/3/all/20070215/8407797/1.

Spyrou, Constantine. "Netflix's Revolutionary New Film 'Okja' Is Causing People to Go Vegan." *Foodbeast* (blog), July 5, 2017. https://www.foodbeast.com/news/okja-reactions/.

Ssinek'ŭra. "*Koemul*: Koemurŭi chŏngch'e! (Pong Chunhoga sumgyŏnoŭn sangjingdŭl)" [*The Host*: The identity of the monster! (The symbols Bong Joon Ho has hidden [in the film])]. *Naŭi yŏnghwap'yŏng* [My film reviews] (blog), June 15, 2007. http://m.blog.naver.com/melt21/140038980340.

Starostineetskaya, Anna. "*Okja* Release Spikes 'Vegan' Google Searches by 65%." *VegNews*, August 6, 2017. https://vegnews.com/2017/8/okja-release-spikes-vegan-google-searches-by-65-percent.

Statistics Korea. "Ch'wiŏpcha su/shirŏmnyul ch'ui" [Trend in the number of the employed/unemployment rate]. *e-narachip'yo* [E-national index]. Accessed November 8, 2015. http://www.index.go.kr/potal/main/EachDtlPageDetail.do?idx_cd=1063.

Sung, Jinsoo. "Tongsitae Hankuk yŏnghwaesŏ chakkachuŭiŭi sangŏpchŏk suyong yangsang" [The commercial embrace of auteurism in contemporary Korean films]. *Yŏnghwayŏn'gu*, no. 63 (2015): 161–194.

Telotte, J. P. "Science Fiction Reflects Our Anxieties." *New York Times*, last modified July 30, 2014. http://www.nytimes.com/roomfordebate/2014/07/29/will-fiction-influence-how-we-react-to-climate-change/science-fiction-reflects-our-anxieties.

Toffler, Alvin. *Future Shock*. New York: Bantam Books, 1970.

Wainstock, Dennis D. *Truman, MacArthur and the Korean War: June 1950–July 1951*. New York: Enigma Books, 2013.

Ward, Simon. *Okja: The Art and Making of the Film*. London: Titan Books, 2018.

Weber, Lindsey. "Let's Talk about the Ending of *Snowpiercer*." *Vulture*, July 11, 2014. http://www.vulture.com/2014/07/snowpiecer-movie-discussion.html.

Weber, Max. "Politics as a Vocation." In *Max Weber's Complete Writings on Academic and Political Vocations*, edited by John Dreijimanis, translated by Gordon C. Wells, 22–23. New York: Algora, 2008.

Wells, H. G. "Preface to the 1921 Edition." In *The War in the Air: And Particularly How Mr. Bert Smallways Fared While It Lasted*. Harmondsworth, U.K.: Penguin, 1967.

Wŏn, Hŭipok. "5·18 Kwangju minjung hangjaeng, Han'guk minjujuŭi undongŭi pich'i toeda" [May 18 Kwangju democratic struggle becomes the light of Korea's democratic movement]. *Kyunghyang Shinmun*, July 13, 2015. http://news.khan.co.kr/kh_news/khan_art_view.html?art_id=201507111446581.

Yim Pil-sung. "Chejagilchi: namgŭgilgi" [Production diary: *Antarctic Journal*]. *P'illŭmmeik'ŏsŭ K'ŏmyunit'i*, May 14, 2005. https://www.filmmakers.co.kr/production_2004010500/23821.

Yŏnhamnyusŭ. "'Okcha' Pong Chunho gamdok manhwa 'K'onan yŏjaai pŏjŏn mandŭlgo ship'ŏtta'" [*Okja* director Bong Joon Ho, "I wanted to make a girl's version of the cartoon *Future Boy Conan*"]. *Hankyoreh Shinmun*, May 21, 2017. http://www.hani.co.kr/arti/culture/culture_general/795537.html.

Yuk, Sŏngch'ŏl. "*Sarinŭi Ch'uŏk* kamdok Pong Chunho, kŭ-ga kunggŭmhada" [Let's get to know Bong Joon Ho, the director of *Memories of Murder*]. *Wŏlgan Ch'amyŏsahoe*, June 1, 2003. http://www.peoplepower21.org/Magazine/715011.

Žižek, Slvoj. "The Lessons of Rancière." In *The Politics of Aesthetics: The Distribution of the Sensible*, by Jacques Rancière, translated by Gabriel Rockhill, 65–76. London: Continuum, 2007.

INDEX

Page numbers in *italics* refer to figures.

ABOUT THE AUTHOR

NAM LEE is an associate professor of film studies at Dodge College of Film and Media Arts, Chapman University. Before receiving her PhD in critical studies from the University of Southern California, she worked as a film critic and journalist in Seoul, South Korea.